BUSINESS ENTE

Managing People in a Small Business

JOHN STREDWICK

RECOMMENDED BY
INSTITUTE OF DIRECTORS

KOGAN PAGE

This book has been endorsed by the Institute of Directors.

The endorsement is given to selected Kogan Page books which the IoD recognises as being of specific interest to its members and providing them with up-to-date, informative and practical resources for creating business success. Kogan Page books endorsed by the IoD represent the most authoritative guidance available on a wide range of subjects including management, finance, marketing, training and HR.

The views expressed in this book are those of the author and are not necessarily the same as those of the Institute of Directors.

First published in 2002

Apart from any fair dealing for the purposes of research or private study, or criticism or review, as permitted under the Copyright, Designs and Patents Act 1988, this publication may only be reproduced, stored or transmitted, in any form or by any means, with the prior permission in writing of the publishers, or in the case of reprographic reproduction in accordance with the terms and licences issued by the CLA. Enquiries concerning reproduction outside these terms should be sent to the publishers at the undermentioned addresses:

Kogan Page Limited
120 Pentonville Road
London N1 9JN
UK

Kogan Page US
22 Broad Street
Milford CT 06460
USA

© John Stredwick, 2002

The right of John Stredwick to be identified as the author of this work has been asserted by him in accordance with the Copyright, Designs and Patents Act 1988.

The views expressed in this book are those of the author, and are not necessarily the same as those of Times Newspapers Ltd.

British Library Cataloguing in Publication Data

A CIP record for this book is available from the British Library.

ISBN 0 7494 3622 0

Typeset by Jean Cussons Typesetting, Diss, Norfolk
Printed and bound in Great Britain by Clays Ltd, St Ives plc

Contents

Preface v
Acknowledgements vii

1. **Introduction** 1
   Providing the leadership 6; Essential starting points 14

2. **Getting the best people** 19
   Human resource planning 19; Recruitment 21; Establishing whether a vacancy exists 23; Defining the vacancy 24; Attracting the applicants 27; Shortlisting 45; Interviewing 46; Selection tests 54; References 58; Making the offer 60; Staff retention 62

3. **Improving performance** 66
   What makes people perform well 66; Making the work interesting 70; Making sure the work is challenging 73; Recognising people's efforts 78; Constructing a fair environment 86; Regarding people as important 91; Team working 91; Encouraging flexible working 96

4. **Training and developing employees** 108
   Introduction 108; Induction 110; Identifying training needs 116; Methods of training 118; Investors in People 122; Government-sponsored training 125

5. **Rewarding employees**   128
   Introduction 128; What are rewards for? 129; Effects of legislation 129; Creating a salary structure 133; Do bonus schemes work? 146; The right collection of benefits 158

6. **Communication, consultation and involvement**   166
   Introduction 166; What is there to communicate? 168; Communication methods 173; Should trade unions be encouraged or recognised? 181; Handling grievances 186

7. **Equal opportunities**   191
   Introduction 191; Legislation 191; What is discrimination? 193; Disability cases 194; Equal Pay Act 195; Practical advice 196; Sexual harassment and bullying 200

8. **Health, safety and welfare**   205
   The legislation and obligation on employers 206; Practical advice 215; Occupational stress 222; Conclusion 223

9. **Discipline, dismissal and redundancy**   225
   Introduction 225; Discipline 225; Dismissal 237; Redundancy 252

10. **Getting the changes you need**   265
    Introduction 265; Understanding the change process 265; Who is in favour of change? 270

Index   278

Preface

'People are our greatest asset!'

Oh, yes? So why do businesses often keep a much closer eye on their other assets – their brands, their buildings, their stock, their vehicles and their finances? Why are employees treated as though they are at the end of the queue when it comes to careful consideration of their needs and aspirations? Why do the actions of companies continually contradict this charming, if hackneyed, expression?

In 30 years working and teaching in human resources, it has never ceased to amaze me that many of the most crucial business decisions have been taken without any thought of the implications for employees, either long term or short term. Too often, it has been left to the human resources department, where one exists, to try to make last-minute adjustments and sort out the difficulties. Interestingly, this state of affairs is true both in small organisations and in the largest global corporations.

It is interesting because, for small organisations, people are sometimes the *only* real asset they possess and so the effect on their people of business decisions should be the first consideration, not the last. Of course, there are many exceptions to my broad generalisations. I am being unfair to many businesses, especially small ones, that have put their employees at the forefront of their business strategy. They have inspirational leadership; they invest heavily in training and development; they motivate their staff to higher performance and reward fairly and generously. It has been a joy to work in and with such organisations where the employee morale is high and where the businesses expand and prosper.

What is more, the directors and owners of these organisations regard their staff as the providers of skills, expertise and flexibility that give the organisations their competitive advantage. Without these attributes, the organisations are lost and will undoubtedly lose the battle for survival.

This book, then, is a broad guide on all matters affecting the management of people in small businesses. 'Small' is loosely defined as a business with fewer than 250 employees. The book has three main focuses. Firstly, it is a guide to the technical aspects of managing people – the **options and techniques available** on recruiting, training, rewarding and motivating employees. Secondly, it addresses the need for **complying with the law** in all of these areas as well as in the areas of health and safety and equal opportunities. However, the law is changed every day through decisions by judges and tribunal chairpersons in this country and in Europe as well as by legislators, so you will always need to be careful to check up-to-date sources. Thirdly, the book includes some discussion of broader issues that relate to the **long-term development of managing people**, such as managing change and successful leadership.

Whether you own or help to manage a very small business just starting out or a more developed organisation with over 100 employees, I hope that you will find some relevant and thought-provoking material that will help you to improve the way you manage your people.

Acknowledgements

Scattered throughout the book are a host of practical examples that have come from many sources. I am very grateful to friends, colleagues at Luton Business School and numerous students who have passed through our portals to take human resources courses over the last decade. Two have been especially helpful in providing cases, namely Melanie Broad and Dave Streeter, and my thanks go to them for making special efforts on my behalf. Also I need to thank my long-suffering wife and family for putting up with yet another summer in which I was writing a book.

1 Introduction

George runs a small service-related business with 100 employees, and today has not been a good day.

Sheila, his best administrator, who has been off on maternity leave for five months, contacted him to say that she wanted to return to work next month but could only cope with a half-time job, and was that all right?

Part of the morning was spent in interviewing potential applicants for a supervisory position and he found it difficult to identify whether any of them were strong candidates – they all seemed about right but he had lurking doubts. He wished he knew whether there was interviewing expertise he could use or tests of some sort so he could be more sure of his decisions.

Kevin, a promising new member of staff, handed in his notice. When George asked him in for a chat about why he was leaving, Kevin said that the training was non-existent and that he had been thrown in the deep end and left to drown.

First thing this morning George received a small delegation of administrative staff who asked, politely but firmly, whether their pay rates could be looked at, as Jones Brothers up the road and others close by were paying at least 10 per cent more than George was.

His secretary passed on a rumour that one of the recently joined female staff members was considering taking up a claim against the company for both equal pay and sexual harassment. The latter claim was due to a series of risqué comments by one of George's fellow directors.

Just before lunch George received a call from one of his area supervisors to say that Dave, a site wiring operative, had fallen off a ladder, breaking his arm and damaging the customer's equipment, putting the customer out of action for hours. George was particularly worried because Dave had worked 15 hours non-stop and put in around 80 hours this week already.

Passing through the main office, George overheard one of the older members of staff talking on the telephone saying, 'Well, communication has always been awful in this place; what do you expect? Anyway, it might be better when we get the union recognised.'

People problems – they don't stop coming. With all the employment legislation over the last 20 years, managing people is becoming more, not less, difficult. For small organisations without specialist staff to handle the people side, the problems, like those faced by George, can be even more severe and potentially fatal. If the best employees leave, if the wrong ones are taken on, if pay gets out of control or if the company is taken to court or tribunals or is faced by damaging union problems, then the chances of a business going under become much greater, especially as the financial resources that large organisations have accumulated to help in weathering the storms may not be present.

No business, large or small, can succeed and thrive without having the right people, with the right skills and attributes, who are motivated towards achieving the organisation's goals.

How would you like people to work in your organisation?

One company has no doubt. In a report to shareholders a few years ago, Jack Welch, Chairman of General Electric, let it be known that:

> We want to become a company where people come to work each morning wanting to try something they woke up thinking about the night before. We want them to go home from work wanting to talk about what

they did that day, rather than forget about it. We want factories where the whistle blows and everybody wonders where the time went and somebody wonders aloud why we need a whistle. We want a company where people find a better way every day of doing things; and where, by shaping their own work experience, they make their lives better and your company the best.

Grand ideas, you may think, for a huge organisation with unlimited resources. Not especially relevant to a small organisation. Well, let me continue Jack Welch's report: 'Far-fetched? Soft? Naïve? Not a bit. This is the type of liberated, involved, excited, boundary-less culture that is present in successful small companies. It is unheard of in a company our size but we want it and are determined we will have it.'

In other words, Jack Welch is envious of the opportunities and advantages that small organisations have of motivating their employees successfully. Evidence from the UK 1998 Workplace Employee Relations survey found that employees in small organisations had higher levels of job satisfaction than those in larger organisations. Statistics show that labour turnover and absence also tend to be lower in small businesses. So staff must see some distinct advantages in working there rather than in multinationals or in large units in the public sector.

Why do people like to work for small organisations?

Some of the reasons are:

- *Small organisations provide an instant and ongoing challenge.* It is clear to everybody working there that they need to work hard just to stay in business.
- *People enjoy the speed of the decision and communication processes.* Decisions can be taken very quickly in small organisations. The normal barriers to decision making apply much less.

There are few layers of management to hold up the process. Decisions on spending money do not need to be accompanied by a lengthy written justification. The decision maker is far more accessible so it is easier for persuasion to be effective. Budgets may be more flexible. Good ideas, then, can be taken up much more quickly and put into action. Similarly, it is far easier for management to communicate important matters to staff. There is often only one site, so a face-to-face meeting with most employees can be arranged quickly. Questions can be fielded and hard decisions justified by the decision maker. From an employee viewpoint, this is much better than receiving a generalised e-mail.

- *People are closer to the power in the business.* The owners are usually visible and approachable, and often friendships can be struck with the owners' families. The owners are human, not like anonymous shareholders, or a Japanese or US bank. It is interesting to note, when an owner buys a new company car, that employees are more likely to take a genuine interest in the car selection rather than regard the purchase cynically or enviously. Incidentally, one owner in a small manufacturing company was so taken by the interest shown in the purchase of his upmarket sports car that the car was loaned for the weekend once a month to employees nominated for their contribution to the organisation.

- *Small organisations can provide outstanding development opportunities.* Your efforts and abilities are easier to recognise in a small business. This is partly because employees' jobs are more visible and small businesses carry no passengers. So when you perform well, it may well open up doorways to progression faster than you think. This can be especially true for employees with few qualifications and little ambition before finding themselves in an organisation that starts to take off. In the case of Everest Double Glazing, four of the glass-cutting team in the original 30-strong factory went on to set up new factories around the country as the organisation grew, despite no managerial experience prior to joining Everest. It was a combination of their ability to assimilate new practices, their cultural awareness and willingness to lead by example that led them all successfully to run factory sites with an output exceeding £10 million.

For those who are qualified and experienced, a once-in-a-lifetime opportunity can arise to take on a substantial management position without having to climb up the greasy management pole of the large organisation. There are numerous examples of graduates entering a small concern and being general manager within five years.

- *Small organisations may not be bound by so many rules.* They tend to have more informal working practices, more familiarity between staff, and fewer rules to have to follow. Employees have a certain degree of freedom to make the rules up as they go along – up to a point, of course!

Not everybody wants to work in small businesses. The employment tends to be even less secure than in a larger organisation, the pay is often poorer, the benefit list can be very small and the facilities may be severely lacking. You find no on-site squash courts, and only very rarely palatial offices or health club subscriptions. For some, the status of working for a household name is an important draw, and the greater security of working in the public sector influences employment decisions for others (although much less so nowadays as outsourcing continues apace).

For many people, however, the advantages outweigh the normal drawbacks inherent in most small businesses. The excitement, the uncertainty, the rapidity of change and a higher degree of recognition for their efforts can have an addictive effect. But none of this happens unless the leadership is there – and it has to be the right sort of leadership. It needs to inspire, motivate, develop and transform. As well as providing all this, small business owners and management also have to see to the small matter of running the day-to-day business.

Providing the leadership

Introduction

Small businesses, then, can have some immediate advantages in the area of managing people. Building on these advantages is not always easy and is very dependent upon the quality of leadership. Traditionally, leadership used to be called 'management' and concentrate on command and control techniques. Hierarchies would be established, procedures laid down and people trained to operate within these control systems. People's responsibilities were clear and narrowly defined. Where a situation arose that was not specified in existing procedures, then decisions would be referred upwards. Staff would *comply* with the system and, if they did not like it, they would leave. Most call centres still operate in this way and it is not surprising that staff turnover is huge – 60 per cent or more is the norm.

In the last 20 years, the culture of compliance has lost out badly as the business environment has rapidly changed and competition has become more intense. Hierarchies are expensive, so organisations have become flatter with fewer managers and supervisors; the emphasis has changed from following procedures to achieving higher performance, from maintaining existing products and services to innovation, and from system rigidity to flexibility. Moreover, the better educated and more confident and egalitarian labour force are far less prepared to be compliant. Work for them needs to be far more than routine and repetitive labour. They are waiting to be inspired and led towards the satisfaction of achievement.

What organisations need to develop, then, is a sense of *commitment* from the workforce, not compliance; and leadership, not management, is the pathway to achieving this. Martin and Nicols (1987) in their research in the late 1980s produced a set of models of commitment (see Figure 1.1) showing the component parts:

- The *sense of belonging* to the organisation builds loyalty, and is created by ensuring employees are informed and involved and share in success.

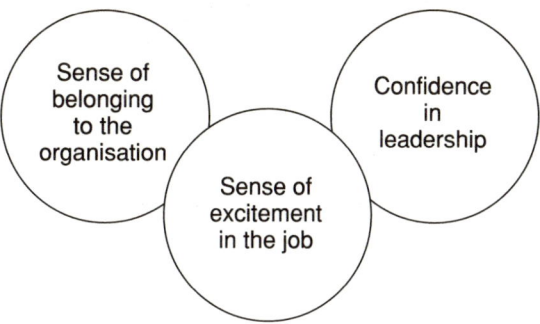

Figure 1.1 Martin and Nicols' models of commitment

- *A sense of excitement* in the job can improve results through high levels of motivation. This can be achieved by communicating to employees the leader's own excitement and vision, and appealing to the inherent needs of all employees to have pride in their work, to have a sense of trust for authority and to want to be accountable for results.
- None of this is possible unless employees have *confidence in the leaders* and respect for their authority, dedication, competence and ethical approach.

Leadership traits

So what traits should good leaders show? John Adair (1997) developed his theory of leadership over 25 years and has spelt out eight main features:

- *Enthusiasm* – a consistent and energetic enthusiasm that employees find attractive and addictive.
- *Integrity* – so employees can trust their leaders' judgement and know where they stand.
- *Toughness* – being resilient and unafraid of making unpopular decisions.

- *Fairness* – treating people consistently and equitably.
- *Warmth* – caring about employees and showing it. Warmth can also be shown through sharing the grief when unhappy events happen to employees, to themselves or to the organisation. Employees can respect cold, calculating and reserved leaders but they rarely warm to them.
- *Humility* – having an ability to be approached and a willingness to listen, to take ideas on board and to understand that having their mind changed is not a defeat (as long as it does not happen too often and is not seen as vacillating!).
- *Confidence* – a clear demonstration of their inner belief and conviction that their basic direction is right and they will get to where they want to go.
- *Adaptability* – being able to change their tactics in response to the demands of a quickly changing external environment.

Some of these traits are built-in features of an individual's personality from adolescence onwards. Purveyors of psychometric tests would go out of business if they could not identify these traits with their test designs. But having the traits and using them effectively are different matters. To be good at leading you need to be aware of the leadership requirements, identify and be conscious of your own strengths and weaknesses in these areas, build on your strengths and try, if you can, to remedy your weaknesses. Training and reflecting on learning experiences are the two most effective methods of both building your strengths and remedying weaknesses. You cannot go forward, however, unless you do know yourself. In Chapter 3, the importance of feedback to employees as to how they are performing is emphasised. For a leader in a small organisation, getting feedback is not easy and it does need to be worked upon.

Providing the vision

Without a vision, an organisation becomes directionless. Happily, small businesses generally have no difficulty in providing the vision.

They are in business usually because the founder had a simple idea and sufficient confidence to leave the comfort of paid employment and step out into the dangerous world of setting up and developing a business.

Those who run the business will know what the vision is, but they do not always articulate it or communicate it to the employees. It is not necessary to convert it into a formal 'mission statement', although many do so, especially those organisations trying for Investors in People where it is, in effect, a requirement. What is necessary is to emphasise the fundamental strength of the business – the idea, the products, the services – and make sure employees know about it. This can be done through the induction process (see Chapter 4) or through a regular review involving all the staff that looks at performance, new products, services and opportunities.

The vision can be encapsulated into a few statements:

- what events got the business under way – the storytelling of how it all began, which employees always find interesting (William Hewlett and David Packard, for example, started their business in a garage in 1939. So keen is Hewlett-Packard to encourage the culture of creativity in unusual surroundings that it continues to feature that garage in internal literature and external advertisements);
- what makes the products or services unique, especially quality issues;
- how the organisation is going to develop and expand – products, locations, staff numbers;
- what part the employees play in this programme of development.

This is all part and parcel of inspiration leadership. Reliving and reinforcing the vision is vital or it gets stale. It is useful for directors to incorporate the vision into some of their day-to-day work and take every opportunity to remind others of the link. Quarterly performance reviews, for instance, could be used to show how departments are contributing to the vision. Lively articles in an internal newsletter could serve to remind employees, and the vision should always feature highly in any internal conference or training course. Some large organisations even put their vision on to their letterheads or on all internal communications ('Becoming Number One' is an example). Whatever happens, all leaders have to 'walk the talk' and make sure their colleagues do the same. Nothing kills a vision more quickly than a couple of cynical executives who make it clear it really means nothing.

Creating a culture

Even with a well-understood and internalised vision, the organisation and its staff will not be able to reach their potential without an effective and supportive culture within which to operate. A culture establishes the values that are important to the organisation, and the combination of values tends to be unique to that organisation. An example of a set of values for a small computer consultancy is set out in the box below.

Set of values for small computer consultancy
- Have fun and enjoy work.
- Always put the client first.
- Make quality a part of everything we do.
- Share knowledge with others.
- Work as a team.
- Develop your full potential.
- Make decisions; don't refer them.
- Take ownership and resolve problems.
- Learn from mistakes without fear of recrimination.

A number of these values are very conventional, such as those referring to teams and quality. However, the first and last ones are crucial in identifying the true culture. The first tries to encourage job satisfaction and enjoyment – you cannot enjoy work if the job provides no satisfaction – and the second aims to avoid a blame culture by encouraging a learning environment.

Blame cultures are terrible to work in. People are so careful to avoid the blame for things that go wrong that they either do not take decisions at all or they waste time attempting to blame others for their mistakes. It is a corrupting environment where mistrust and lying are commonplace. Such a culture must be avoided at all costs. Linda Holbeche (1998) tells the story of a young executive given responsibility for a major business unit who promptly lost $10 million in the first 18 months. When he went to the chief executive to hand in his resignation for performing so badly, this was brushed aside with the comment, 'Don't you think of resigning. We've just spent $10 million training you!'

A positive culture should encourage employees to take decisions and initiatives and, if things go wrong, to work out why this happened and what to do for the best next time. This should be done in an open and frank manner, with the person concerned willing to admit to mistakes and to learn from them, with support from the manager and colleagues.

Other interesting examples of published values include:

- Have a can-do attitude.
- Communicate with our customers in a style and language they can understand.
- Make realistic promises – and keep them.
- Coach and encourage others at any level to develop their talents and give their best.
- Look first for agreement, not for differences of opinions.

If you want to create a set of values for the first time, do make sure you ask your existing staff to help you draw them up. By all means get in a consultancy to facilitate the process, but do not ask them to do all the design work. The culture must come from inside and, if staff have played a big part in drawing up the values, they are much more likely to want to see those values implemented and working properly. If you impose the values, you risk condemning them to the waste-paper basket.

A good summary of the importance of culture in improving performance comes from Chris Watkin (2001), who has researched the subject of *organisational climate* and concluded that up to 70 per cent of climates can be traced to the leadership or management style. Good managers create good climates while poor managers create poor climates. His checklist for a positive climate is shown in the box below.

Positive organisational climate indicators
- *Flexibility.* There are no unnecessary rules, procedures, policies or practices. New ideas are accepted easily, and management's focus is on getting the best people together to do a job rather than establishing long lines of authority.
- *Responsibility.* Employees are given authority to accomplish tasks without constantly having to seek approval. They are encouraged to take calculated risks without fear of blame.
- *Standards.* Challenging but attainable goals are set for the organisation and its employees with the individuals taking part in the goal-setting and planning process.
- *Rewards.* Encouragement is used much more often than criticism, and rewards should be in direct proportion to the quality of employees' output.
- *Clarity.* Employees know exactly what is expected of them and how they can contribute to the organisation's goal.
- *Pride.* People are proud to belong to the organisation.

An example of a culture-driven small organisation is shown in Case 1.1.

Case 1.1 Sportasia Community

Since its beginnings selling sweatshirts to a handful of schools in Sheffield in the late 1980s, Peter Beeby's company Sportasia has grown into a £5 million turnover enterprise with over 5,000 customers and 100 employees. From the early development of the organisation, Beeby wanted to motivate employees through ensuring that they shared the values of the organisation, had opportunities for personal development and felt inspired, respected and appreciated.

As well as 'walking the talk' in the workplace, Beeby has formulated what he has called the Sportasia Community Company model – something of a mouthful, but a culture that is easier to disseminate when written down. It has six 'pillars' as its foundation:

- *Information and involvement.* Employees have the right of access to information and involvement in decision making but must be responsible for open and honest participation. Employees are expected to air their grievances openly rather than infect others with their cynicism.
- *Shared prosperity.* Employees have a right to share the company prosperity through profit-sharing and share ownership schemes but a responsibility to make a full contribution to the community effort.
- *Employment protection.* Employees have a right to employment protection but a responsibility to be flexible and adaptable in the work they do.
- *Organisational values.* Employees have the right to be treated with fairness, consistency, respect and support but the responsibility to treat management and their fellow employees and customers with the same values.
- *Fair reward.* Indecent salary differentials should be avoided and employees need to demonstrate honest endeavour and commitment.
- *Development opportunities.* Employees have strong rights to personal development but responsibilities to meet training objectives and to develop in harmony with the needs of the community.

This balance between rights and responsibilities is at the heart of the culture and extends to all levels of the organisation. Two of its core values are the importance of listening and the belief in humour. Managers expect their decisions to be openly challenged, especially if decisions appear to go against the espoused values. Researchers into the organisation appear convinced that there really does appear to be a sense of community and this is reflected in the firm's lack of formality in dress code and in ways of doing business. The company has tried to build links with suppliers that share the same values.

Because of the emphasis on community and discussion of problems, Beeby sees no need for unions. Collective bargaining is anathema to an organisation that has sought to break down the sense of 'us and them'. (Source: Trapp, 2000)

Essential starting points

Commitment and compliance

So far this chapter has concentrated on how a good employer in a small organisation will try to inspire employees so they become **committed** to that organisation. This is a proactive process by the organisation to help it get a competitive advantage. There needs to be a constant balance between the drive to obtain this commitment and the need for **compliance**. From an employer's viewpoint, this means keeping on the right side of employment law, which has become extensive. From the employee viewpoint, compliance can mean keeping to the employer's rules and doing what you are told (but no more).

The two strands of commitment and compliance intertwine throughout the book. Chapters 7, 8 and 9, on equal opportunities, health and safety, and dismissal and redundancy respectively, concentrate mostly on the compliance aspects, including all the employment rights brought in through legislation. The remaining chapters centre more on increasing commitment through proactive policies and initiatives in the fields of increasing performance, training, pay and communication. There is some law in these chapters that needs to be taken into account. By the same token, the introduction of some of the legal aspects provides you with the opportunity to turn legislation to your own advantage through additional initiatives and fielding the 'business case' for equal opportunities or health and safety.

Employee rights

Employees have a lot more rights these days than they used to. Advances in employment law have come thick and fast, mostly initiated from Europe in an attempt to develop a level playing field in employment terms and conditions, so that one nation does not try to undercut another.

Here is a starting list of employment rights, most of which will be dealt with in more detail in later chapters:

- right to a written statement of the main terms and conditions (see Chapter 4);
- right to a minimum wage (see Chapter 5);
- right to an itemised pay statement (see Chapter 5);
- right to a guarantee payment (see Chapter 5);
- right to equal pay (see Chapter 7);
- right to maternity leave and maternity pay (see Chapter 5);
- right to take part in union activities with a union of choice (see Chapter 6);
- right not to be discriminated against on the grounds of sex, marital status, race or disability (see Chapter 7);
- right to a minimum period of notice (see Chapter 9);
- right not to be unfairly dismissed or unfairly chosen for redundancy (see Chapter 9);
- right to a redundancy payment (see Chapter 9);
- right to a written statement of reason for dismissal (see Chapter 9);
- right not to be forced to work in excess of 48 hours a week (see Chapter 3);
- right to work in a safe environment (see Chapter 8).

This is by no means a comprehensive list. There is a right to retain existing terms and conditions when a change of ownership of the organisation occurs or where the job is transferred from one organisation to another. The law under these circumstances is known as TUPE (Transfer of Undertakings (Protection of Employment) Regulations) and is so complicated and changes so often under case law that a whole chapter would need to be devoted to it to do it justice. There is no room in this book, so you are advised to get legal advice if jobs or work are transferred.

Employee handbook

At the heart of an employment contract are the terms and conditions under which an employee works. Most organisations, from an early stage, bring these common terms and conditions together into the form of a handbook that is issued to all employees. This will include sets of rules that are the basis for employee compliance:

- *Safety rules.* These are a vital part of the employer's duty of care to protect employees. They cover the operation of plant and equipment, wearing of safety gear and limiting access to areas of work, tools and machinery unless trained or qualified.
- *Performance rules.* These relate to many aspects of an individual's performance including attendance, timekeeping, flexibility on hours, working practices and location, levels of performance, willingness to work overtime and the requirement to take part in bonus schemes or raise suggestions for improvements.
- *Behaviour rules.* Included here are rules that concern the relationship with customers and fellow employees, such as the need to be courteous and responsive to customers, to wear certain regulation uniform and to take part in team processes.
- *Rules evolved through custom and practice.* Not all rules are written down. Rule books would be far too long if they had to include every conceivable situation so common sense assumes that, for example, certain violent behaviour would not be allowed. Nor do written rules apply if they are not implemented by management. For example, the rules may clearly indicate that employees may not take out of the premises any materials belonging to the organisation. In practice, employees may have been taking small quantities of certain low-grade materials for their own use with the knowledge of management so the original rule is regarded, at law, as being amended to take this custom into account.

A checklist for inclusion in the handbook is given in Chapter 4.

Should a small organisation employ a human resource specialist?

Recent research indicates that organisations employing over 200 staff consider they need at least one human resource specialist, while around 60 per cent employ a specialist if they employ more than 150 staff. Some organisations with the need for an important skill, such as selection or training, employ such a person even though they may have less than 100 staff.

The *advantages* of employing a specialist are as follows:

- Specialist advice can be vital in legal areas, such as equal opportunities and dismissal, advice that may be expensive to obtain from outside.
- It is difficult to uphold a value that people are an important asset if there is no manager with responsibility for recruiting, developing and rewarding employees.
- A specialist will provide you with much unbiased information on employee performance, appropriateness of pay rates and organisation structure.
- Specialists are invaluable for crucial projects such as salary reviews, disciplinary issues, rapid build-up of staff and redundancies.
- Employees should benefit from having a sympathetic person to turn to for advice and help.
- Longer-term development in human resources needs the input of a knowledgeable expert to cover effective training, employee relations and job design issues.

The *disadvantages* of employing a specialist are as follows:

- If you recruit from outside (and you probably will to bring in human resources expertise and a qualification), the person will need to adapt to the normal culture of the small organisation – quick changes in direction, small budgets and lack of promotion opportunity. It is not always easy to find such a person.

- The candidate must have some experience in a small organisation to see what works well and what does not. Ideas and innovations that have been successful in a large organisation do not always translate into a small company culture.
- The additional cost has to be weighed against the benefits. It can be regarded as another 'unproductive overhead' unless the person proves his or her value quickly. It is possible to outsource most of your human resource activities to a human resource consultancy on a flexible contract, which may be cheaper.

References

Adair, J (1997) *Leadership Skills*, IPD, London

Holbeche, L (1998) *Managing Employees in Lean Organisations*, Butterworth-Heinemann, Oxford

Martin, P and Nicols, J (1987) *Creating a Committed Workforce*, IPM, London

Trapp, R (2000) The Society of Fabric, *People Management*, 12 October, pp 36–37

Watkin, C (2001) How to improve organisational climate, *People Management*, 28 June, pp 52–53

Further information

Chris Watkin can be contacted at chris_watkin@haygroup.com.

2 Getting the best people

Small organisations are not particularly imaginative when it comes to attracting, motivating and retaining staff, as a 2001 MORI survey, 'People management in growing companies', showed. The response showed that organisations believed that finding and keeping staff was as important as attracting and retaining customers but considered that pay was the overriding factor in achieving this. Little thought was given to job satisfaction, employee involvement or the company's external image.

So how do we go about getting the right people? There are two stages here. Firstly, we must carefully define the group of people that we want: the numbers, the skills, the attributes and competencies, and the timing. In modern parlance, this is called 'human resource planning'. Secondly, we have to go out and find the people. We need to trawl the market sources, short-list the possible candidates and then select appropriately.

Human resource planning

In general, most organisations apply 95 per cent or more of their time to the second of these with little or insufficient consideration to the first part. Sadly, logic demands that the first of these is by far the most important. Unless you have a clear picture of both your short- and long-term requirements, you may finish up with an unstable group of employees who have a mixed bag of skills and personalities that neither gel together into a team nor provide the required responses to customer demands.

As part of the business plan, all organisations should have a clear vision *of how many people should be employed over the year*. This will take into account whether the organisation is growing or static, or whether cutbacks are necessary. A simple calculation, taking previous staff turnover into account, will give a good indication of the recruitment requirements for the year. An example of a business planning a 20 per cent growth plus a 5 per cent productivity improvement would be:

Existing staff number		200	200
Less average annual staff turnover – 25 per cent		(50)	
Number without recruitment	(a)	150	
Business growth rate of 20 per cent			40
Less productivity gain of 5 per cent			(10)
Total required	(b)		230

The difference between (b) and (a) is the staff to be recruited: 230 – 150 = 80 staff.

The next part of the planning is to take into account the skills and competencies required of all the staff to meet the business plan:

- An *analysis of training needs* may be useful here, and this is explained in Chapter 4.
- You may want your workforce to adopt skills and working practices that make them, and the organisation, much more *flexible*, and ways this can be done are shown in Chapter 3.
- You may decide to take *major initiatives in areas such as quality, customer care or better communications*, and you will need to enhance the skills of employees in these areas.
- Finally, you may want the organisation to work better together through enhancing *team working*.

Teams may have immense individual talent, and some people may have the skills to make them appear bargain buys, but there are endless examples of how the results can be disappointing without an underlying comprehensive team planning policy. The benefits of effective team working are shown in Chapter 3.

With a clear, simple but flexible HR plan, we can now consider the practical processes involved in the recruitment and selection process.

Recruitment

Firstly, we must consider: *what are we trying to achieve*? The selection process is all about trying to be good at predicting the future. We are trying to bring somebody into the organisation who will fit in, perform well and stay for at least a reasonable period. Despite all the attempted developments of recent years to make the selection process more scientific, most employers still take this important business decision on the basis of a short précis of a person's life and a 45-minute discussion. It certainly is an important decision. If you get it wrong, it can be very costly. Let us take a real example of recruiting a salesperson that proved unsuccessful by the end of the first year. The costs were calculated as follows:

Salary cost	£25,000
Car, pension and benefits	7,000
Recruitment costs (advertising, agency, etc)	3,000
Training costs	1,000
Management costs (recruitment, training, monitoring, mentoring, motivating, etc)	2,000
Rectifying errors (rebates, cancelled sales, etc)	10,000
Total costs	48,000
Less estimated value added by salesperson over the year	15,000
Real costs	£36,000

22 Managing people in a small business

Remarkably, there are still managers, owners of small businesses even, who recruit on the basis of 'Well, we will give them a try and if it doesn't work out, we will get rid of them.' That attitude is like standing in a shower, tearing up £10 notes.

So, it is vital we should do what we can, within reasonable time and costs, to get the decision right. Some interesting research has shown that some techniques get better results than others in predicting success. Figure 2.1 shows a summary.

1.0	Perfect prediction	
0.9		
0.8		
0.7		
0.6	Assessment centres – promotion	0.68
	Structured interviews	0.62
	Work samples	0.55
0.5	Ability tests	0.54
0.4	Assessment centres – performance	0.44
	Personality tests	0.38
0.3	Unstructured interviews	0.31
0.2		
0.1	References	0.11
0	Astrology	0.0
	Graphology	0.0

(Source: Anderson and Shackleton, 1994)

Figure 2.1 Predictions of success in recruiting

It can be seen that few techniques achieve even a 50 per cent success rate but some are much better than others. For example, let us dispose at this early stage of astrology and graphology. Although these are used

Getting the best people **23**

fairly extensively in France and a few other countries, this research indicated that you might just as well toss a coin for the success they achieved.

We will look more closely at some of the techniques in this chapter. There are a number of steps we will look at in turn:

- establishing if a vacancy really exists;
- defining the details of the vacancy;
- attracting the applicants;
- short-listing;
- interviewing;
- testing;
- references;
- making offers.

Establishing whether a vacancy exists

Vacancies occur essentially for two reasons. Either it is because of the organisation's growth and development (expansion into new products or areas or winning new contracts) or because an existing job incumbent has left the post. Before leaping into the recruitment process, it is well worth considering the alternatives:

- *Can the work be outsourced competitively?* If certain work is not a core part of the business, then outsourcing it can both save money and reduce management time.
- *Can the work be reorganised?* Is it possible to replace the post by separating different parts of the work, eliminating those that are unnecessary and farming out the rest within the department or around other departments? It is possible to consider the concept of job enrichment here. For example, when a supervisor leaves, do not replace him or her but, instead, extend the work of existing employees to cover more responsibility and decision taking. This is not only more efficient but it may provide

employees with more challenge and satisfaction in their work. There are pay implications here, of course, as employees will generally not be very willing to take on these extra duties without an increased reward but paying seven or eight staff a 5 per cent increase still shows a substantial cost saving overall on top of the recruitment costs saved. There is more on work design and empowerment in Chapter 3.

- *Can the hours be reorganised?* If the work outlook is uncertain, it is worth considering covering the work through overtime until the position is clearer, or employing somebody on a part-time basis, which allows a degree of flexibility should the volume of work increase in the future. Overtime, however, can be expensive and the culture of long hours is rarely successful in the long run.
- *Can the work be automated?* There have been massive strides in office automation in recent years, following on from those achieved in manufacturing and logistics. Although it is seldom possible to replace one employee through mechanisation, the arrival of a vacancy can provide an opportunity for a total rethink of the work structure and processes.
- *Finally, does the position add any value anyway?* It is still surprising how many jobs exist, even in smaller organisations, where the value of the work has never been seriously questioned. This should happen whenever any vacancy arises.

Defining the vacancy

The essential elements of vacancy definition are a **job description**, setting out what duties and objectives are involved in the job, and a **person specification**, which clarifies the skills, competencies and attributes required from the successful job holder.

Job descriptions can take two main forms. They can be task-oriented or accountability-oriented. Examples of these are shown in the boxes on the next two pages.

Task-oriented job description

Job Title	Secretary, Sales Office
Reports to	Sales Office Manager
Location	Head Office
Hours	Full time

Summary of position

To carry out secretarial duties, including word processing of letters and sales reports, telephone work, filing, essential hospitality and general assistance with meetings.

Main activities

1. To produce sales reports from information provided by the regional sales teams.
2. To word-process letters, circulars, etc for the sales managers and supervisors.
3. To deal with essential e-mail circulation to sales staff.
4. To handle telephone queries relating to the sales report and commission issues.
5. To file documents, letters and reports and any other items for the department.
6. To help with hospitality at times of conferences and weekly meetings.
7. To take minutes of sales meetings and help initiate any action pending from these meetings with the appropriate manager.
8. To carry out any other necessary duties associated with the sales office.

Accountability-oriented job description

Job Title	Senior Library Assistant
Reports to	Senior Librarian
Location	Main Library
Hours	Total of 38 per week on shift rota basis

Main accountability

To implement library procedures in respect of book ordering, cataloguing and loans within the appropriate time span and within costs allocated.

Key result areas (extracts)

1. *Book ordering.* To place orders for books as requested, to check their arrival within the agreed time span, to complete the certificate and pass all documentation to the senior librarian to authorise payment within three days.
2. *Cataloguing.* To ensure that books delivered are catalogued correctly and on the shelves within eight working days.
3. *Library loans.* To handle applications for, and safe return of, all inter-library loans within the stipulated time period. To chase up any non-returned books if more than two days overdue, recording accurately all transactions.

Of these two, the accountability-oriented form is far preferable. Although what employees do in their work is important, it is what they are accountable for and what they achieve that is crucial. Remember that the job description is one of the first detailed items that a candidate will see, so it is worth setting those accountabilities out at the earliest stage.

It is not necessary to include every single item of the work or to keep job descriptions rigidly up to date because they are not, in themselves, legal documents. They only indicate the nature of the contractual relationship, and employees are expected to carry out *any* work, within reason, over and above anything detailed in the description. However, it is both good practice and helpful in building a good degree of mutual trust if descriptions resemble the essence of the work to be carried out, and they should certainly be updated when a vacancy occurs. They can also play a part if an employee takes the organisation to a tribunal. Finally, they are useful in the performance management process and in establishing training requirements, both of which are dealt with in the next two chapters.

At this stage, you will need to clarify the terms and conditions of the position, including the salary, hours, holidays and benefits. Do not follow the course of action of 'seeing what salary the best candidate is asking for'. This will lead to confusion in your salary structure and may involve a tendency to discrimination. A further discussion of salary issues takes place in Chapter 5.

Person specifications inform potential candidates of the traits and characteristics required for the job. They should act as a self-selecting process, reducing the number of unsuitable candidates. We will see that they should be an essential feature in the short-listing process in that candidates can be measured against the specification to see which ones should be taken forward to the next stage. Without a person specification, the short-listing becomes much more arbitrary.

Until the advent of equal opportunity legislation, specifications used to include factors such as 'physical make-up', 'interests' and 'circumstances'. Today, these factors could be considered discriminatory. Selecting on the ability of a candidate to relocate or work extended shifts has recently led to successful tribunal cases from female candidates, and most physical requirements (height or weight) have been abandoned.

Today, the specification should be centred on the qualifications, experience, skills and competencies that the organisation considers necessary for the successful candidate to be able to do the job well. A typical example is shown in Table 2.1.

Attracting the applicants

Now we have defined the job and clarified the type of person we are looking for, we can start the search for the right person.

An internal candidate may be an unlikely solution, especially in a small organisation where all the talent is well known, but this solution has numerous advantages:

Table 2.1 Person specification – Employment Agency Branch Manager

Requirement	Essential	Desirable
Education and qualifications	– educated to A-level standard	– good grades in English and maths
Work experience	– two to three years' experience in a supervisory role within a customer service or sales environment	– agency experience – sales experience – managerial experience
Abilities	– good verbal communication – managerial skills – analytical skills – planning and organising skills – computer literate	– good written and numerical skills – good business acumen
Motivation	– self-motivated – competitive – results-oriented – prepared to invest in staff development	– desires career advancement – ambitious
Personality	– socially confident in all situations – empathetic – persuasive – able to cope under pressure – adaptable – creative and innovative	– diplomatic – able to direct and control others

- The employee knows the organisation, its culture and its products.
- There are no expensive recruiting costs involved.
- It sends a loud message to the workforce that promotion and progression are encouraged.
- There are few delays in the process, and adjustments should take less time.
- From an employee's viewpoint, there are probably fewer risks involved than in moving to another organisation.

However, let us assume that there are no suitable internal candidates and that there is a belief that new blood is welcome, bringing a wider variety of skills and experiences into the organisation. The choice now is whether to jump in and advertise directly or whether to seek help from a third party.

Third parties come in the following forms:

- *recruitment agencies*, which will handle the entire recruitment process up to short-listing, providing candidates from their own sources or advertising on your behalf;
- *advertising agencies*, which help devise a single advertisement or complete campaign and advise on the advertising media;
- *executive search agencies* (sometimes known as 'headhunters'), which will search for senior staff on your behalf, approaching suitable candidates directly, often with considerable secrecy;
- *Job Centres*, which can give energetic support, especially if the organisation is either moving into the area or has an expansion programme with multiple vacancies, particularly at operative or clerical and administrative level.

They each have a number of advantages and disadvantages, as shown in Table 2.2.

For many smaller organisations it is so much easier for a manager to pick up a telephone and ring the agencies than go through the sometimes complex process of designing and placing advertisements and handling the response. In many large cities, where the local

Table 2.2 Use of third parties

Third Party	Advantages	Disadvantages
Recruitment agencies	– Can provide candidates at speed using their database. – Save considerable time on dealing with large numbers of applications. – Some specialist agencies have a very good knowledge of the vacancy market. This applies to accounting and IT staff especially.	– Charge a fee from 10% to 20% depending on level of vacancy and competitive situation. – May not provide appropriate candidates especially if they have not been briefed adequately – Staff recruited through agencies have a tendency to move on more quickly. Although the agency that provided them cannot supply them with further job details for ethical reasons, they are almost certainly bound to be on the books of other agencies, which are under no such restriction.
Advertising agencies	– Experts in copywriting, especially with eye-catching headlines, use of colour and house style. – Provide high-quality artwork, which the media cannot usually provide. – Know the media options well with up-to-date prices.	– Charge fees for the service although less than may be expected as they negotiate discounts on the actual advertisement space with the media concerned. – May persuade you to spend more on the advertisement than you originally intended.
Executive search	– When secrecy is important for internal reasons, such as a restructuring, they are discreet agents.	– They charge high fees, from 25% to 50% of the first-year salary. Some of the fees are chargeable

Getting the best people **31**

		even when the appointment is not made. – They can be of variable quality so it is important to use one referred to you who is of high reputation.
	– They know where to look in a very limited market, such as for a head of research for a pharmaceutical company. – They save on all the time and effort involved in responding to advertisements.	
Job centres	– Central and convenient places for applicants to use providing a high response rate. – They offer a venue for mass interviewing. – They usually do not charge a fee.	– No sifting takes place so much of the response can be unsuitable. – Response can be weighted towards the unemployed rather than a wider market place.

newspapers are limited in number, often owned by the same company, and where the advertising rates are high, it makes sense to stick with agencies.

Here are a few common-sense suggestions on dealing with agencies:

- Build up a relationship with one that can get to know your business, have some idea of your culture (Is it fun to work there? Are the staff generally younger or older? Are the working conditions good?) and will respond quickly and efficiently to your needs.
- Do not forget to try to insist on a reduced commission, especially if the volume of work is rising.
- A national name, such as Blue Arrow or Manpower, will tend to provide you with a consistent quality service, but a more aggressive local newcomer can provide the edge on price and response time.
- Take care to clarify their detailed terms and conditions. Ask if they make separate charges for advertising costs. Find out the charging arrangements for employees who do not stay more than a few weeks. Most agencies have a sliding scale of rebate for

32 Managing people in a small business

employees who stay less than six months. For example, Enterprise Personnel, a small agency working out of Biggleswade and Luton, give 100 per cent rebate if the employee stays less than two weeks, scaling down to 25 per cent if the employee leaves between six and eight weeks.

- Make sure you are aware of the law in respect of employees who have been working for you on a temporary basis, who were provided by an agency and to whom you have offered permanent employment. In 2001, the government proposed a new law that would stop any agency fee being charged when a temporary worker takes up permanent employment *eight weeks* after the original hiring has finished.

Agencies, however, remain costly. Assuming a 15 per cent fee, the costs for taking on two clerks at £12,000 equals £3,600. A very reasonable advertisement can be bought in many media for considerably less than this. It may be worth while to test the response of a dedicated advertisement occasionally or even regularly.

Advertising

We shall look at a few general issues first, then move on to designing an advert and finally touch on some innovative technical advances linked to the Internet.

When advertising for most staff, you will generally be using the local paper. For more senior or specialist staff, however, the local paper will simply not have a sufficiently wide circulation to attract enough suitable candidates. Here, it may be more appropriate to use the regional or national press or specialist publications. Table 2.3 gives some possible suggestions on media to use and examples of costs in 2001.

These are spot rates, and discounts can be negotiated. It is essential that these costly advertisements are carefully designed with high-quality artwork, and you are extremely unlikely to have the in-house resources to cope with this. Desktop publishing has come a long way

Table 2.3 Examples of media and costs

Vacancy	Possible Media	Mid-2001 Costs
Computer Programmer	*Daily Telegraph* – display	£142 per single column/cm
Marketing Director	*Marketing Week*	£1,140 for quarter page
Manager – Housing Association	*Guardian* – Wednesday	£50 per single column/cm
Human Resources Manager	*People Management*	£3,900 for quarter page, full colour

but the artwork offered is still very limited and few individuals have the creative ability to blend design, text and artwork for a one-off advert. As the audience you are trying to reach is a critical one, it is best to leave this work to the experts, namely an advertising agency. They will come up with designs that take your specific needs into account. They may say that this design work is free but there is often a 'production' charge each time the advertisement is published. You need to clarify this with the agency beforehand because the charges can add up. You have to recognise that the type of people you are recruiting do not come cheap, and the advertising cost is a relatively small proportion of their annual salary.

For advertisements in the local newspapers, you have a choice as to whether to design your own advertisements or simply provide the copy (and perhaps a logo) to the newspaper and let them set the advert out themselves. They do not charge for this service but the results are often hit and miss, depending who is given the work and how much time that person has. It is preferable to take charge yourself as long as you have somebody who can master some basic DTP operations. This does allow you time to consider various text drafts and to play around with borders, the position of the logo and any basic artwork, as well as the size and general appearance of the advert.

Designing an advertisement

Are there any hard-and-fast rules in drawing up an advert? There are certainly three key objectives of a good advertisement that you should always keep in mind:

- It must attract attention.
- It must create and maintain interest.
- It must stimulate action.

We shall look at each of these in turn.

You must **attract attention** to compete successfully with other job advertisements in the media. This can be achieved by:

- using bold and unusual headlines that catch the eye (see the box below for examples);
- clearly displaying the job title, salary and location;
- using an effective illustration or striking artwork (see Figure 2.2 for an example);
- using full or part colour, although there are cost extras involved here;
- agreeing with the publisher a prominent location of the advertisement, again with a supplementary cost.

Bold and unusual headlines

Opportuni   Responsibili   Flexibili

To get what you want, just add tea
(Advertisement by the Tetley Group)

'It was the day my grandmother exploded'
(Advertisement for retail staff for Books Etc)

Rise and Shine
(Advertisement for graduates for Cambridge City Council)

A further point on salary: all the research in this area indicates that the inclusion of salary in the advert increases the quality of the response. Without a salary, many applicants are put off, as they are unsure whether they are wasting their time, while others with wrong salary expectations will waste their time and yours with an application. In any case, what have you got to hide? It is almost impossible to keep salaries secret in the workplace today, and those who attempt to do so usually come unstuck. You can keep some of your options open by following any of these examples:

- Salary in the range of £16,000 to £18,000.
- Salary up to £18,000.
- Salary OTE £25,000. (This is where bonuses are normally added to the basic salary, relating to satisfactory performance in a sales or commercial environment, with OTE standing for 'on-target earnings'.)

If a company car goes with the job, then it is essential to insert that in the advert.

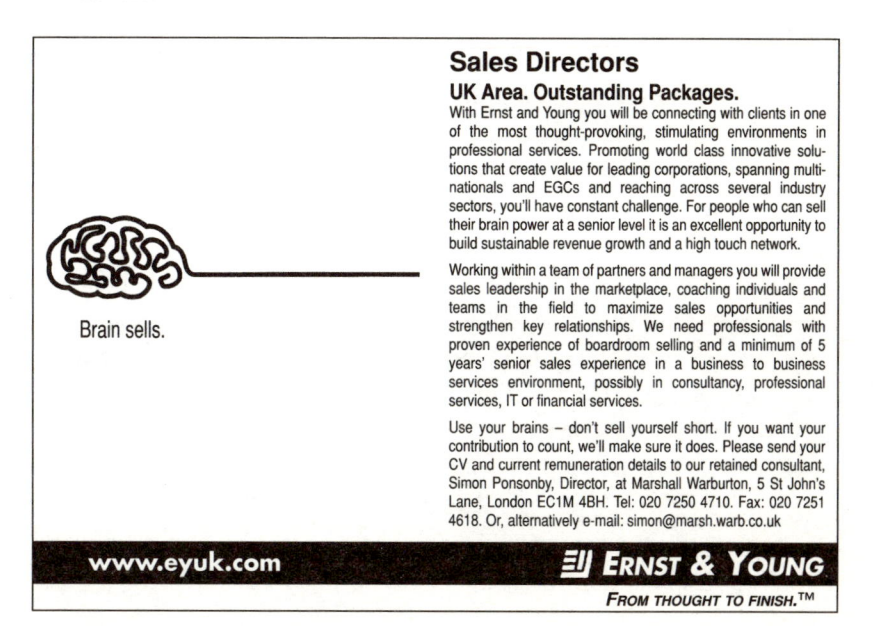

Brain sells.

www.eyuk.com

Sales Directors

UK Area. Outstanding Packages.

With Ernst and Young you will be connecting with clients in one of the most thought-provoking, stimulating environments in professional services. Promoting world class innovative solutions that create value for leading corporations, spanning multi-nationals and EGCs and reaching across several industry sectors, you'll have constant challenge. For people who can sell their brain power at a senior level it is an excellent opportunity to build sustainable revenue growth and a high touch network.

Working within a team of partners and managers you will provide sales leadership in the marketplace, coaching individuals and teams in the field to maximize sales opportunities and strengthen key relationships. We need professionals with proven experience of boardroom selling and a minimum of 5 years' senior sales experience in a business to business services environment, possibly in consultancy, professional services, IT or financial services.

Use your brains – don't sell yourself short. If you want your contribution to count, we'll make sure it does. Please send your CV and current remuneration details to our retained consultant, Simon Ponsonby, Director, at Marshall Warburton, 5 St John's Lane, London EC1M 4BH. Tel: 020 7250 4710. Fax: 020 7251 4618. Or, alternatively e-mail: simon@marsh.warb.co.uk

ERNST & YOUNG
FROM THOUGHT TO FINISH.™

Figure 2.2 Eye-catching artwork

It is not enough to grab the passing attention, however. That **interest has to be maintained**, so the advert has to communicate accurate information about the job, the company, the rewards, the nature of the job and the type of person wanted, and do all this in an interesting and attractive way. It needs to include the following:

- *A very brief introduction to the organisation*, such as:
    - Oyster, the leading company in waste management in the Midlands.
    - Georgetown is a fast-growing computer consultancy specialising in networking solutions.
    - GTS is a young but highly influential company providing services to energy markets.
- *A brief description of the position*, clarifying what is actually involved in the job. It is a fine judgement to put in sufficient to make the position attractive without costing too much. Here are some better examples:
    - Leading a team of five engineers and analysts in the design and testing of manufacturing software to tight deadlines.
    - You will work with a range of community groups to support and develop community-led regeneration initiatives.
    - You will manage a research project to assess the sports development impact of the 2002 Commonwealth Games and contribute to the team's review of ethical policies and procedures in national governing bodies of sport.
- *Details of what will make up the successful candidate*. This will be essentially extracted from the person specification, and will include skills, qualifications, experience and personal attributes. An example, for a Building Quality Control Inspector, is shown in the box opposite.
- *Other crucial information*, which might include attractive benefits, such as a relocation package, flexible hours and subsidised mortgages, and caveats, such as a non-smoking working environment.

> ### Building Quality Control Inspector
> - A sound practical knowledge of current building techniques/requirements in the construction of new flats and houses.
> - An HND or equivalent in building and construction with at least three years' experience in the trade.
> - The ability to communicate effectively with site management, subcontractors and, most importantly, our purchasers as part of our customer care scheme.
> - The confidence to make important decisions relating to quality control in order to achieve a first-class product and to deal effectively with after-sales enquiries.
> - A clean driving licence.

The final part is to **stimulate action** – the message must be sufficiently strong for potential applicants to read it to the end and then make the time and effort to respond in the required way. Essentially, the choice is between getting applicants to send in their CV or for them to telephone or e-mail for a job information pack, which would include an application form. The pack would also include the job description, person specification and some information about the organisation, such as a company brochure.

There are evenly balanced arguments between asking for candidates' CVs and using application forms. Applicants generally prefer simply to send in their CVs with a covering letter, believing that all the relevant information is included. They may choose to make an application to organisations that make an application easier rather than one that insists on the laborious process of completing a long application form.

From the organisation's viewpoint, however, it may be preferable to insist on an application form because it is simpler to select a short list from a set of identical application forms. CVs may leave out negative areas such as no current driving licence or dismissal from previous employment. Applicants may also leave out their age or not put their experience in chronological order, which could hide a crucial time gap. In fact, there is research evidence that around 25 per cent of CVs have significant lies or omissions. If candidates are not prepared to complete an application form then they show little commitment to the application.

A compromise is to ask initially for CVs, on which a short-listing decision can generally be taken quickly, but then ask candidates invited for interview to bring along with them a completed application form. This form could then clear up any areas of doubt or omission.

It is sometimes useful to specify the name of a person on the advertisement who can be telephoned for an informal discussion. If there are a number of vacancies, then it is an option to consider organising an open day at a local hotel to which applicants simply turn up with their CVs.

There is also a technological development that can combine applications and screening at the same time, although it is costly to set up and therefore likely to be inappropriate for most smaller companies. This is where applicants call a freephone number and are given a unique identification number that sets up a file for them. Candidates then have to answer a number of multiple-choice questions using the telephone keypad. When this is finished, the system calculates candidates' scores and, if they are high enough, organises interview times and sends out application forms.

Application forms

The purpose of an application form is to provide full, relevant and consistent information on which to base decisions on recruitment and selection. It should also be designed to be user-friendly, with a clear and simple layout and unambiguous questions, and it should not be too lengthy. That is a lot to ask, and most application forms fail miserably in that they are badly laid out and far too long.

Will one form be sufficient for the organisation? For a straightforward clerical position, the information required in general is essentially factual – personal details, education, qualifications and work experience are usually sufficient. This can be achieved in a two-page form. An example is given in Figure 2.3 – a two-page form spread over three pages.

COMPANY NAME – LOGO etc. ....

APPLICATION FOR EMPLOYMENT

Job applied for   Full-time........ Part-time........

PERSONAL DETAILS

Name.. Telephone.............................
Address ....
....
.... Post code ....
Date of birth .... Current driving licence?   Yes/No
Details of any current endorsements
....
....
....
Do you need a work permit to be employed in the UK?
....
Have you worked for this company before?   Yes/No
If yes, please give details.

Have you had any criminal convictions?   Yes/No
If yes, please give details.

EDUCATION AND TRAINING

Secondary school   From   To   Examinations taken   Results with grades

College

Other educational establishment

Figure 2.3   Application form

Details of any short courses taken or skills achieved

Year	Course provider	Length of training	Subject

EMPLOYMENT HISTORY

Please start from your current job and work backwards

Employer	From	to	Job title	Brief job description	Final salary	Reason for leaving

THE CONTRIBUTION YOU CAN MAKE

Please use this space to write anything that would help your application. For example, indicate any special skills that you would bring to this job, any previous experience that you think is especially relevant and any special interests that you have. You may wish to indicate any achievements at work or outside the workplace.

Are you willing to work Night shift......... Away from home......... Abroad.........

Figure 2.3 *continued*

YOUR HEALTH

Please indicate your current general state of health (tick)
Excellent......... Good......... Satisfactory......... Poor.........

Give details of any handicap or impediment that the company should be aware of and would need to make adjustments for in the workplace.

Please give details of any absences from work due to illness over the last two years.

I confirm that the information I have given is true and complete in all respects. I understand that I may be asked to give details of references at interview. Should any information be found to be false or incorrect in any way, then any offer of employment will be voided.

Signed .... Date.......................................

TO BE COMPLETED BY INTERVIEWER

Interviewed by .... On ....

Interviewer's comments

References provided

Figure 2.3 *continued*

For more senior positions, it is usually necessary to allow applicants to reflect on their experience to date, explain their motives and ambitions and explain why they believe they can match the requirements of the advertised post. This usually necessitates a four-page form.

Having two forms can create some confusion, however, especially when jobs are on the border of seniority. Keeping to one long form, however, means requiring all applicants to plough through the sections on motives, ambitions and justifying their applications, which can well put off a number of good applicants. On balance, two forms are the best solution, even for a small organisation.

Given the developments in equal opportunities, it is difficult to justify personal questions, such as those about marital status and number of children. These should be avoided.

A few don'ts on advertising

- Don't insert unnecessary copy such as:
  - 'Grants is a subsidiary of RYE Engineering.' Who cares?
  - 'The position requires a good standard of timekeeping.' Will this put off a poor timekeeper?
- Don't detail minor benefits, such as life assurance or sickness schemes. In reality, nobody ever joined an organisation for these benefits. If they are interested, they can always ask at interview.
- Don't try to cram too much information in – you only need to attract enough attention to get applicants interested enough to apply. You cannot hope to get in everything you want.
- Make sure the type is large-enough size – small type looks penny-pinching.
- Try to ensure the advert fits the image you want to portray – an advert for a charity would be simple and to the point while one for a small consultancy should be creative, even flamboyant.

Alternatives to advertising

There are other traditional methods of attracting new staff that can be used alongside or instead of newspaper advertising, including word of mouth, approaching previous applicants and mail-shots. They can be very effective but should be used with care, as indicated in Table 2.4.

Do not forget other low-cost stalwarts such as vacancy noticeboards outside your site or even putting postcards in local shops. They may not attract hundreds but you may find a few local staff this way. Do make sure your receptionist knows about these vacancies and how to deal with them, for example by having vacancy packs (or at least an application form) available to random callers.

High-tech recruitment

Web-based recruitment is used today by IT organisations and most large companies. It is especially suitable for large-scale recruitment, such as graduate entry, but can be used just as effectively for one-off positions. Click on to any household name and you are likely to find a 'positions vacant' icon that leads to descriptions of the positions currently on offer and an invitation to complete the online application.

This facility is not too difficult to set up and is easy to use, with electronic responses to the applicants being very speedy. Your Web site development software consultant will organise it. Applications received this way can be short-listed quite easily (see later). The basic problems are threefold. Firstly, most potential applicants will not know where to look for small company vacancies, so the hit rate could be small. Secondly, applications are not so timely as those in response to an advertisement. That is why the medium is good for ongoing recruitment in an expanding organisation, especially for IT, high-tech and finance positions, or for graduate recruitment, where you recruit throughout the year for one starting date. Thirdly, it is highly important to keep the site up to date, and experience shows that this rarely happens in practice.

That is not to write off such facilities. Some organisations have been pleasantly surprised by applications from customers using the online service, who just happened to look at the site through curiosity after completing a purchase. It very much depends on the nature of your product or services, how well known your name is and the nature of your customers and others who can use your Web site.

Table 2.4 Alternatives or additions to newspaper/magazine advertising

	Advantages	**Hazards and Difficulties Encountered**
Word of mouth, including relatives	– Very cheap and simple. – Can be bolstered by offering a bonus to a member of staff who introduces a successful applicant. – Likely that the applicant will have a reasonable knowledge of the organisation and the job. – Should fit easily into the culture and ways of the organisation. – No need to plough through a large response.	– If used as a sole method of recruitment, then the staff will only come from a narrow range. – Outside applicants may not know about opportunities so the source is limited. – Can be, and has been, regarded as a discriminatory approach in practice, as females or males and ethnic minorities can be excluded from the process in a predominantly white, single-sex organisational environment.
Approaching previous applicants	– Very cheap and simple. – Applicants may already have been interviewed but just missed being selected on the last occasion so an appointment can be swift.	– The post and its conditions may have changed since the applicant applied. – The applicant may no longer be interested, having been suited elsewhere. – It is necessary to maintain an effective database of such applicants with a time cut-off point.
Local mail-shot through commercial leaflet distributor	– Can be targeted at specific areas in the locality that are convenient for travel and have produced quality applicants in the past. – Relatively low cost.	– Cannot be certain of 100% delivery rate. – Not necessarily thought of highly by potential applicants.

An alternative, of course, is to make use of an independent recruitment site such as www.monster.co.uk or www.stepstone.co.uk from which responses will be channelled directly to your site. Stepstone claims to have over 10,000 jobs advertised at one time while Monster believes it has over 9 million job seekers who surf its site. Most jobs are advertised for 60 days, and clear instructions are given on how to design the advertisement you want. Fees vary considerably from month to month so you will need to go to the sites to find out the applicable costs.

Shortlisting

Shortlisting involves reducing the number of applications received to an appropriate-sized list of candidates to be invited for interview. The correct process here is to compare candidates to the person specification. Those who do not meet the *essential* requirements specified should be discarded for the position (although they may be considered for other vacancies). You must be quite sure here that you do not reject on discriminatory grounds, such as sex, marriage, disability or age (more details of this in Chapter 7).

Those who have not been discarded will make up a shorter list. Perhaps the pile has come down to a manageable interview list, say between four and seven for each vacancy. If you have the happy situation where the numbers still exceed that total, you will then have to exercise an *inclusion* process, which involves setting up a scoring process. It might look like this:

Experience	up to 20 points
Key skills	up to 20 points
Qualifications	up to 10 points
Location	up to 5 points
Others	5 points
Total	60 points

It is best for two people to carry out the actual scoring independently and then compare any discrepancies. The top scoring five or six candidates are then invited to interview. It may appear a long-winded process but experience indicates that this part of the process actually takes little time, and it is crucial to get it right. Moreover, organisations have been increasingly caught out in tribunal cases where they have claims from applicants of having been excluded on the grounds of sex or race. Use of this method is usually a sufficient defence, if it has been carried out properly.

A few organisations have adopted screening by telephone or through the Internet. Here the applicant is asked a series of multiple-choice questions to which they respond by using the telephone keypad or keying in a numbered response. The questions generally relate to applicants' experience or skills although some are behavioural questions asking applicants to choose the correct solution to, say, a customer complaint. On the basis of their answers, the system will select or reject each applicant. It will then automatically fix an interview time for those selected, and send out further details. An even more sophisticated system is the automated screening of CVs and application forms, which can rank candidates on skills, experience, etc. Such a system is clearly expensive to set up so rarely suitable for small organisations, except those in the high-tech field.

Interviewing

The interview has been the standard form of selection for hundreds of years. It has survived as the main method of selection because it is relatively low-cost and can be carried out by anybody, with or without training, and because an exchange of views and information is essential before agreement is reached over any job. Most interviewers are confident that they possess an inherent skill but few correctly hold this belief. Here is a selection of ways that interviewers often get it wrong:

- *They take a decision intuitively.* The 'I have a gut feel about this person and I do not need to look at any objective evidence' school of interviewing has numerous adherents. This is generally based on the experience of one past success that has eradicated the memory of the numerous failures obtained through this method.
- *They prefer candidates who are like themselves.* Again, research evidence shows that most interviewers give higher ratings to candidates who have similar traits, interests and approaches to themselves, rather than matching the candidate against the person specification.
- *They stereotype candidates.* Despite the illegality of judging candidates on the basis of their sex, race or age, interviewers, often unknowingly, allow these views to cloud their judgements.
- *They take instant decisions.* Studies show that the average length of time between a candidate entering the interview room and a decision being made is just under four minutes. Interviewers jump to conclusions rather than taking a cool and collected look at interviewees' skills and experience against the job requirements.
- *They talk too much.* An interviewer should be talking for about 20 per cent of the time and listening for the remaining 80 per cent. Only by listening can an interviewer make the necessary judgements. Of course, the job should be 'sold' and questions should be answered but this can be done in that 20 per cent time frame.
- *They fail to probe sufficiently.* Chiefly because they talk too much, they do not take enough time to probe carefully an employee's experiences and attitudes. It is vital to ensure that a candidate's stories 'add up' and that no skeletons remain in the closet. Is there a gap in the CV? Why did the interviewee leave the job when he or she seemed to be doing so well? Why did the interviewee have difficulty working for his or her last manager? Are there any hesitations in responses to facts or opinions asked for?

- *They select under pressure.* Interviewers are aware that a further delay will ensue if a candidate cannot be found from the interview list so they often reach a state of panic and upgrade what they see as the best candidate even when that person has a number of crucial faults and does not meet the specification.
- *They cannot take on board all the information provided.* Carrying out an interview is far more difficult than it seems. Interviewers have to think where they are going, listen carefully to answers and remember key details, and most brains simply cannot cope with this. That is why a single interviewer should rarely take the decision alone.
- *They give no structure to the interview.* Far too many interviews are too informal and discursive, switching from job requirements to candidate skills, mixed in with anecdotal evidence from both parties. We shall look at the format of a structured interview shortly, as having a formal structure is key to success.
- *They are badly organised.* They may be late starting or finishing, they may allow interruptions, they may lose the candidate's CV, they may forget about expenses or they may be simply rude – all of which may terminally put off the candidate from accepting any offer from the organisation.

So what do you need to do to get the interviewing process right? A few pointers are given in the following sections.

Have two people involved in the interviewing process

One person alone may be satisfactory for initial interviews but inadvisable as the lone decision taker. The candidates may be rather more likely to open up and respond to careful probing, but few interviewers will be likely to be able to listen to the answers, take notes and think of the next question at the same time. In recent times, moreover, there have been a series of tribunals where unsuccessful applicants have made accusations of racial or sexual bias, which, with only one interviewer present, have been difficult to rebut. A panel interview (more than two people) is unwieldy, costly and logistically difficult to arrange. Two people, including the immediate manager of the successful candidate, can generally do the job best.

Prepare properly

This includes the following:

- The two interviewers should work out how the interview will be approached – who is to lead on questions in which areas and the system of note taking.
- The application form/CV should have been examined carefully with any missing areas noted so questions can be mooted in these areas.
- The schedule of interviews should be realistic. Few interviews take less than 30 minutes and those for sales, technical, supervisory or management should be allocated at least 45 minutes. Some will take longer, but usually one candidate cancels at the last minute, which generally evens up the schedule. You should not plan to see more than five candidates in one day. It is tiring, and even the best interviewers tend to get them mixed up if that number is exceeded.
- In terms of identifying the candidates, you may ask them to include a passport-sized photo with their application or you can arrange to take a quick photo before the interview starts. Neither is wholly satisfactory from the candidate's viewpoint and some may regard this as having the potential for discrimination, but it does help the interviewers in taking their final decisions.
- The room should be prepared, and it should be ensured that there will be no interruptions. An informal setting is best rather than questions across desks. A place for candidates to wait should be fixed.
- You should try to ensure that the best candidate on paper is seen first. This gives you a good benchmark with which to compare the remaining candidates.

- The interviewers should agree a system of rating each candidate, based on the person specification, similar to that carried out for short-listing.

Make sure the interview is structured

Figure 2.1 at the start of the chapter shows that structured interviews have a far higher predictive success than unstructured ones. Structuring means a planned, logical process of questions that tease out the required answers. They are used in a similar, if not identical, fashion for each candidate, and it makes the comparison of candidates so much easier. There are two aspects to this process.

Firstly, the *order* of questions should be agreed. The normal method is to take each position that the candidate has held, starting from the existing or last one, and work backwards over the previous three or four. (Three or four is usually sufficient.) For each position, you need to establish carefully the facts of the job (what the candidate did, for how long, what career progression took place, etc) and then establish how this experience matches that required for the vacancy and how the person matches the specification. You will also need to try to measure the success of the candidate in these positions and the reasons for the change of job. You may wish to include training and qualifications achieved in each job or take these as a separate subject area. You will finish with questions concerning the candidate's current motivation and career plans.

Secondly, the structure of the questioning needs to be planned. To establish more exactly whether the candidate matches the requirements, you may need to ask situational or hypothetical questions. Here, you set out a specific scenario, usually related to the work that the successful applicant will be carrying out, and ask the candidate how he or she would act in that situation. You could also ask whether the candidate has faced such a situation in previous work and how he or she actually acted. You can then judge the response in relation to what you regard as the correct approach. An example is given in the box opposite.

Example of a situational or hypothetical question

The hypothetical question

You have constructed the following hypothetical question to be used at interviews for the position of Marketing and PR Manager for a small furniture manufacturing company:

> It is 9.30 in the morning. You have a meeting at 10.00 of your regional sales team that takes place every three months with some of the team travelling long distances and with important policy issues to discuss. You have arranged for the financial director to be present at 11.00 to talk over budgets for the next year. The meeting finishes at lunchtime, after which you need to talk to three of the team individually about matters in their region before they go. You have an appointment with the managing director at 3.30.
>
> You have just received a phone call from a magazine journalist who is writing a feature article on furniture and wants to include your products. She needs to have more details and especially is concerned with a hostile article she has found that was written a year ago criticising your quality. She asks if you could fax some of the answers and courier the latest brochures (she is only a few streets away) and she will ring you again for an extended discussion at 10.30. Her copy deadline is the end of the day. What do your do?

The response

As with all situations, there is a great deal of additional information that would be useful to know before coming up with an answer. Credit would be given to an applicant who asks pertinent questions (Have you talked to the journalist before? How important is the magazine? Could anybody else run the meeting? How important is the meeting with the managing director? etc).

You have decided that the ideal solution is as follows:

> You need to fax and courier the information the journalist needs. Because the article could be make or break for the business, you need to put all your resources that day into ensuring the best impression is given. You should suggest that she and you meet up, perhaps over (an early) lunch, to talk it all through, especially about how things have changed very much since that critical article – you could point out awards that have been won, etc. The rest of

> the day has to revolve around the journalist's response. You would need to start off the meeting, explain what is happening and allocate responsibilities for running parts of the agenda to members of the team. Ensure the managing director and financial director know what is happening – the financial director may be able to chair the meeting. Rearrange times to see the three members of your team, and also rearrange the meeting with the managing director. Choose a high-quality restaurant nearby.
>
> Applicants can be scored on their own response to this situation on a scale of 1 to 10.

You need to remember how to use both **open and closed questions**. Closed questions are used to elicit specific facts:

- When did you obtain your accountancy qualification?
- Were you dismissed from your last job?

If you want candidates to expand on information they have given and generally open up more, then you ask open questions:

- Why did you want to leave that employment?
- What do you enjoy about customer service work?
- Which do you consider to be your major strengths in managing people?
- Tell me about the difficulties you faced when you became a supervisor.
- How did you cope with moving from a local authority to working in the private sector?
- When did you really discover that your career should be in training?

The more experienced you become in interviewing, the more is learnt about how to mix a majority of open questions with the occasional closed question. For example, when interviewing for a supervisory position, you would ask a number of open questions relating to the candidate's experience of supervision and his or her views on how it should be done well. You would intersperse these questions with some closed questions relating to how long the candidate has acted as a supervisor or whether he or she has disciplined an employee for poor workmanship, attitude or timekeeping.

If you want to get into fine detail about a candidate's work history, behaviours or attitude, you ask **probing questions**. For example, if you have noticed a slight discrepancy between the starting date of one job and the leaving date of the previous one and have sensed that the manner of leaving may not have been too happy, you probe this situation with questions such as:

- You seem to indicate that you were not entirely happy working at Johnson Brakes. For how long were you looking to leave the employment?
- Did you have any indication that your manager found your work unsatisfactory? I should add that we may want to take up a reference with her.
- Did you finally leave the employment voluntarily?
- Was there any gap between leaving Johnson Brakes and starting at Melsum Exhausts?

Experienced interviewers often probe simply by asking candidates, when they pause at the end of explanation, to 'go on' or 'tell me more' or ask them, 'Was there another reason?', leaving a pause for the candidate. This often results in either the fundamental truth of the situation coming out or candidates getting themselves caught up in the knots of their own deception. This is another good reason why it is important for two people to be present at the interview, so one person can continue probing while the other takes notes. This may seem too much like 'the Bill' but it is a vital insurance against missing key facts that can impact on the final decision.

One last point on interviewing: throughout, interviewers must be courteous. They should not interrupt candidates or put words in their mouths, except where candidates are young, nervous or inexperienced and where genuine help is needed. Unnecessary or aggressive probing can have a negative effect on interviewees, who will not want to work for an organisation that appears to be rude or suspicious or both. The courteousness should be extended to the ending of the interview where candidates should be asked if they have any further questions, informed clearly of the next stage and thanked for attending. For those who appear to be prime candidates, a quick tour of the premises may be appropriate, especially if it is a manufacturing environment.

Selection tests

What sorts of tests are available?

There are essentially three types of tests – ability, aptitude and personality.

Ability tests measure the candidate's existing ability, which can be mental, logical and physical, including numerical, sensory or motor skills and mechanical ability. They can be job-specific, such as relating to typing, bricklaying or assembling. There are a number of off-the-peg tests for most common situations or it is possible to construct your own where you have regular vacancies.

Aptitude tests similarly measure ability but in a predictive framework, indicating whether candidates will be good at, say, computer programming or engineering skills.

Personality or psychometric tests attempt to measure the emotional tendencies that make up an individual's personality. This includes traits such as self-confidence, self-discipline, conscientiousness, innovative thinking and emotional stability. It should be noted that there is no 'pass' or 'fail' on these tests. Candidates are asked to respond to statements such as 'Once I make up my mind, it is important not to change' by either agreeing or disagreeing or by scoring on a five-point scale between agreeing strongly and disagreeing strongly. Most of these tests are now computerised, so candidates key in their responses, which allows a print-out of the result to be available very quickly.

To test or not to test?

A starting point here is to look at Figure 2.1 again, where you will see that tests score highly in their predictive ability. They also have the following advantages:

- They can provide objective information that is difficult to draw out at interview. Candidates may try to convince you that they are well organised, caring, forthright and innovative but an authoritative psychometric test has a much better chance of getting to the truth.
- Candidates will regard the selection procedure as more rigorous if selection tests are utilised, and tests certainly can provide a professional image.
- Because many tests have been used for some time, they can provide accurate norms for occupations such as selling or for supervisory roles.
- Some ability and aptitude tests are quite cheap and can be carried out quickly and easily.

However, there are disadvantages:

- Most test providers, especially where psychometric tests are involved, insist on individuals being trained and licensed to offer the test. This means that they can be expensive to use.
- Giving feedback, especially to poor performers, can be difficult and time-consuming.
- Tailor-made tests can look amateur, and doubt will remain as to how valid they are.

So tests should be used sparingly and when you are quite clear as to the test result outcomes that will distinguish good candidates from your viewpoint. For ability and aptitude tests, you should decide on the acceptable level that candidates must reach unless they are to be rejected. For psychometric tests, you should take the far more difficult decision of setting out the personality profile(s) that you are looking for so that you reject those candidates who are some distance from the preferred profiles.

Here is an example. A well-known brewing company decided to identify the personality profiles for their best innkeepers, following a growing incidence of high turnover, fraud cases and low profitability. The results surprised them. Far from having the strong outgoing, relaxed and warm-hearted traits that were previously looked for in a typical innkeeper, the most successful innkeepers were found to be practical, careful, tense and calculating. On reflection, the company saw that profitable pubs were those that successfully dealt with peak weekend periods, provided good value and varied food, and managed the finances well, including the arrangements for casual staff. From that time on, they used psychometric tests to identify candidates who possessed the ideal profile, which resulted in a substantial reduction in staff turnover and fraud, and an increase in profitability.

If you are using an agency, then, to help you recruit specialised staff, make sure you have the profile clear first before a test is agreed. The agency may help you decide on this, of course. A test result without a profile specification first is a waste of time and money.

A final word of warning. You may receive in the usual junk mail offers from so-called experts to carry out exciting new ranges of tests at very reasonable prices. Before accepting any such offers, make sure the organisation concerned is licensed to administer and interpret the tests, and also ask them to provide information on the *validity* of the test. Validity means that the test does actually measure the characteristic it is supposed to measure, and the predictive validity is the key measure here. This requires a study of the performance of employees some time after they have been tested, and is concerned with the extent to which predictions of performance made on the basis of test results have been confirmed in practice. The British Psychological Society quotes typical values of 0.35 for ability and aptitude tests and 0.15 for personality tests so you should aim for tests with a value that is equal to or greater than this level. You will need to ask test producers to produce norm data and the validity level. It is also useful for them to provide you with names of businesses currently using the tests so you can contact them and gauge their experience. Avoid test producers who are cagey on providing you with this information.

When should tests take place?

Testing and interviewing go hand in hand in the selection process. Sometimes an initial interview takes place and promising candidates are then invited to take appropriate tests. Alternatively, candidates short-listed for interview are given tests when they arrive and the results of the tests are discussed as a starting point for the interview. It does not matter too much which way is chosen. The important point is that selection tests should be used only as a selection aid. They should not be relied on solely in the decision to make an offer to the candidate.

Assessment centres

For managerial and graduate recruitment, a concentrated one-day session of interviews and tests can be used, called an assessment centre. This may include work simulation, a battery of ability, aptitude and psychometric tests, team working exercises and a group presentation. The programme can be set up for you by a licensed psychometric test provider at a cost of between £800 and £2,000 (plus expenses) depending on the number of candidates and tests used. It will be necessary for two to three managers to be present to help with some of the assessment processes.

Assessment centres have a high degree of prediction success (see Figure 2.1) and can be great fun, if a little stressful, for both participants and staff concerned.

An example of using an assessment process and integrating it with the company culture is shown in Case 2.1, which deals with easyJet procedures.

Case 2.1 EasyJet assessment

In 2001, easyJet employed 250 pilots and benefited from the intimacy of its early pioneering days, seeing itself still as a small and focused organisation. However, to meet the planned expansion programme of 25 per cent a year, the company will have to recruit 140 new pilots each and every year.

Applications online are strongly encouraged, and around 100 speculative applications are received each week. The company runs challenging assessment days for candidates and builds up an extensive database of suitable pilots, some of whom are young and may hope to join in five years' time. The key to the selection process is an interview that assesses personal qualities as well as technical competence. Qualities looked for are a respect for procedures coupled with a sense of independence. A key part of the assessment process is to filter applicants by their ability to fit into easyJet's culture.

This refers to the unusual approach of constantly involving employees in the learning process. There is a 'culture committee' that draws in staff from all sides of the business. It is seen as an opportunity for employees to learn a method of thinking creatively, as well as functioning as an employee representative council.

Pilots are asked to spend some time working at Luton, and existing pilots are encouraged to take new recruits out for a drink and introduce them to the easyJet ways of working. Behind all the informality and autonomy that the employees seem to enjoy, however, there is being built a learning structure in which management can proactively develop learning events rather than simply providing courses. The insight programme, for instance, is a five-day individual development course that includes components on understanding yourself, being innovative and analysing how other sectors solve problems.

(Source: Pollock, 2001)

References

The offer of employment should not be made, even informally, until references have been obtained.

Once a decision is reached on the chosen candidate, it is normal to make approaches to past employers to check the accuracy of information provided by the applicant and to ensure that there is no 'skeleton' lurking in the applicant's past that has not been revealed.

References are one of the most unsatisfactory aspects of human resources in practice. Most organisations make attempts to obtain written references but the actual results are woefully inadequate. Either the requested reference never arrives, or it provides a set of platitudes that can be unconvincing, or it is incomplete, leaving out some key information that may affect the decision to offer employment. You may need to try to read the coded message. ('A sociable and gregarious individual' means the candidate drinks too much, for example.) Referees may feel they run the risk of being sued if they provide too much detail although the greater risk is one of being sued for negligence by the organisation for which the reference was provided. So avoid attempting to obtain written references except where the work involves security or working with children and vulnerable people where exhaustive written references are required. It simply is not worth the time or effort.

Nor is it worth approaching the candidate's existing employer. It is not unknown (although highly unprofessional) for an existing employer to give an employee a less than glowing reference because it does not want the employee to leave. The employer may also not know that the applicant is looking for another job. It may give an outstanding reference because it wants to be rid of the employee! Although such cases are in the minority, you cannot be sure that the information is accurate.

The best system is to obtain at interview the names and telephone numbers of the managers that the applicant worked for in his or her *previous* employment. You sometimes find that by telling the applicant that these people will be approached for a reference, the applicant becomes much more open about why he or she left that organisation!

You can then telephone those referees, explaining that you are on the point of offering a certain position to the applicant, and ask a few simple, quick questions. Firstly, you need to clarify the applicant's employment dates and job title. Then find out the reason why the applicant left and whether the referee would offer him or her employment again. Finally, ask if there is any reason why the applicant should not be offered the position you have in mind. Listen carefully for any hesitation in the answers and probe if you need to. It could be serious and influence your decision.

It is not wise to make an offer until such information is received. Despite recommendations about making offers of employment 'subject to satisfactory references', it is a very unpleasant process actually to withdraw an offer when a poor reference is received. The applicant may have already handed in his or her notice to the existing employer, and the reference received may just be vindictive or out of date. It is far better to ensure the reference is obtained before the offer is actually made. Finally, except for school leavers, it is not worth considering references from the applicant's friends or colleagues, who are unlikely to be able to make an unbiased judgement.

Having said all this, references should be treated as just one part of the jigsaw. Just as with selection tests, a decision should not be based on the reference alone; a reference will always be a subjective and incomplete item, representing a period in time. Individuals change over time, and younger ones will often blossom, given a supportive, encouraging and developmental environment.

Making the offer

You have now completed all the interviews, carried out the tests and found at least one candidate who meets the requirements of the person specification and obtained a satisfactory reference. If you haven't found such a candidate, do not take the 'best on the day' – that is a huge risk and you will regret it in most cases. Bite the bullet and advertise again, after reconsidering the specification. The ultimate choice, if more than one candidate is available, should lie with the person who will manage the successful candidate, to make sure the 'personal chemistry' works.

If you consider that team working is vital in the area of the appointee, it may be appropriate to involve the rest of the team in the decision-making process. The short-listed candidates can be invited to meet the team and make a short presentation, and team members can be consulted on the appointment. This generally leads to a greater sense of commitment from the team to the new member.

The offer should be telephoned to the successful candidate, his or her verbal acceptance obtained (or any last-minute negotiations on salary or benefits carried out) and a starting date agreed. This should be followed up with a written offer containing the following details:

- job title;
- starting date;
- starting salary and any agreed details on salary progression and how it is determined, especially during the first year;
- help with relocation, if appropriate;
- company car level and arrangements for petrol, if appropriate;
- details of confirmation of the offer (the candidate is usually asked to sign his or her agreement on one copy of the letter, returning it to the company in the envelope supplied);
- other company benefits, if not given beforehand, as appropriate (including medical and life assurance, staff discounts, parking arrangement and pension scheme);
- a request to bring his or her driving licence on the first day, as well as any qualifications claimed for which the organisation has not yet obtained confirmation, if appropriate.

The offer will, when accepted, need to be followed up with a formal 'contract of employment', which needs to be given to the employee within two months of the start of employment. Unsuccessful candidates should be informed at this stage, perhaps indicating by telephone to the 'first reserve' how near they were to receiving an offer. It is both courteous and a good insurance policy in case another such vacancy arises.

Informing unsuccessful candidates

There have been two contrary developments in recent years in this area. Firstly, some organisations have simply not bothered, telling all candidates that, if they have not heard within three to four weeks, they can assume they have been unsuccessful. This approach certainly saves a bit of money, but is discourteous and reflects a pretty negative attitude to people generally. If you do not have the time or resources to write individually to each candidate, then send a pre-printed card apologising for the lack of personal touch due to a very high response but assuring the candidate that his or her application will be kept on the file in case any suitable opportunities arise.

The second development is for unsuccessful candidates to be given feedback on why they did not succeed. Although this can be very worth while for the candidate, it is a difficult job to handle and can be a logistical nightmare where large numbers of candidates are involved. For small organisations with few resources, it is to be avoided.

Keeping inside the law

You will find guidance on employment contract requirements in Chapter 4 (induction) and on inherent dangers relating to equal opportunities in Chapter 7.

Staff retention

Good selection practices will get you the right people but those people may not necessarily stay with you. The rest of this book is concerned with ways to ensure your staff stay on board and make a positive contribution. But the box below gives a checklist produced by Robin Davies to start the ball rolling.

How to boost staff retention

- *Build a sense of belonging.* Take time out to engage new recruits' commitment and energy. Allocate a work colleague who has the time and personality to make them feel welcome and explain how things work.
- *Avoid information overload.* Map out a formal induction period with the information spread over time rather than front-loaded, so recruits have a solid context in which to place the information.
- *Pay the going rate.* Make sure you meet recruits' expectations in terms of individual worth and comparison with the market place.
- *Start early.* Prepare for the first day, make sure recruits have the resources they need, get them a copy of the latest newsletter and confirm any changes to their role since the last interview.
- *Create a development plan*, based on their abilities and needs. It helps to cement long-term commitment from both parties. This can include involvement in assignments outside of their immediate job, such as project groups, secondments or the organising of one-off events.
- *Be flexible.* Remember that satisfaction is linked not only to the nature of the tasks set but to each individual's lifestyle. Flexible workers tend to be more committed, adaptable and resilient.
- *Don't ignore values.* Employees may have been attracted by the values explained at interview so make sure they exist in reality.

(Source: adapted from Davies, 2001)

Postscripts

Should you give expenses for interviews?

For local interviews (30 miles or less), certainly not. However, if candidates are asked to travel some distance at their own expense (ie they do not have company transport) then there is an argument that it is only courteous to make some arrangements. An easy rule of thumb is to pay for candidates travelling over 80 or 100 miles and all candidates who stay overnight, but each case tends to be individual. It is wise to try to avoid overnight stays by ensuring that those travelling some distance have their interview slot after 11 am. You may wish to enquire of most candidates if they have any expenses, because few will claim any, especially if they are keen on obtaining an offer.

Should you give an employee a probationary period?

It sounds sensible to have a probationary arrangement, but it isn't. If you are uncertain whether you have taken on the right person, then you should not have given that person the job, in reality. It is too much of a risk, and the costs of failure are too great. The message given by a probationary period is one of uncertainty. Research has shown that some employees leave in the early months because they think they may not 'pass' the probationary period and they want to get out before their employment is terminated. Once you have decided that applicants pass your selection criteria, then treat them as though they are going to work for you for a long time.

Of course you need to keep a close eye on them in the first few months and you need to give them regular feedback as to their progress (more about this in Chapter 3). If they are successful, then make sure they know this. If they appear not to be performing as well as expected, then take remedial action quickly to get them back on track. But do not present another hurdle for them to get over. If the worst happens and improvement is not forthcoming, and you realise you have made a mistake, then you have to cut your losses and give the employee notice – you do not need a contractual probationary period to carry this out.

References

Anderson, N and Shackleton, V (1994) Informed choices, *Personnel Today*, 8 November, p 33

Davies, R (2001) How to boost staff retention, *People Management*, 19 April, pp 54–55

Pollock, L (2001) The bigger easy, *People Management*, 22 March, pp 48–50

Further information

Clegg, B (2001) *Instant Interviewing*, Kogan Page, London

Maitland, I (1997) *Recruiting: How to do it*, Cassell, London (a useful manual with examples of application forms and selection tests)

Roberts, G (1997) *Recruitment and Selection*, IPD, London

For a useful resource for training managers in recruitment and selection, see *Recruiting and Keeping the Right People: Practical activities for managers* (www.fenman.co.uk).

For an article on recruitment online, see Prigg, M (2001) Find who you need online, *Sunday Times*, 29 April, p 12.

For an example of a successful use of recruitment online at Standard Life Insurance, see *People Management*, 28 May 1998, p 11.

For online recruitment Web sites, see:

- www.totaljobs.com;
- www.monster.com;
- www.sap.com.

For a detailed analysis of selection testing, see Toplis, J, Dulewicz, V and Fletcher, C (1997) *Psychological Testing: A manager's guide*, IPD, London.

Test providers and trainers include:

- SHL, which has designed and tested a wide range of tests, at www.shlgroup.com;
- Oxford Psychologists Press at www.opp.co.uk;
- Occupational Psychology Services Ltd at www.opsltd.com;
- Stuart Robertson and Associates at www.sr-associates.com.

3 Improving performance

This could be regarded as the most important chapter in the book. Your people have to perform well, not just work hard. They have to improve continually or the competition will catch you up. So motivation and performance improvement are key factors for your workforce. This chapter will start off with a brief summary of what motivation means, how you can identify it and whether the huge amount of academic theory surrounding the subject is of any use in practice. The next part will cover the way you can set targets for employees within a simple framework for measuring performance together with ways of feeding back this information to those concerned, a process which is called 'performance management'.

The next section investigates techniques of improvement building, including an emphasis on team working, increasing flexible working practices and systems of empowerment.

What makes people perform well

It is quite easy to recognise a well-motivated workforce. You can often notice it as soon as you come into an organisation. You see signs like:

- People seem to be enjoying their work.

- They appear to work well as teams, and are co-operative in getting things done.
- They are focused on achieving results.
- They celebrate one another's successes and avoid blaming others when a failure occurs.
- They are energetic, enthusiastic and involved in their work.
- They are knowledgeable and, where they do not have the immediate facts or information, they know how to get hold of them quickly.
- They are prepared to put themselves out for customers, their colleagues and their managers – to 'go the extra mile' when it is necessary.
- Nobody ever says, 'Sorry, that's not my job' or 'No, I really can't help you there.'
- They never let a phone ring unanswered in their department.
- The staff take an interest in their surroundings – they clear up after themselves and keep the place tidy.
- They keep their promises – when they say they will do something, they produce the goods.

An ideal world? Perhaps; you are unlikely to see all of these features at one time too often but it does occur, especially in small organisations going somewhere fast.

What are the drivers for this dreamt-for situation? There used to be simple motivation theories that held that people acted in this way through either the incentives of high pay or fear of losing their job, the carrot and the stick, but these have been discredited for 50 years or more. It has been clear for some time that employees are motivated by much more than tangible rewards, such as pay and benefits (sometimes called **extrinsic** rewards). The **intrinsic** rewards (recognition, job satisfaction) are just as important, perhaps more so. That is not to say that tangible rewards are not important. Employees want a fair reward, and a small minority are genuinely motivated by the thoughts of obtaining a great deal of wealth. If employees are dissatisfied with pay, they are unlikely to be motivated, but pay alone will not be sufficient.

Recent theories have shown that an educated workforce is looking for a more complex mix of tangible and psychological benefits and relationships. Researchers have come up with many different blueprints for success and then disproved one another's theories. What is more, research has shown that everybody is different, not just as people but at different times in their working careers. The motivation for a young aspiring manager looking for a fast-track career can be very different from the motivation for that same person with two young children and working part-time or for that person in his or her late 50s.

Can we generalise at all, then? It *is* possible to draw out some research evidence from a collection of US theorists who published books and articles on the subject between the 1940s and the 1980s that today has a degree of general consensus:

- *People are looking for interesting jobs.* Herzberg (1968), in his two-factor theory arising from interviews with 28,000 employees, found that the nature of the job was an important influence over their degree of motivation. The degree of control and responsibility for the work being carried out, the inherent interest in the work itself, the challenges the work produced and the interaction with colleagues who shared the interest and the belief that the work was important were all important factors.
- *People respond well to having goals for which to aim.* Work cannot be meaningful without having a target to work towards. Locke found that employees strive to achieve goals in order to satisfy their desires and emotions and they regulated their effort depending on the nature of these goals. If goals were lacking or too easy, people did not perform as well as people with unambiguous, stretching goals.
- *People want their efforts to be recognised.* Maslow (1954) produced a theory where an individual's needs quickly moved from simple physiological and safety needs (represented at work by a basic salary and job security) up to 'higher-order' needs, which included recognition for a job well done. Subsequent research has supported the concept that a sense of achievement

allied to appropriate praise and recognition from colleagues and superiors is a vital cog in the motivation wheel. In a recent US survey, 98 per cent of managers agreed that receiving positive encouragement helped them perform at a higher level. Certainly, positive feedback and reinforcement has been seen by trainers as essential to the learning process that builds up performance.

- *People like to work within a fair environment.* People will always compare the way they are treated with the way their contemporaries are treated, be it their siblings when they are young or their classmates at school. In the work situation, it becomes very demoralising when unfair advantages appear to be given to undeserving colleagues in the areas of work allocation, pay or promotion. This has been confirmed in research by Adams (1963), who identified the employee's need for **procedural justice** – having a system in place that determines that decisions should be taken under fairness conditions – and **distributive justice**, where fair decisions are actually taken in practice according to the agreed rules and culture. This thinking also ties in with recent findings by Kohn (1993) that employees associated fairness with safety through the support and encouragement they expect to get from their manager.
- *People want to be regarded as important.* It is not just the job they do that is crucial for employees these days. Recent research has shown that, as employees become more self-confident and the old class division between the 'bosses' and the 'workers' has all but disappeared, employees want to be respected as individuals – to be people in their own right. They want to be informed of important developments, they want to be consulted on decisions that may affect them and they want to be involved in activities connected to their job but not necessarily part of it. They do not want to be dismissed as a 'labour cost' or to be easily dispensable when times become hard.

Understanding the theory of motivation is one thing; putting it into practical effect is another. The next part of this chapter explores the opportunities available to organisations to meet the motivational needs of the employees.

Making the work interesting

One has to say that not everybody wants an interesting job. There will be some employees who see work as *instrumental* – they do it simply to get the money to pursue their real interests in life. These could be a serious hobby (like golf, gardening or writing), or family life, including looking after children or sick relatives. Some are happy to switch off when they come to work, 'hang their brains in their locker' and not care what happens to their work as long as the time passes. Despite what many managers think, such employees have always been in the minority and their numbers are rapidly diminishing. This is due to the widening of horizons and the greater opportunities for all, no matter what their background or location. An increasing number of young people are continuing to further education and a lot more are going on to higher education. More people are setting up their own businesses, and every community has role models of men and women who have started their own businesses from humble beginnings and made a success of them. Many employees who left school at 16 are looking to come back into part-time education to obtain a qualification at a later date.

In any case, you should only want people who work for you to have some motivation to do better for themselves and for the organisation.

A second viewpoint often expressed is that there are still many jobs that are inherently boring and there is nothing you can do to make them interesting. There is some truth in this, but not much. Most of these jobs are unskilled, manual work, operating basic machinery, and most will not last beyond another 10 to 20 years in developed countries. Competition from poorer countries with much lower pay rates will destroy a good majority – manufacturing, in any case, is continuing to decline in all advanced economies – and the remainder will be automated out of existence. (It is true that in automating some jobs you actually deskill them but that is a more complex argument and varies from one situation to another.)

In any case, if you accept the fact that some people like tedious jobs and some jobs are going to be tedious, the people in those jobs are not going to be your well-motivated, involved, committed employees who make the difference between success and failure.

Let us assume, then, that we return to the premise that jobs have to be interesting to motivate employees and see what can be done to make progress in this area.

Job design

Jobs can become more interesting and challenging in three ways:

- *Broadening their scope*. Rather than employees carrying out a limited number of tasks, they can be rotated through many tasks. This rotation can be through a management-inspired rota or through a rota worked out by the team themselves (see the section on team working later in this chapter). This will help with covering for holidays and absenteeism as well as reducing boredom. Care has to be taken, however, that this rotation adds value and is not seen as a succession of boring jobs where responsibility is diluted even further.
- *Broadening the skills*. Often linked with rotation is the need to train employees in new skills so they can cover these new tasks (this is covered in more detail later in this chapter in the section on encouraging flexible working). At a 3M factory in Durham, a set of skills was identified for each task and operation, and employees were trained, tested and accredited when they had reached the required standards so that they could cover a wide range of work. Research carried out in the plant found that the vast majority of employees found this system far better than being stuck on one monotonous job. There are training cost implications but these are always outweighed by the improved productivity arising from a properly implemented new system.

- *Broadening the responsibilities.* Herzberg is credited with thinking up the term 'job enrichment' although the more common name today is 'empowerment'.

Empowerment

Employees want to feel they are valued and that they contribute to the success of the enterprise in which they work. Many want to take decisions, devise solutions to problems, exercise their initiative and be accountable for results. Though they may not be considered 'management material' they are quite capable of taking responsibility for their actions, behaviour and performance at work.

Empowerment can be seen as a mix of practices and behaviours that encourage people to realise their ambitions for a meaningful working life. The main idea in this concept is to give employees more responsibilities for controlling their jobs, although it is linked with other employee policies that encourage customer focus, team working and trust between management and employees. In short, empowered staff have ownership of the work they do, trust their managers and exercise their initiative appropriately and without fear of recrimination. Let us look at a few examples:

- In a retail company, service staff were empowered to decide whether customers would be given replacements for items they considered faulty rather than having to refer them to the manager.
- Supervisors at Rank Hovis were empowered some years back to run budgets and negotiate terms with suppliers, rather than rely on standard national arrangements.
- Call centre staff at a credit card company were empowered to authorise a reduction in fees and charges when dealing with customer complaints.

Empowerment can include allowing a work team to decide when they take their breaks, how they rotate workstations, and holiday and shift rotas. One small jobbing sheet-metal company empowers its operatives to carry out all contacts with the client once the contract has been signed so they, not the manager, discuss delivery and any technical changes or quality issues and have the specific responsibility to get the work to the client on time within specification.

A by-product of effective empowerment can be the lowering of stress levels because it has been found that most people who suffer from stress today are people who do not feel that they are in control of their lives.

Develin & Partners have devised a checklist for an organisation to identify how far the empowerment concept operates. An extract from this list is set out in Table 3.1.

Making sure the work is challenging

Employees like working towards goals but those goals have to be the right ones. The starting point is to have some form of **performance agreement** with each of your employees or teams. This agreement, which need not be too complex a document – a page or less is sufficient – will set out the agreed level of performance expected and how it is to be measured. It will include the stages detailed in the following sections.

Ensure the agreement ties in with your organisation's goals

In Chapter 1, it was emphasised how important communicating the organisation's vision was, so it is common sense to take the organisation's goals arising from that vision and cascade those down the organisation, so that they link up with each employee's own goals. This is straightforward in the sales and production areas, where sales and manufacturing targets can be divided up amongst sales and production teams and then down to each salesperson or production operative. In other areas – purchasing, quality control, customer service – it takes a little more time, but it is just as important. If the goals do not seem to

Table 3.1 Empowerment checklist (extract)

	Empowerment Characteristics	Score (1–5)
	Morale	
1	Employees see that the organisation is trying to make the best use of their abilities	
2	Employees are clear about what the organisation expects of them	
3	Employees are keen to take responsibility when they feel able to do so	
	Management Behaviour	
4	What managers do is the same as what they say	
5	Managers freely share information with their staff	
6	Managers place great emphasis on encouraging, supporting and listening to their employees	
	Control	
7	Employees have influence over the way their work is done	
8	Employees take responsibility for the quality of their work	
	Working Practices	
9	Team working is the norm	
10	Cross-functional process improvement is the norm	
11	Promotion, rewards and recognition go to those who practise what the organisation preaches	
	Culture	
12	Customer satisfaction is everybody's uppermost concern	
13	Praise is more frequently heard than criticism	
	Innovation	
14	Employees spend a proportion of their time seeking better ways of doing their job	
15	Employees share their skills and knowledge with their colleagues	

(Source: Develin & Partners)

Scoring: from 1 (strongly disagree) to 5 (strongly agree)

If you score:

over 47	you have a high level of empowerment
25–47	you have some way to go but you have a reasonable foundation on which to build
under 25	indicates a long way to go

---

fit in with what the organisation is trying to achieve (they are not 'aligned', as it is known), then confusion in direction may set in.

Agree the individual performance plan

The goals should be set out in SMART mode:

1. Goals should be **Specific** and **stretching**. Specific means that they are transparent and not open to dispute. To set stretching targets supports further aspects of goal theory stating that motivation and performance are higher when goals are difficult but accepted, support is given to achieve them and feedback is regular and valued.
2. Goals should be **Measurable** so that all sides can agree when they are achieved (or not). Measurable targets also make interim feedback so much easier.
3. Goals should be **Agreed** and **achievable**. If employees disagree with the goals because they find them too difficult to achieve, then they may well set out to prove this by determining to fail. It is unwise simply to lay down employees' goals without allowing the employees any input. They will have far less commitment to the goals if they have not contributed to their construction. Contributing also provides employees with the opportunity to suggest constructive and innovative ideas as to how to improve their own performance.

4. Goals should be **Realistic** and **relevant**, which makes them more attractive to all the parties. Goals are relevant when they fit in with the organisation's aims and an employee's own development, and realistic when the employee has helped to put them together. This will include the right number of goals, and this is sometimes difficult to judge. If an employee has a large number of goals, say 25 or 30, then the process of monitoring and measuring performance becomes insuperably complex. If there are only one or two goals, then an employee can become too narrowly focused. Experience has shown that a total of between a minimum of four and a maximum of 10 goals has proved to be the most successful.
5. Goals should be **Time-related** so that it is clear at what point they should be achieved.

Some examples of SMART goals are set out in Table 3.2.

Table 3.2 Examples of SMART goals

Unsatisfactory Goal	SMART Goal
To introduce a new computer system for the purchasing department.	To research, agree proposals and successfully implement a new computer system for the purchasing department that will achieve a 10% savings in administrative costs within a budget of £15,000 by 31 December.
To improve customer satisfaction.	To research into the reasons behind the current dip in customer satisfaction, get proposals agreed for action to be taken that will lead to satisfaction rising by 5%, and test-run these proposals by 1 August.
To innovate successfully.	To come up with at least three ideas that have a clearly proven outcome of cost-saving or quality improvement.

The system of measurement should be established carefully. You will usually need to include both **quantitative** and **qualitative** measures. For example, a goal for call centre operators to increase the number of calls they take must not be at the expense of the quality of the calls. Similarly, an increase in the output of a production section must not lead to an increase in waste or decline in safety standards. Costs may also play an important part in defining the goals.

Qualitative measures are quite a difficult area. Certain goals, especially those where you want an employee to act or behave in a specific way, are very difficult to convert into measurable chunks. The competency movement has tried to get round this difficulty by creating a set of words that describe behaviour at certain levels, which can help in the measurement. An example of qualitative measures is shown in the box below.

Measures of responsiveness towards customer

Level 1   Limited awareness of customer needs or the effect of own actions. Adds no value to the relationship.

Level 2   Performs own job without proper regard for customer opinion. May understand what is required but needs constant reminding about customer skills.

Level 3   Reacts to customer requirements and understands customer's viewpoint but does not always get it right.

Level 4   Seeks to anticipate customer requirements. Listens to customers and influences their views. Gets it right the great majority of the time.

Level 5   Anticipates customer requirements and works with customers to develop the business relationship. Is seen as an ambassador.

On the other hand, care has to be taken that the goals and their measurement do not get too complex and unwieldy. It could be said that a performance agreement seems a lot of extra work for a busy manager and will take up productive time that could be better spent elsewhere – but that would be wrong. Sitting down at least once a year and planning what key tasks employees are going to be focusing on is one of the most important jobs a manager can do. It is the people equivalent of financial budgeting – have you ever heard an accountant say that budgeting is a waste of time?

Throughout the concept of managing people properly runs the issue of trust. Not everything that is agreed needs to be written down, and basic assumptions on standards can often be assumed between the parties. It is the essential understanding that is vital and this can often be best achieved by getting the employees themselves to draft out the goals for discussion and produce the final arrangement.

The agreed goals making up the performance agreement should be written down on some simple document running to no more than two pages at the very most. The same principles in constructing goals apply to teams as well as individuals. We will look more closely at this area later in the chapter under team working.

Review the targets

It is not enough simply to agree the goals. The external environment is constantly changing and goals may need to be reassessed in the light of these changes. This is not to say they should be altered on a monthly basis, but no goal should be sacrosanct, especially in a fast-moving environment. In a world where you try to be fair, sales targets can be altered both up and down if the outside environment takes a major shift.

Recognising people's efforts

People like to be told how they are doing and they like to be recognised when they have done well, so feedback and recognition are both crucial if you want to get the best out of employees.

Feedback

Giving feedback to employees can be excruciating. Tom Peters, a US business guru, once reported that most managers would prefer to go to the dentist than to give annual feedback to employees through an annual appraisal scheme!

Giving feedback to employees is generally seen in its traditional form: the manager sits down once a year and tells the employee how he or she has been doing. There are many dangerous currents and hidden reefs for the unwary feedback mariner that can cause feedback sessions to be wrecked. We will look at this system first and then consider later in the chapter some of the problems that can lead to an employee considering this process to be unfair. We will examine an alternative method (360-degree feedback) that is gradually being adopted because it can be regarded as fairer and more productive.

Dangers to look out for in giving feedback include the following:

- *Feedback is irregular.* To give feedback just once a year is insufficient. Twelve months is a long time from setting goals to talking about the results, so feedback sessions need to be more frequent. It is preferable for an informal meeting to take place every three or four months with a quick run-through of achievements to date. One small organisation in the training sector asks managers to carry their set of goals in their briefcase so they can be discussed informally at any appropriate time.
- *It turns into a combat.* In research carried out by the CIPD in 1998, over a quarter of respondents reported that they were dissatisfied with the way the manager carried out feedback meetings. Too often, and especially where a pay review hangs on the meeting, the feedback session is seen as a combat where the contestants, armed with their data (and a few examples or excuses), fight hard to ensure their point of view prevails. By having interim discussions, this should be avoided, but the manager has to work hard to ensure that there is a real balance between praise for the areas of success and a serious discussion

on areas that can be improved. Again, this turns on the degree of trust between the employee and the manager.
- *It has no meaning.* Alternatively, both sides may be embarrassed by the ordeal and not want to risk their relationship by drawing out any unpleasant truths, so little of value is said. Without a real discussion, real feedback does not exist, leaving employees uncertain of their performance and the manager unhappy with the way it has been handled. It can also put off the day of reckoning, if one is necessary.
- *Opinion takes the place of fact.* If the manager believes that there are areas of performance that do need improving, then that manager must have some facts to back the belief up. The manager's decisions must not be mere opinions made in an arbitrary fashion. Meetings should also concentrate on identifying the causes of the problem and realistic ways it can be solved – not arguments where the blame is moved around by the parties.
- *There is concentration on the negative.* Research has also indicated that too much time is taken up by negative aspects, and a conscious effort should be made by the manager to ensure the positive areas do get sufficient attention. Where there are a string of difficulties, concentration should be on the two or three most crucial ones.

Well, we have concentrated too much on the things that can go wrong, so let us look at what good should come out. The successful outcomes should be:

- *Agreement on the level of performance achieved.* This is best achieved by getting employees to estimate these points themselves. It is useful to ask employees to prepare for the meeting by reviewing their own achievements in respect of the goals.
- *Agreement on the facts that influenced this level of performance.* It is important to listen carefully and question them in respect of the difficult areas. Examples are:

- 'Do you think you could handle the situation any better next time?'
- 'The figures for Jones and Brown appear a little better than yours. Can you suggest ways you can bring your own figures up to theirs?'
- 'This was clearly a difficult area for you. What help do you need for next year to improve this situation?'
- *Outline agreement on the challenges and goals for the next period.*
- *Agreement on what support and/or resources need to be arranged for employees.*

Recognising employees

We all like to think we recognise the achievements of our employees but the facts seem to dispute this. A US survey by consultants Kepner-Tregoe in 1995 found that only 40 per cent of employees received any form of recognition for doing a job well while only 50 per cent of managers agreed that they actually gave recognition for high performance. Perhaps we assume that getting things done properly is just part of the job, which it is, but the lack of encouragement can put that job in jeopardy on the next occasion. On the positive side, a Harvard Business School research report indicated that, in the most innovative companies, there was a significantly higher volume of acts of recognition than in companies of low innovation.

Why do we hold back on recognition? Psychologists tell us that praising others means we have to open up our emotions, sometimes in public, and for some people that is not always easy. Another reason is that we fear an accusation of having favourites by praising the good performers, while a third problem is that it may take up too much time to do it properly. Furthermore, we sometimes believe in the myth that good managers ought to be cool, aloof and analytical. In practice, as motivational managers will confirm, giving encouragement is one of the easier jobs (far, far easier than trying to discipline somebody). If we carry it out properly, it rarely leads to jealousy among the team and it takes up very little time. And, although we have respect for leaders who keep their distance, we are much happier working for somebody who is more human and demonstrative.

How well are you doing in encouraging employees in your organisation? Try judging yourself against the list of questions in Table 3.3 before moving on to the next stage.

So what is it that employees do that we should recognise? It could be something like this:

- coming up with a specific idea relating to the job, something that is quite innovative;
- going that extra mile to satisfy a customer;
- producing work of a very high quality;
- using a new method that saves money, time, effort or waste.

If these achievements link in with specific organisational objectives set out in the 'Vision', such as 'exceeding the customer's expectations' or 'above all others in quality', then there is even more reason to make the recognition visible.

More mundane, but just as important, contributions include:

- the time and effort that have gone into a particular piece of work – a report, an analysis or a set of proposals;
- spending extra time, perhaps late into the evening or weekend, to complete a project.

It is just as important, some would say more so, to recognise the achievements of teams, especially if your organisation is specifically emphasising how important team working is in the organisation's success.

Types of recognition

Recognition comes in two formats, the formal, where a scheme is specifically set up, and the informal, where recognition happens on a day-to-day unstructured basis.

Table 3.3 Do you encourage and recognise your employees?

		Score (1–5)*
1	I make certain we set a standard that motivates us to do better in the future than we are doing now	
2	I express high expectation about what people are capable of accomplishing	
3	I pay more attention to the positive things people do than to the negative	
4	I clearly communicate my personal standards and professional standards to everybody in the team	
5	I make it a point to give people feedback on how they are performing against our agreed-upon standards	
6	I spend a good deal of time listening to the needs and interests of other people	
7	I personally acknowledge people for their contributions	
8	I express a positive and optimistic outlook even when times get rough	
9	I find creative ways to make my recognition of others unique and special	
10	I make sure that our teams celebrate accomplishments together	

(Source: adapted from Kouzes and Posner, 1999)

* Score 1 for almost never, 2 for rarely, 3 for sometimes, 4 for often and 5 for almost always.

You should feel satisfied with a score of more than 38, and there is plenty to do if your score is less than 20.

Although mostly devised for larger organisations as part of a culture change process, a **formal recognition scheme** can well suit an organisation with 150-plus employees. The essential elements are:

- Employees are encouraged to come up with good ideas and

innovations (the Japanese concept of Kaizen that replaces outdated suggestion schemes).
- Training is provided in how to think through and put forward an idea.
- Schemes are assessed quickly by a review body, and feedback and advice on acceptance given quickly.
- For those schemes accepted, the employee gets a proportion of the estimated payback, around 20 to 40 per cent, some paid immediately and the rest after the changes have been implemented for a year.
- For each genuine idea, an immediate payment (say £20 to £30) is made by the supervisor or manager.
- Successful ideas are publicised through noticeboards, newsletters and public awards.
- Ideas from teams are strongly encouraged.
- Awards can be taken as money or from a list of alternative prizes.

Further encouragement to get everybody involved is through every idea being put into a prize draw with a major prize, such as a long-haul holiday, for the lucky ticket holder. Many organisations that have run such schemes have spoken highly of their success in getting employees to be more committed to improvement and innovation. After all, if your team has proposed some major action in your department and the proposal is accepted, you are going to be highly motivated to make sure the proposal works. It will give you more money but it will also give you considerable job satisfaction. Recognition schemes, then, act as a vehicle for motivation, involvement and commitment all at the same time.

Alternatively, a simpler concept is a scheme that regularly recognises an employee or group that has done well (such as an employee-of-the-month scheme). The scheme can operate through nomination by colleagues and managers.

Nature of recognition

Recognition can take the form of tangible or non-tangible rewards. Those that are tangible include:

- one-off bonuses;
- incentive travel;
- vouchers for holidays, luxury goods or groceries;
- a celebration dinner or party;
- days out – go-carting, health centre, luxury hotel;
- a prominent parking position for the employee of the month.

The important thing to remember is that it is not the cost of the event that makes it memorable; it is the memories of the event by the participants. One event recounted to me five years after it took place was of a day out by coach to the New Forest for all 85 employees and their partners to celebrate a successful year by the owner of a small manufacturing company. Not a great deal happened apart from a good dinner, short speeches and a short walk in the forest, but the person still remembered this happy day for a long time. He also emphasised that the unexpected nature of it and small personal gift to each employee led to a much greater sense of commitment to the organisation. Employees sincerely felt their efforts had been appreciated.

Another example on an individual basis is of the owner of a street-lighting company who gives the employee of the month his company Jaguar for the weekend. He does have other cars, of course, but it is inherent trust in such a decision that is appreciated by the employees.

The intangible rewards can be more subtle but just as long-lasting:

- recognising employees in front of their colleagues – the presentation itself is important;
- recording appreciation in writing – in newsletters or on noticeboards;
- asking employees to coach new employees – because they are good at their jobs and can pass the skills on to others;

- asking employees to use their skills and knowledge by taking part in projects;
- writing congratulations to employees' home addresses so it can be shared with the family.

There are some difficulties associated. Awards have to be ones that the recipient wants otherwise they are wasted. Words of congratulation have to be carefully drafted so as to ensure they do not offend. After a successful event, what do you do next year? Employees may be disappointed if nothing happens the next year or even by a repeat. Employees' expectations may be raised too high by the excitement. Even so, whatever you do in terms of recognition is worth the risk because it is far too risky to do nothing.

Constructing a fair environment

It is very important to employees to believe that they are treated fairly in the workplace and that this fairness is demonstrated in the performance feedback process and in decisions over pay and promotion.

Fairness in feedback

A number of dangers relating to feedback have already been discussed but here are a few more that relate to treating the employee fairly:

- *The goalposts have been moved.* During the year the changes in the business environment may cause some substantial shift in direction affecting many staff. This means that goals will be affected. Activity may need to stepped up or scaled down. This can lead to arguments with employees as to whether goals have been achieved or not. The best approach here is either to reach agreement on a new goal (if that can be done without compromising some rewards) or to ignore that goal in terms of the final assessment of employee performance. This depends very much on the importance of the goal (for the organisation and the individual), how dependent the reward system is on that particular goal and how easy it is to reach agreement on the change.

- *Goals are not evenly matched.* It is all too easy for some employees to be regarded as having 'soft' goals – too few or ones that are too easy to achieve. Getting equality of goals across a number of very different jobs is almost impossible but it is worth while to have somebody monitoring the arrangements made, casting their eye over everybody's goals to see if any stick out like a sore thumb, before they are finalised. If this is apparent, further discussion could take place between the manager and the individual to tighten up on the list. It will take a little time but it is a worthwhile exercise to help prevent disillusionment setting in.
- *Some employees only concentrate on their goals.* There may be a temptation for some employees to concentrate all of their efforts on the goals on which they appear to be measured. It has to be made quite clear that goals are only part of an employee's work direction. Ensuring routine elements are carried out effectively, supporting their colleagues and having a flexible approach to their workload are equally important.
- *Managers make bad judgements.* Giving feedback implies some degree of judgement, especially where goals are not so easy to measure. Managers may be affected in their judgements by their personal relationships where friendship diverts them from a full and frank discussion of declining performance. Alternatively, employees who do not get on well with the manager may believe that they are being criticised unfairly. There are dangers in 'recency', where discussions centre on a recent unfortunate incident that is fresh in the manager's mind and good work done the rest of the year is forgotten. Another danger lies where a manager is unreceptive to an employee's new ideas, liking things to be done the way they have always been done. All managers need to be aware of these inclinations.

There are so many difficulties associated with the feedback process that training or coaching managers to carry out performance feedback must be considered essential if it is to work well. This is one of the circumstances where bringing in an experienced consultant is probably the best approach, somebody who will have an independent viewpoint. They can help in fine-tuning your feedback system and setting up a short training programme, which will include role-plays. Experience has shown a substantial improvement in the system and employees' respect for it, when management has made such an investment in training.

360-degree feedback

Because top-down, one-to-one feedback has so many problems of fairness associated with it, there has been a growth in recent years in experiments where feedback comes from a number of sources. This is especially relevant where staff provide services for other departments and where measurement is not easy.

There are a number of models currently in practice, some of which are highly bureaucratic and unsuitable for small organisations. The principles, however, are the same and can be adopted on an informal basis:

- *Sources of feedback.* They can be quite wide, as shown in Figure 3.1. It is best not to have more than six or seven in total, and to involve the employee in the choice. Most sources in practice tend to be internal ones and will always involve the employee's manager.
- *Are all staff involved in the process?* 360-degree feedback can be very time-consuming so some organisations restrict the process to managers, certainly at first, to make sure it works well. A few organisations have extended it to all employees. Some have made the process voluntary, although questions tend to be asked when managers do not volunteer!
- *What does the feedback look like?* Sometimes rating scores only are given to save time on processing, while other schemes have

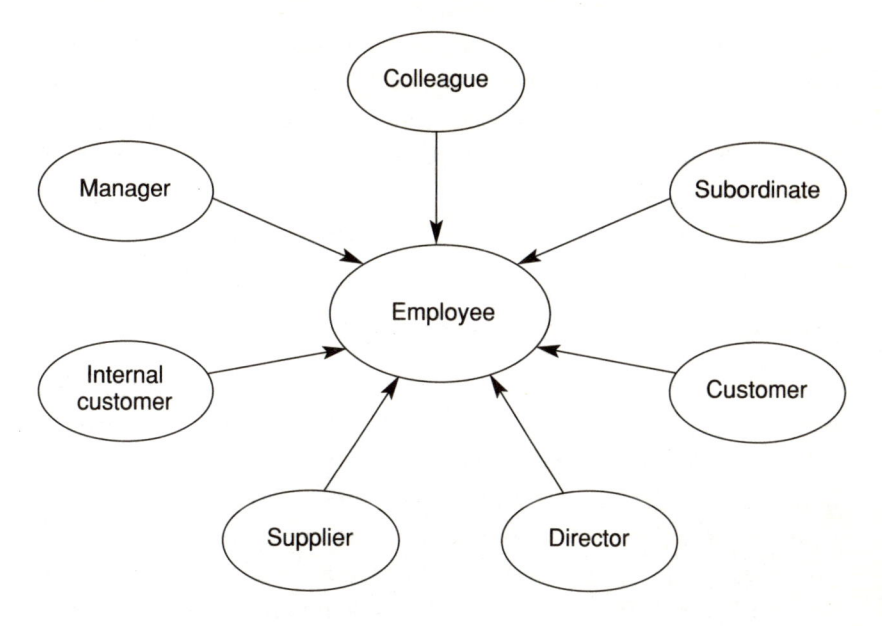

Figure 3.1 Sources of feedback

opportunities for personal comments. It is important that the feedback source remains anonymous, although all the research evidence indicates that those providing the feedback do so honestly and with a balanced response, usually because they are part of the scheme and want feedback to themselves to be like this.

- *How is the feedback given?* Not by the manager, generally speaking. To make sure the scheme is scrupulously fair, the actual feedback results tend to be given by an independent third party, usually a consultant with HR experience. This is because the information provided can be so powerful. It is one thing to be fed back poor results from one's manager, because they can be written off in the employee's mind if the personal relationship is not good. However, if the broader feedback is poor, then it cannot be questioned.

360-degree feedback has been shown in a number of studies to be a powerful tool that can cause employees to change and, with training, to improve their performance – which is the whole point of feedback. It is well worth considering such an approach, after getting advice from an expert, if you are confident that your organisation is one that wants to become 'feedback-rich' and where honest advice is welcomed.

Fairness in pay decisions

Chapter 5 deals with payment systems, including performance pay, but the important word here is **transparency**. Employees want to know the basis of decisions on pay to ensure that those decisions are fair ones. It is not an easy process because trying to ensure transparency has led many organisations down the path of increasingly complex schemes involving pages of calculations. There are certainly arguments in favour of simple pay determination models for small organisations. If the system of performance management is a robust one and feedback is carried out well, then more than half the job is done.

Fairness with developing their own skills

Most employees regard their own personal development as one of their highest priorities so it important that they are not denied the chances to develop. Development needs emerge naturally from the feedback process, so a discussion on these needs is an essential way of leading into the goals for the next period. In the next chapter, we look at effective development methods that are relevant to the individual and the organisation.

Fairness in promotion processes

Transparency is a word that also should apply to the promotion process. If there are opportunities available, it makes sense to publicise these in the organisation to make sure your pool of applicants is as large as possible. At times this may seem a waste of time and effort, with one obvious outstanding candidate, but surprise candidates can emerge, and the process of a short internal news item on the intranet or newsletter is informative and promotes the culture of transparency.

Using assessment centres to select managers or identify potential is also worth considering. Their use for selection purposes has been outlined in Chapter 2, and the same format and system can be used to select for promotion purposes.

Regarding people as important

The final notch on the motivation ratchet is to make sure employees understand what is happening in and around their jobs, and to get them involved in improving the performance of the organisation as a whole. The subject is dealt with in detail in Chapter 6, including effective methods of communication, consultation and involvement, all of which should be far easier in a small organisation where the communication chain is so much shorter.

Team working

Nobody doubts the importance of teams these days. Having a collection of highly talented individuals working for you is no guarantee of success, as many a football manager knows. Teams have been shown to be more effective in helping to solve problems and in achieving higher performance; the growing dependence on technology requires fewer employees in total but greater interdependence between those employees or the systems will break down. Teams also score highly on creativity, as this thrives on interaction between people with different viewpoints and experiences.

The reduction in management and supervisory levels in larger organisations, called delayering, has meant that teams need to work together with far less supervision, and the creation of customer-focused teams, especially in retailing and financial services, has happened because of the need to provide an integrated service that meets the immediate needs of customers and tries to preserve their loyalty.

What do effective teams look like?

Mike Woodcock (1979) attributes nine types of behaviour that contribute to team cohesion and effectiveness. These are:

- They are clear about what they want to achieve.
- They confront issues and resolve them in an open way.
- They have an atmosphere of support and trust.
- They can use both cooperation and conflict to get results.
- They have clear procedures for taking decisions.
- They are led in a way that suits the task, the team and its members.
- They review what they are doing regularly and learn from this.
- They encourage team members to develop themselves.
- They work well with other teams.

A good start for improving team performance, then, is to get teams to identify their strengths and weaknesses against Woodcock's measures. Then the team can move on to improving its performance.

Improving team performance

Ways to improve team performance include:

- *Making sure team goals are clear.* This is just as important for teams as for individuals so all the same conditions apply as detailed earlier in the chapter, with the link to organisational goals even more important.
- *Making sure the mix of team members is right.* The team should include the range of specialist or technical expertise needed for

the tasks – members should be selected for their expertise, not their seniority. Sometimes the most junior members are the best informed on a subject or come up with the best ideas. A variety of personal styles can also work wonders. One of the best-known models of team performance through effective membership has been produced by Meredith Belbin (1981). A summary of his team types is shown in Table 3.4. It is very useful to have somebody who matches each of these characters in a team so that the team becomes well balanced.

Table 3.4 Belbin's team types

Types of Employees	Qualities
Chairperson – gets the team to work together to produce results.	Strong sense of objectives; welcomes all contributors.
Company worker – turns ideas into action and sees they are carried forward.	Hard working and self-disciplined; has common sense and is organised.
Shaper – challenges team's ideas constantly.	Outgoing, dynamic and energetic, if frustrating at times.
Plant – A constant source of new ideas.	Strong imagination, intellect and knowledge.
Resource investigator – develops new contacts and initiates new projects.	Responds to challenges; good networker; enthusiastic.
Teamworker – supports other team members.	Sensitive, sociable and supportive.
Monitor–evaluator – evaluates ideas and analyses problems.	Hard-headed, realistic, prudent and unemotional.
Completer–finisher – takes care of details.	Time-obsessed, painstaking and conscientious.

- *Supporting transparency.* A theme running through this chapter is the need to bring issues, information, changes in policy and decisions out into the open.
- *Making sure conflict is handled well.* Effective openness and co-operation will work towards reducing the harmful and destructive effects of conflict that can sour relationships between team members. However, active co-operation will encourage positive types of conflict where open debates about the interpretation of facts or different courses of action can take place. This is the essence of good problem-solving techniques. It is up to the team leader to ensure that team members are working from the same sources of information, that all team members have the opportunity to contribute to the debate and that decisions are taken in a transparent way – not necessarily by vote, of course, but by a process where the decision can be justified. It is also vital that the dignity and self-respect of team members are preserved in the process.
- *Ensuring regular reviews take place.* They are vital, and help the team to assess their own progress, ensure time-scales are adhered to, allow celebrations to take place and allow learning from experience in, it is hoped, a no-blame culture.

An example of a small organisation successfully moving towards self-managed teams is shown in Case 3.1.

Case 3.1 Self-managed teams at Vesuvius

Vesuvius is a specialist ceramics factory in Ayrshire employing 275 staff, of whom 185 work on the shop floor. In the mid-1990s, following a change of ownership, the company took a long, hard look at its people management policies and then embarked on a change programme under the banner of the business excellence model developed by the European Foundation for Quality Management (EFQM). This programme was designed to create a culture in which all employees took responsibility for improved performance, and centred on the introduction of self-managed teams.

'The view was that, if you gave people responsibility, they would be keen to grow themselves and the business, so it was a case of giving them the trust to go out and manage business processes,' explained HR Manager, Steve Simpson.

Over three years up to 1997, new working practices were negotiated with the trade unions. A single wage structure was introduced together with complete flexibility across jobs and departments. Production staff were given training that enabled every member of every team to do all the jobs within that team. Team meetings came in for each area and, as a symbol of trust, clocking-in was abandoned.

A certain amount of opposition came from shop stewards and traditional supervisors, who felt that power and authority were slipping away. Within a short time, however, most employees recognised the new way of working as a good way of overcoming the day-to-day problems that stood in the way of their work, which they could solve themselves with their colleagues rather than having to run to the supervisor for a decision. The recognition that no jobs would be lost overall also helped the situation. To support their training, all employees worked towards and achieved at least NVQ level 1.

The supervisors became facilitators, involved in planning, safety, quality and training, and they all gained level 3 qualifications in NVQs. Some older supervisors found the change quite difficult but the majority coped well with the change and found that it strengthened, rather than weakened, their authority and status.

The results were extremely encouraging. Using the EFQM assessment techniques, the overall employee satisfaction measure rose from 70 per cent to 90 per cent over three years for quality and productivity, company image and employee involvement. Satisfaction with health and safety rose even more, from 53 per cent to 90 per cent, suggesting that staff were becoming more convinced that the company cared about their environment and working conditions. Similarly, the company results as a whole improved, with turnover up 50 per cent over five years and a decline in customer complaints. Cost savings through self-managed teams (mostly the reduction in the number of supervisors and improved productivity methods) saved the organisation £500,000 a year.

(Source: Arkin, 1999)

Another approach to team building through action-centred leadership is shown in Case 3.2.

Case 3.2 Action-centred leadership at Clamason Industries

Clamason Industries, a West Midlands-based family-owned business, 220-strong, producing high-precision metal pressings and associated electrical assemblies, hit hard times in the mid-1990s. It recorded a loss and only half the orders were delivered on time with very poor service to major customers such as Toyota and Rover. It was turned round by a new chairman, Michael Jukes, who invested in John Adair's long-established technique focusing managers' and supervisors' minds on three key issues: achieving the task, building and maintaining the team and developing the individual.

Everybody involved in managing people, including directors, went on the three-day residential action-centred leadership (ACL) course at the time that the company was restructured into a tighter management grid. Subjects on the course included communication, delegation, target setting, conflict management and counselling skills. For supervisors, top-up leadership development was offered through Dudley Tec, leading to the award of NVQ level 4 in management.

In practice, management had to change its culture from one of cracking the whip to get the job done to one of building teams and developing individuals, and then letting them get on and take responsibility for the job. The thirst for training that emerged from this initiative has now permeated to the shop floor where 80 employees were working towards NVQs by the end of 1998 and a further 20 had signed up to subsidised non-vocational courses. By the beginning of 1999, the workforce had shrunk to 180 but the company was in a much more secure position with a far better record of service to customers and a higher reputation in the market place.
(Source: Chadda, 1999)

Encouraging flexible working

Small organisations should have the built-in advantages of flexibility. Being small, they should be able to adapt more quickly to the business environment and to changes in the market place, and their employees need to understand thoroughly how important this is if the organisations are to survive and prosper. Customers want service increasingly round the clock. Sudden peaks and troughs of work need to be accommodated, new skills need to be brought on stream quickly and the major changes in working within e-commerce provide opportunities that cannot be missed. At the same time, a tightening of the labour market in recent years and the gradual switch of work from manufacturing to service industries have meant the need to offer more flexible hours and conditions of work so as to attract a wider range of applicants, especially those with caring responsibilities. It is certainly true to say that the tapping of this labour force has done much to keep the lid on general pay inflation over the past 20 years.

There are four different types of flexibility:

- *temporal flexibility*, which is centred around differing hours of work;
- *numerical flexibility*, which allows numbers of staff to rise and fall quickly;
- *geographical flexibility*, which allows employees to work away from the workplace;
- *occupational flexibility*, which encourages adaptability of skills and responsibilities.

Temporal flexibility

Job-shares are a growing form of part-time work, which used to be restricted to routine administrative posts but are gradually moving into higher positions. They can be very successful but need to be thought through carefully before being implemented. The proposal needs to be costed, it needs to start on a trial basis and procedures for decision making and communication need to be clarified to all concerned.

Flexitime used to be very popular but organisations have become less keen, for reasons given in Table 3.5. Under this arrangement, employees are allowed to choose their time of work, as long as they attend for a core time, say 10 am to 4 pm, and attend their agreed total hours within each month, although hours can be carried over or made up later within specific limits. Time worked over the maximum can be taken off as holiday. Every hour worked has to be recorded.

Annualised hours are relatively modern, but can be quite complex. Employees are contracted to work an annual rather than a weekly or monthly number of hours, and the number of hours can vary each week or month, although employees receive the same monthly pay. The rota may involve more hours in summer than winter (in frozen food production, for example). The hours are often divided into 'core hours', which are rostered, and 'unallocated hours', which are worked when required due to absenteeism, machine breakdowns or variation in work flow.

A short example of a small company's approach to flexibility is shown in Case 3.3.

Case 3.3 Flexible working

Kevin Coleman, Managing Director of office refurbishment company Swift Construction, won the 2001 Boss of the Year in the Parents at Work/Lloyds TSB annual award. Coleman, who employs 15 people in his Surrey-based business, was recognised for his commitment to flexible working and the importance he places on work-life balance.

Despite the size of his company, Coleman offers formalised job-shares and flexible working hours and has shown his commitment to maternity and parental leave.

(Source: *People Management*, 28 June 2001)

A summary of advantages and disadvantages is shown in Table 3.5.

Table 3.5 Advantages and disadvantages of temporal flexibility

Flexible Practice	Advantages to the Organisation	Disadvantages to the Organisation
Job-share	– Helps reduce absenteeism: one person will cover for the other. – Holiday cover built in. – High level of continuity. – Two employees bring a wider range of skills.	– Colleagues have to deal with two different employees. – Handover may not be seamless. – Manager may not like the arrangement because it can be complicated.

		– At peak periods, there could be an extra pair of hands.	– Double the number of appraisals and payslips. – Policy decision taking could be difficult when split. – Compatibility between the two parties has to be very good.
	Flexitime	– Absenteeism tends to drop as employees who have transport problems do not ring in sick but arrive later instead. – Can be an attractive recruitment aid. – When working well, it can provide a wider coverage for phones and customer-facing activities.	– Managers sometimes find it difficult to arrange cover when employees' arrival and departure times are unpredictable. – Employees can be tempted to manipulate the system, counting every hour they work. – It does not always encourage employees to 'go the extra mile', but rather to go off early or work later to build up their hours.
	Annualised Hours	– Can eliminate overtime payments. – Ensures employees' time is utilised effectively. – Unallocated hours are only worked when required so employees will try to ensure they are not required by reducing absenteeism, machine breakdowns, etc. – There have been recognised improvements in team working under annualised hours.	– Schemes can be complex and not family-friendly, especially when unallocated hours are required at short notice. – If unallocated hours are used up, then overtime has to be paid, which negates some of the value of the scheme.

Part-timers and the law

The Part-Time Workers Regulations came into effect in July 2001, which implemented an EU Directive. This made it illegal to distinguish in any terms and conditions between full- and part-time employees, no matter how few their hours. (Until 2001, you could differentiate terms for those working less than 16 hours.) Part-timers have to be provided access to the same benefits, which can be tricky for big items, such as company cars and private health insurance. It is not a defence to argue that the benefit cannot be provided on a pro-rata basis but it is possible to convert the benefit into cash calculated on a pro-rata basis.

Numerical flexibility

There has been a large increase in the number of employees on **fixed-term contracts**. Although having a pool of employees whose service is limited can be useful should redundancies be necessary, it has to be remembered that a succession of continuous short-term contracts generally counts, at law, as being one continuous contract with all the accompanying rights to redundancy payments and claims for unfair dismissal. Since 2001, the right has been abolished to include an unfair dismissal or redundancy waiver in any fixed-term contract. Another detail is that you should not take it for granted that you can select employees on fixed-term contracts for redundancy in preference to permanent employees. This may be regarded as discriminatory if the majority of such employees are female or from ethnic origins.

Where short-term contracts can be very useful is in the employment of year-out students, especially those who take the third year out from their college course. They are more mature than 18-years-olds taking a year out before going to university and they can also bring into the organisation some specialist knowledge in areas such as computing languages or law. Employers' experiences have almost always been positive in this area and there is always the possibility of the students returning to you after graduation with no recruitment or induction costs. Year-out students are also quite cheap!

Agency staff have always been utilised for temporary positions but there has been a gradual movement towards **using agencies** in a more strategic way. This means contracting with one agency to provide all the temporary needs at a preferential rate and keeping such staff for longer periods of time so they replace permanent staff. This allows considerable flexibility, avoiding possible redundancy costs or unfair dismissal claims. Agencies are so competitive these days that the cost may be no higher then direct employment. Against these benefits must be weighed the difficulties of permanent and temporary staff working side by side on different pay rates.

Some family-friendly benefits, such as part-time working and career breaks, can provide further flexibility benefits (although mostly for the employee). These are detailed in Chapter 5.

Geographical flexibility

With the advent of new technology, more and more jobs can be done from a home or satellite office, and **teleworking** and **working from home** have shown considerable growth over the last 10 years. There are few full-time teleworkers, but large numbers of employees who are spending an increasing amount of time working from home, only coming occasionally into the office or base. The most suitable posts for teleworking are those that are self-contained and involve no face-to-face contact, such as IT development, routine clerical work or some forms of research. For the employer, there are considerable advantages:

- saving of office space;
- a wider pool of potential employees, as they do not need to live close to base;
- staff able to stay on while bringing up a family.

For the employee, there are also advantages of the reduction in travelling time, bother and costs, and the flexibility of working time – having more choice in mixing work and leisure.

Care does have to be taken in setting up a teleworking operation, however, with considerable cooperation from both sides, as detailed in the box below.

> ### Advice on setting up a teleworking operation
> - Make sure the employee's home situation is physically and socially suitable for carrying out extensive work. A spare bedroom is best, rather than a part of the dining room (although improved portable equipment makes this less of a problem).
> - Ensure health and safety requirements are met – cables, electrical equipment, workstations, etc, as if the equipment was in the office.
> - Make sure arrangements are in place for servicing and insuring equipment.
> - Agreeing work expectations is essential – targets, time-scales and quality of work.
> - Agree regular contact times – meetings to keep in touch and extended calls for updating.
> - The employee should receive all the communications and invitations to attend meetings that staff working in the office do – a sense of isolation and missing out on social contacts at work has been found to be the greatest reason for teleworking to be abandoned.
> - Employees should not be overlooked for promotion because they are not often seen.

Working Time Directive

An important factor to remember with all systems of flexible working is the operation of the Working Time Directive. There is considerable complexity in these regulations but the main clauses are:

- *Working hours.* Employees are not obliged to work more than 48 hours a week averaged over a period of 17 weeks.
- *Rest breaks.* Employees must have 11 consecutive hours of rest in any 24-hour period and a 24-hour rest in every seven days. They must also have a 20-minute break if the workday exceeds six hours.

- *Holidays*. Employees are entitled to a minimum of fours weeks' paid holiday a year. This can include the statutory days of holiday.
- *Derogations*. At the time of writing, employees can agree with their employer to opt out of these regulations, and around 25 per cent of employees have done so according to a recent report. However, the European Union will be re-examining this provision and it is likely to be stopped in 2003. Employees who have autonomous decision-making powers, such as senior managers, are also exempt from these regulations.

Occupational flexibility

Keeping job descriptions loosely defined is a key to flexibility and something that small businesses are good at doing. It is important that employees understand the ethos of setting their hands to any job that needs to be done – as long as they are competent to do so. This aspect of competency is crucial. All too often, the willingness of the employee mixed with a lack of training can lead to deadly results – as the figures on deaths and serious injuries amongst young people on building sites show. Flexibility should be consciously sought out and supported by appropriate training. Details of how the training processes can be carried out are indicated in Chapter 4. The importance of training cannot be overestimated.

Horizontal flexibility is a term that describes **multi-skilling**. Although specialist skills can be very important, they can cause barriers to providing a complete and speedy service. For example, getting an interactive Web site up and running involves a number of IT skills. A large provider may have teams of staff each with a specific skill but co-ordinating this activity costs time and money. The small provider will have the edge if it has staff who can complete all the tasks themselves and handle the customer relations as well.

An example is D W Windsor, a manufacturer of traditional street furniture, such as lamps and bollards. Within their 30-strong assembly force, the emphasis is on each team member being able to carry out at least six different jobs. As much of the work is made specifically to orders from local authorities and housebuilders, the make-up of the work is unpredictable so it is vital that employees can switch from one type of work to another at short notice. The speed of reaction to customer orders is recognised as a key competitive advantage. In addition, the employees enjoy the variety of the work. There is a strong link with empowerment, as employees need to be trusted to pay attention to the high quality required (the products are expensive) and co-ordinate their work so that the jobs are completed on time often without close supervision.

Many large organisations are trying to mimic the small business through multi-skilling. Manufacturers have set up production 'cells' instead of assembly lines, with employees trained in most of the jobs in the cell. Insurance companies are restructuring so that one department of multi-skilled administrators can provide a service to brokers or customers on sales, new products or claims, rather than having to deal with different departments.

Staff should also be **skilled vertically**. This means being able to handle some supervisory or managerial decisions (a type of empowerment mentioned earlier) as well as carrying out routine or even menial work (keeping their work area clean and tidy rather than hiring in cleaners).

Checklist of things to avoid in flexible working
- *Failing to ask the workforce.* Do not let managers, fresh from a flexibility seminar, rush into a heady cocktail of new concepts – nine-day fortnights, annualised hours, etc. It will fail because they have not assessed sufficiently whether the arrangements are appropriate to the work in their department and have not involved employees in the change process.
- *Creating a paper mountain.* Do not spend an inordinate amount of time being hyper-cautious by being swamped in a sea of committees, focus groups and paperwork. Set a specific time not too far ahead when a decision will be taken to act.

- *Leaving it to the experts.* Any new system has to have IT support but it must not be driven by IT convenience or expertise; the human issues are far more important. The danger is that you may have a brilliant system for, say, homeworking, but everybody has lost interest.
- *Allowing too many exceptions.* With certain flexible practices, such as annualised hours, flexitime and hot-desking schemes, it is important that procedures are followed by everybody. So take care that some departments do not make up their own rules that entirely negate the purpose of the flexible practice. Departments should be allowed some latitude but ensure they keep within the limits.
- *Not checking on the outcomes.* Unless the flexible practices produce the planned results, you are wasting your time. So ensure that the cost savings are made on homeworking, that annualised hours reduce overtime, that the flexible hours system reduces staff turnover and that service delivery has improved.
- *Resting on your laurels.* The systems appear to be working well so no effort is made to fine-tune them or move on to the next stage and get even bigger benefits.

(Source: Adapted from Lake, 2001)

A further example of how initiatives in flexible working have turned around a small business is shown in Case 10.1, the Pindar Set case.

References

Adams, J (1963) Towards an understanding of equity, *Journal of Abnormal and Social Psychology*, **67**, pp 442–36

Arkin, A (1999) Peak practice, *People Management*, 11 November, pp 57–59

Belbin, M (1981) *Management Teams: Why they succeed or fail*, Butterworth-Heinemann, Oxford

Chadda, D (1999) Pressing ahead, *People Management*, 11 February, pp 50–51

Herzberg, F (1968) One more time: how do you motivate employees?, *Harvard Business Review*, January–February, pp 53–62

Kohn, A (1993) *Punished by Rewards*, Houghton-Mifflin, Boston

Kouzes, J and Posner, B (1999) *Encouraging the Heart*, Jossey-Bass, San Francisco

Lake, A (2001) How to foul up flexible working, *People Management*, 26 July, pp 36–37

Maslow, A (1954) *Motivation and Personality*, Harper and Row, New York

Woodcock, M (1979) *Team Development Manual*, Gower, Aldershot

Further information

For a wider application of team working, see:

Clegg, B and Birch, P (1998) *Instant Teamwork*, Kogan Page, London

Hardingham, A and Royal, J (1994) *Pulling Together: Teamwork in practice*, IPD, London

For detailed information on the Working Time Directive, see the Incomesdata.co.uk Web site.

For a useful short publication on empowerment, see *You Can't Give It, People Have to Want It* from Develin & Partners (tel: 01895 820202).

For a guide to recognising employees, see Kouzes, J and Posner, B (1999) *Encouraging the Heart*, Jossey-Bass, San Francisco.

If you want to read more on motivation, see:

Holbeche, L (1998) *Motivating People in Lean Organisations*, Butterworth-Heinemann, Oxford

Whetton, D and Woods, M (1996) *Effective Motivation*, Harper Collins, London

Of the many books on performance reviews, see:

Armstrong, M (2000) *Performance Management*, Kogan Page, London

Bee, R and Bee, F (1998) *Constructive Feedback*, CIPD, London
Gilley, J, Boughton, N and Maycunich, A (1999) *The Performance Challenge*, Perseus Books, London
Hartle, F (1997) *Transforming the Performance Management Process*, Kogan Page, London

Flexibility is covered by:

Reilly, P (2000) *Flexibility at Work*, Gower, Aldershot
Stredwick, J and Ellis, S (1998) *Flexible Working Practices*, IPD, London

For advice on flexible working, contact HOP Associates at www.flexibility.co.uk. They have a free publication, *The Complete Guide to Flexible Working*.

4 Training and developing employees

Introduction

We have seen many ideas in Chapter 3 on how to improve the performance of employees either as individuals or as teams. Training comes into the picture in three ways. Firstly, employees will not be able to perform well unless they have the essential skills and knowledge to do the job. Secondly, training will be required in how to operate some of the systems that have been suggested; for example, managers need training in how to run an effective project team, performance management system or system of annualised hours. Thirdly, the monitoring and control methods in place should indicate when training is required to get performance back on track.

Of course, training comes into each of the other chapters. Managing change, handling equal opportunities, health and safety or redundancies all have a training input, and all chief executives who commence any initiative without thinking through the training implications do so at their peril. We should also consider one of the latest government buzzwords – 'lifelong learning'. This points out that we should never stop learning, whether as individuals or as businesses. The day we stop learning, we fade away. This is why a number of large, progressive employers are encouraging their employees continually to develop themselves – to look for new skills and more knowledge – so that the employees continue to add value to the organisation.

Some small businesses are very negative towards training. 'If I train my employees, they promptly take the qualification or skill to another organisation and get more money – what is the point?' If I have heard that once, I have heard it a hundred times. There is a grain of truth in it, but there is also just as much truth in the complaint from larger organisations that the people they train are promptly poached by small organisations who cannot be bothered to train!

The answer is, as always, something of a compromise. Many small organisations simply do not have the resources to train for one-off jobs and need to import certain skills they do not have in technical and managerial areas. But if training is avoided altogether, the culture of the business becomes one of 'easy come, easy go', with little or no loyalty. Employees who appreciate the time, money and effort spent on their training are much more likely to be loyal, positive and committed to the business. Those who leave have been known to come back later on with even more skills and experience, or to be customers or suppliers with respect for the business. Avoiding training is no real option.

This chapter will concentrate on identifying a number of key training areas that apply across all aspects of managing people. This includes:

- *induction* – getting people started, which incorporates the use of an employee handbook;
- *identifying training needs* – where training is necessary;
- *types of training you can carry out* – internal and external;
- *Investors in People* – whether you need this;
- *help from government bodies for training in small businesses.*

Induction

There is no better starting point than induction. No matter how successful your selection processes, all the value will be lost if new employees decide after a short period that the organisation is not for them. Research has strongly indicated that the first three to four months have a decisive impact on an employee's decision on whether to stay. It is also clear that a well-prepared induction has a large influence on that decision. On the more negative side, there have been a number of high-profile cases where young employees have had accidents in their first few days at work because management skimped on the induction process.

That is not to say that inductions should be complex, lengthy and expensive. As with most aspects of human resources, they should simply be appropriate to the job and the new employee. There are some features, however, that will apply for all employees, which will help them to settle quickly into their new positions. These include the following:

- *Basic information on the organisation.* This should cover its products or services, a brief history, key people (including the chief executive!), main customers and suppliers, locations and recent successes such as large contracts or awards leading to good publicity. Included here also should be an organisation chart, mission statement, set of values and details of the system of internal communication. It is worth summarising this information in a small leaflet or including it in the employee handbook, because little will sink in on the first day. Care has to be taken that information on the organisation does not become a boring monologue.
- *Basic information on the department and on the job itself.* Details of how the department is structured and an introduction to colleagues are essential. The employee should have a job description but time should be set aside to extend this into the detail of the department's output, its standards and expectations,

including how the specific job fits into the department's output chain.
- *Health, safety and welfare information.* This should cover fire drills, first aid arrangements, washrooms and conveniences, lunch arrangements and any safety elements related to the job, such as protective equipment, hazardous substances and smoking restrictions. Chapter 8 has more details on safety issues. Much of this information can be given as part of a tour of the premises.
- *Information on terms and conditions.* The offer letter will have set out the essential terms of the job, but legislation (Employment Rights Act 1996) requires a contract of employment, called a 'written statement of particulars of employment', to be issued within two months of the employee starting work. The details to be explicitly given are listed in the box below.

Written statement of particulars of employment

The employee must be notified of the following areas:

- the names of the parties to the contract;
- the date of commencement of employment;
- hours of work;
- location of the workplace plus an indication of whether the employee will be required to work elsewhere;
- rate of pay and frequency;
- job title;
- holiday entitlement;*
- sick pay and sick leave;*
- details of any pension arrangements;*
- details of entitlement to notice and the notice that the employee should give;*
- details of disciplinary and grievance procedures.*

*This information can be provided by reference to standard documents available to the employee (on the noticeboard or in an employee handbook, for example).

How to put an induction programme together

Inductions will vary depending on the employee and the position. It is always easier to carry out an induction when a number of employees are starting at the same time. On the other hand, it is unwise, even dangerous, to start an employee without a formal induction, simply because it is time-consuming to carry out an induction for one person. It is advisable to have the first day mapped out for all new starters and make sure that the reception desk is ready to receive them. An induction for a production trainee in an engineering factory could be planned as in Table 4.1.

A useful way to reinforce the first day's learning is to give trainees a sheet with some very simple questions early in the day and to give them short breaks after each session to answer those questions. Any gaps in trainees' knowledge can therefore be remedied. It is important to stress to trainees that this is not a test, and it should be treated fairly light-heartedly, although questions on health and safety need to be reinforced seriously.

An office induction can follow a very similar pattern, although the premises tour may be much shorter. Induction processes are sometimes ignored for supervisors, technical staff or managers on the basis that they should be able to pick up all the information they want quickly through questioning. There is some truth in this but an opportunity should be scheduled for the four essential elements of any induction detailed above to be covered very early in the employment. In one small service organisation, new supervisors were given a short investigative project to carry out during their first few days at the same time as they were learning their own job. This was to ensure that they obtained a broader view of the organisation than they would normally have obtained.

An example of the effectiveness of an induction programme in a medium-sized organisation is shown in Case 4.1.

Table 4.1 Induction programme for a trainee in an engineering factory

8.30	Reception	Met by Training/Safety Officer – taken to training room
8.40	Training room	Introduction to organisation – take trainee through basic company induction literature
9.30	Coffee in refreshment area	
10.00	Tour of premises	Training/Safety Officer, including introduction to General Manager
11.00	Training room	Health and safety issues. Protective clothing issued
12.00	Lunch	Introduction to Manager and colleagues
13.00	Work area	Manager to outline training that will be given and outline of work that will be carried out
15.30	Training room	Training/Safety Officer – outline of company procedures on holiday, absence, discipline, etc, making use of company handbook. Review of day, reminding trainee of most important features
16.30	Return to work area	Brief details of what will happen as training starts

Case 4.1 Blackpool Pleasure Beach

In 1998, as a result of a rising number of complaints and minor accidents, Blackpool Pleasure Beach designed and introduced a much improved induction programme for all 1,500 temporary summer staff and any new recruits to the 300-strong permanent staff. The course was designed in collaboration with local colleges, which secured an element of public funding from the Further Education Funding Council.

The course consists of a three-hour workshop and supervision of a continuing system of workbooks kept by the trainees. The workshop includes taking employees through the employee handbook, covering such topics as dress code, food hygiene, identifying forged banknotes and suspicious packages. Health and safety is especially important so all staff can deal with minor accidents and major emergencies. Each chapter in the workbook ends with a list of simple questions that employees must answer correctly to gain their certificate.

Customer care is emphasised throughout the induction, as is the belief that excellent service can be delivered if the basic jobs are done well and the spirit of loyalty and co-operation is strong. The induction is delivered in a way appropriate to the staff, many of whom have learning difficulties, chequered work histories and few qualifications. All those who successfully complete the course (the vast majority) are rewarded with a certificate and free tickets.

At the end of the first year of operating the programme, it was found that the number of minor accidents had dropped by a half and the claims for compensation from 125 to 62, dropping further to 50 by 1999. Moreover, the course has motivated staff to pursue further training in areas such as first aid and security. In 1998, 160 employees completed NVQs. It is seen as a major contributor to raising morale, which is vital in the service industry where the employees create the atmosphere that makes customers enjoy themselves and want to come back.
(Source: Littlefield, 2000)

Employee handbook

It saves a lot of time if general information that applies to all employees is included in an employee handbook. For employees, it clarifies details of their employment contract and is a reference point for any area on which they are uncertain. The problem is that it will constantly need updating whenever changes are made. Some organisations get round this by notifying employees when changes are made and then producing an updated version of the handbook, say, every two years, using in-house desktop publishing. On the other hand, with the development of intranets, many organisations place the constantly updated handbook on the intranet, which becomes available for employees to check, and they can print out sections they want. New employees are provided with a hard copy. A checklist of items to be included in the employee handbook is given in the box below.

Checklist of items to be included in the employee handbook

Introduction
This should include:

- a message from the Chief Executive;
- background to the organisation, including a short history;
- products, location;
- company vision;
- communication systems.

Terms and conditions
These should include:

- hours of work;
- flexibility arrangements;
- holidays;
- pay arrangements, including the right to make deductions;
- other benefits (private health scheme, pensions, staff discount, share-save, etc);
- sick pay;
- disciplinary procedure;
- rules governing behaviour;
- dress code;
- grievance procedure;
- notice arrangements;
- health and safety, including first aid;
- statement on the right to change terms and conditions after consultation;
- statement on the right to lay employees off without pay when work is not available (optional);
- statement on confidentiality;
- security issues;
- customer care.

Identifying training needs

Training needs arise at three levels:

- *Business level* – where training is required for everybody in the organisation. This could be in technical areas, especially learning a new computer system or understanding new products, or it could be where the organisation's culture needs to change, such as a drive for higher quality or to improve customer care. Just as with introducing a new computer system, cultural changes are expensive and time-consuming, and need to be handled with great care. When successful, however, they can make a huge difference to the performance of the business – so, in reality, they are inevitable on a regular basis.
- *Department level* – where training is required to meet specific departmental requirements such as a new accounting process or production technique.
- *Individual level* – where training can help individual employees meet their potential, remedy a fault or prepare for promotion.

Sources to help you identify training needs

We have seen in Chapter 3 that **performance reviews** can be a major source for identifying individual training needs. Where employees fall short of expected performance, then carefully identified training can put them back on the right path. Performance reviews can also be useful for identifying where departments are failing and not reaching their targets.

The stimulus for training at the business level must come directly from the board when they are examining the **business plan**. Every move – expansion, consolidation, closure, new products, new locations, new systems – has people implications, and most involve training. The cases in Chapter 10 show how small businesses have incorporated training into their business developments to ensure the required results – without training, the outcomes would have been patchy at best.

A final source for identifying training needs is the **employees** themselves. Through the consultative and communication process (consultative committee, employee surveys, etc – see Chapter 6), ideas may come forward of gaps where training could be beneficial – new employees may bring ideas from their old companies, or it may be quite clear that managers are generally failing in areas such as communication. Listening to employees is important here, and responding to their ideas on training always gets a good reception.

You may want to bring the ideas together into a **training plan**. You will certainly need to cost the ideas to determine which ones can go forward within the budget allowed. Having a laid-down plan means you can review it as it goes forward and evaluate it afterwards to see how successful or otherwise it has been.

The training cycle

It is useful to understand the principle of the training cycle, as shown in Figure 4.1.

For training to be effective, each of these stages needs to be worked on carefully. Evaluation of the training is often omitted or covered simply by a 'happy sheet' issued at the end of a short course to participants. Proper evaluation takes place many months later to identify the long-term benefits of the training experience.

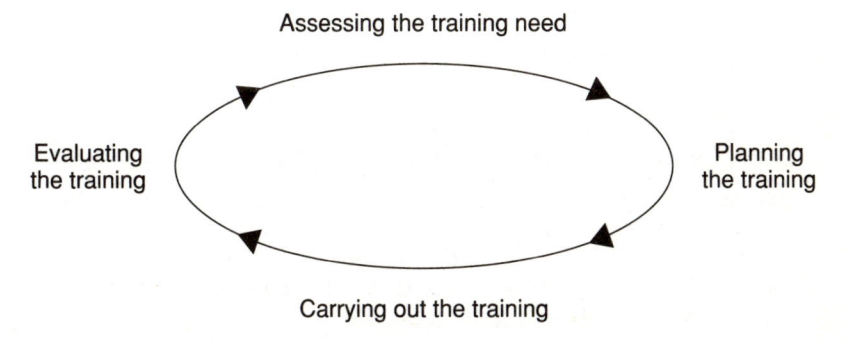

Figure 4.1 The training cycle

Methods of training

A traditional view of training is simply attending training courses outside the organisation. Although this has its part in the whole training scene, it is actually quite a small one in terms of effectiveness. Surveys have shown that, even for the small organisation, internal training is generally much more cost-effective and focused, so we shall look at this first.

Coaching

Coaching is everybody's job. For the new employee sitting next to you, for new starters under your supervision, for all staff whom you control as a manager, you will need to coach them along so they get better in their job. Some people are naturals in this role and are very willing to help when required. Others are more reticent, hostile even, and may resent having to give up their time to help others. Again, it is vital that you develop a culture and spirit of co-operation, rather than individual competition. 'I learnt by being thrown in the deep end, so everybody else should' is an understandable attitude but will be expensive in terms of mistakes, time lost and staff turnover.

Whether the coaching is for a school leaver commencing work as a chicken-gutter or for a Cambridge graduate learning the arcane world of mega-mergers, there are some essential features in the coaching process. These are set out in the box below.

Checklist of essential coaching features
- *Make sure learners want to learn before you start.* If the motivation to learning is not there, nothing will get through. You need to sort any learning problems out before you can achieve any results.
- *Always think about the people receiving the information.*
  - How much do they already know?
  - How good are they at learning?
  - How much can they take in today?
  - What ways do they like learning?

In other words, start from their position, not yours. They are the ones who have to learn and you have to make it as straightforward as possible. This is not spoon-feeding, and you should include challenges they have to meet, but only as part of the coaching process. In itself, a challenge should not be insuperable or one that learners can easily fail because the coaching was led from the wrong position.

- *Provide the coaching in small chunks.* You may like to give a comprehensive view of the whole subject and feel that, if you miss something out, you are at fault. This is wrong. We all have our limits to concentration, and research has shown that the average rate of retention is:
  - 10 per cent of what is read;
  - 20 per cent of what is heard;
  - 30 per cent of what is seen;
  - 50 per cent of what is seen and heard;
  - 70 per cent of what the learner says;
  - 90 per cent of what the learner says and does.
- *Never, never give what could be called a 'lecture'.* Teaching staff waste enough time at universities giving these and are surprised when students do not turn up!
- *Don't start unprepared.* Even for short, informal coaching, make sure you have the necessary materials and equipment to hand.
- *Ensure that learners put learning into practice* through actually carrying out the part of the job they have learnt. Reinforcement through doing is essential.
- *Build on previous coaching.* Make sure learners have retained previous skills and knowledge learnt through recent coaching before progressing – ask questions, encourage the right answers and give tests, if appropriate.
- *Get learners involved.* Constantly ask questions, give opinions, get learners to ask questions, and pause and leave gaps.
- *Check what has been learnt* by finishing with some questions or examples.
- *Break off the session* when it is clear the learning has stopped.
- *Praise success.* Reinforcement of learning is vital, and learners retain much more if the experience is a successful and happy one.

Mentoring

It is always valuable to have a person to turn to who will support your progress and help your development. Of course your boss should do this, but experience has shown that an experienced employee with no formal responsibility over you, who has an interest in helping people develop, can be an invaluable source of advice and knowledge.

Mentoring does not have to be set up formally in small organisations. In the case of younger managers or supervisors or technical staff, it is worth considering asking an experienced staff member to meet up with them from time to time and act as their mentor. This can include helping them with the culture and politics of the organisation (it may be obvious to you but can be a minefield for new employees, especially where relatives of the owner work in the organisation!), encouraging them when they face difficult challenges or go through a bad patch, providing learning opportunities and generally helping them with their career.

You may not be able to reward the mentor specifically for carrying out the job well but a gift or small bonus would not go awry.

Using external training providers

External providers can be useful in preparing and running a dedicated internal course for you or you can sign up for one of their public courses. A provider will charge between £700 and £2,000 per day for an in-company course, which includes preparation costs, although these may be charged separately. The cost difference depends generally on whether the organisation concerned is a one-man band or a well-known national provider. External courses vary between £100 and £800 a day. There are literally hundreds of training providers, and you are, no doubt, continually bombarded with their literature. It is impossible to advise which you should use but keep these points in mind before using a training provider for the first time:

- Get the provider to give you the telephone numbers of two organisations of your size that have used the services recently.

You should try to get in contact to judge whether the provider is right for you.
- Providers will be happy for you to drop into one of their training courses, especially a public one, so you can judge the quality.
- Make sure the providers of an internal course question you carefully about your organisation, its products, history and development, and then give you a very detailed course plan. Otherwise, they may simply be giving you an off-the-peg job that may not be sufficiently relevant for you.
- Providers will always take more time with you if they believe that the relationship will be a long-term one – so always talk to them on this basis.

National Vocational Qualifications

Some small organisations have found that National Vocational Qualifications (NVQs), which were set up in 1986, can be a useful plank in developing employees. They are centred on the outcome of the practical work tackled and are a measure of an employee's competency in that work. The qualifications range from level 1 to level 5:

level 1   Occupational competence in performing a wide range of activities that are routine and predictable.
level 5   Competence at a professional level, with a mastery of a range of relevant knowledge and the ability to apply it in situations that may be unpredictable. It is likely to be accompanied by personal autonomy together with responsibility for the work of others and the allocation of resources.

There are very mixed views on competencies and their values. A number of organisations have found great success in the integration of the system in developing practical skills, especially in construction, engineering and other practical trades and industries, such as catering and retailing. Where it is successful, employees have responded well to building up their skills from level 1 to level 3, and the quality of the product and the service has improved. It has certainly helped employees improve their general literacy and numeracy, which can be vital. Where businesses have found it unsuccessful, it is because of their bureaucratic paperwork, costs of initiating, running and supervising the scheme and the lack of specific relevance to those businesses' specialised product or service area.

So the take-up is patchy, and businesses need to check carefully with their trade association to find a company like theirs that has found it to be cost-effective before going too far down this route.

Investors in People

Investors in People (IIP) has had a very much greater take-up amongst small businesses. It is an award accredited by the Learning and Skills Council to businesses that have met four main criteria:

- a written business plan, including information on how employees will contribute towards achieving it;
- a system of performance management that helps determine training and development needs of all employees;
- evidence of induction training and continuous development for all employees;
- evaluation of training against business goals.

Small businesses have been attracted by the accreditation not only because of the way it claims to improve business performance but also because some large businesses and government departments insist on contractors having the accreditation before being allowed on tender lists. Research has indicated that working towards and achieving the accreditation improves a number of key performance indicators, such as staff attendance, staff turnover and ease of recruitment. It does have some effect on the businesses' public image. More than 40,000 organisations have achieved IIP or are committed towards the accreditation.

An example of an organisation finding benefits through IIP is shown in Case 4.2.

Case 4.2 Investors in People at the Van Hage Garden Company

For 45 years, Van Hage operated its upmarket garden centre from one site in Hertfordshire but a rapid expansion in the late 1990s brought two more locations and an increase in staff numbers to over 300. While integrating the practices across the sites to make sure things were done the Van Hage way, it became clear that there were substantial gaps that needed to be filled. Appraisals were not being taken seriously enough, training was being carried out in a haphazard and unplanned way and many staff did not have the confidence to transfer their skills to employees on the new sites.

After taking advice from various quarters, Investors in People appeared to be the best way forward to ensure that standards in training, development and communication would be improved and a coherent 'people plan' put together to ensure the organisation would meet its expansion and profitability targets.

The first step was to carry out an employee survey to indicate the employees' views on key training and development areas. This took place in 2000 and, although there were some very positive comments on the commitment to employees by the organisation and the quality of the early induction, some serious weaknesses were revealed. Only 20 per cent of managers said they had a clear idea of where the business should be in two or three years' time; 65 per cent of employees said that they were not told about what was happening in training and development; 43 per cent reported that their training and development needs were not regularly reviewed and, for those that were reviewed, only a minority considered that their training was related to future business needs. One specific communication weakness was voiced by weekend staff who read about Van Hage's purchase of a nearby garden centre in the local newspaper.

Clearly action was needed to remedy these weaknesses. IIP workshops for both directors and managers took place in March 2000, led by a training consultant, where all the important issues were discussed and analysed. An integrated training and business plan emerged from these workshops, and agreement was reached on a number of initiatives, which were put in place as part of a coherent training and communication plan:

- Team briefings began in mid-2000 with a brief written every two months by the managing director and cascaded down to all staff within a four-day period. The brief included a business update with information not previously provided to staff, details of all training opportunities and personnel information.
- Manuals were produced for managers on policies, procedures, training and development to help them in all aspects of managing people in Van Hage's, and it was emphasised that managers were responsible for all the training and development of their staff. They received substantial help and assistance from personnel and other sources but they could not delegate these responsibilities.
- Workshops on product awareness were introduced so staff could extend their knowledge across the wide range of plants and gardening materials.
- Skills were developed through a number of employees taking part in the Retail Plant Care Award.
- The induction programme was revamped so that it extended beyond the first one or two days to a clear programme of training and assessment in the first three months, managed by the departments.
- A group training and development officer was appointed in mid-2000 to run a number of regular in-company workshops and to assist line managers in planning the development of their staff. The revised appraisal system played a major part in this planning, and running the appraisal system was the subject of some early workshops.

Melanie Broad, Human Resources Manager, was confident that the company would shortly achieve the IIP award:

> We were always conscious that, as a small organisation, we were unaware of best practices and not always thinking or acting consistently as far as training and communication is concerned. IIP has provided the framework for us to take a hard look at our practices and make the necessary improvements we need as a growing organisation. These initiatives have been very valuable in themselves. The board have been 100 per cent supportive and the results are starting to come through in terms of better customer care, reduced staff turnover and a positive view of the organisation from our staff. We have no doubt that IIP has been a good investment that will bring tangible rewards in the long term.

(Some funding for these activities was available from the local Learning and Skills Council.)

Government-sponsored training

Every UK government has been committed to assisting small businesses to succeed and prosper, and this is also an objective of the European Union. Various schemes are in operation to achieve this end, and this is a small selection:

- *Business Links*. Business Links are made up of Chambers of Commerce, Learning and Skills Councils, Local Enterprise Agencies and government departments dealing with trade, enterprise and education. Small organisations are catered for specifically by Business Links short courses and seminars. As well as courses in finance, sales and marketing, there are those focused on managing people, including:
  - employing others;
  - building a super team;
  - influencing and persuading;
  - interpersonal skills;
  - mastering stress;
  - giving outrageously good customer service;
  - assertiveness;
  - listening skills.

  Some of these short courses are free to businesses with fewer than 50 employees. Contact can be made via the Business Links information line on 0800 500 200.
- *DTI Work-Life Balance Fund*. The DTI has £10.5 million to distribute as grants over three years from 2001 to 2003 for consultancy support to organisations that would like to develop and implement work-life balance policies. Applications from small businesses have been successful in the first year, including one by Watford Football Club.
- *University for Industry*. The University for Industry (UfI) was launched in 1997 to help plug the UK's skills gap and give individuals a second chance at education through e-learning. The government has set a target of 1 million people enrolled on a UfI

course by the end of 2003 and also wants to see employees from at least 12,000 small and medium-sized enterprises on UfI courses by March 2002. There are currently around 400 courses available from basic numeracy and literacy to customer care and IT. By 2001, there were 1,000 Learndirect centres located across the UK in sports centres and shopping malls, churches and community centres. Mobile learning pods are available to be established within company's premises. It is expected that employers will contribute towards the courses to ensure they are affordable, although individuals can use their Individual Learning Accounts. The skills needs of small and medium-sized businesses are one of the UfI's four priority areas. The UfI can be contacted via its information line on 0800 100 900.

- *Small Firms Training Loans.* This is a joint initiative between the employment department and three banks designed to help businesses employing up to 50 staff to pay for vocational education and training. The scheme offers deferred repayment terms on loans between £500 and £125,000 to cover training costs and, subject to a maximum loan of £5,000, consultancy advice on training matters.
- *Individual Learning Account.* Everybody aged 19 and over in the UK can set up an Individual Learning Account of £200, which can be used to part-finance some specific training. The account allows 80 per cent off computer literacy courses, for example, and 20 per cent off a wide range of other courses, such as bookkeeping, food technology and business administration. Discounts can also be obtained from GCSEs and A levels taken in later life. Continuous professional development in technical subjects such as plumbing and electrical subjects also qualifies for a discount. The maximum for one year in these areas is £100. Discounts are not available in training for professional qualifications or on higher education courses.

There have been difficulties associated with fraudulent claims over ILAs and the Government suspended the scheme in England in 2001, although it continues to operate in Scotland and Wales.

Reference

Littlefield, D (2000) Riding high, *People Management*, 17 February, pp 48–49

Further information

For a variety of advice on training subjects, see:

Hackett, P (1997) *Introduction to Training*, IPD, London
Jackson, P (2001) *The Inspirational Trainer*, Kogan Page, London
Meighan, M (2000) *Induction Training*, Kogan Page, London
Thorne, K and Mackey, D (2001) *Everything You Ever Needed to Know about Training*, Kogan Page, London

For more details of Investors in People, see Taylor, P and Thackery, B (2001) *Investors in People Explained*, Kogan Page, London.

Coaching and mentoring are covered in:

Parsloe, E and Wray, M (2000) *Coaching and Mentoring*, Kogan Page, London
Thorne, K (2001) *Personal Coaching*, Kogan Page, London

A further example of how training has made all the difference to business performance is shown in Case 10.2, Hindle Power.

Useful Web sites are:

- www.iipuk.co.uk (Investors in People);
- www.dfes.gov.uk/ila (Individual Learning Accounts).

5 Rewarding employees

Introduction

This chapter is principally about pay. However, it is wise to remember that employees are concerned about all sorts of rewards and especially the concept of fairness, as explained in Chapter 3. Rewards need to be effective in encouraging employees to work towards the needs and objectives of the organisation. This chapter deals predominantly with financial reward, but employers who ignore non-financial rewards make a big mistake, as research has shown that recognition in the workplace can be just as great a motivator as a fat pay packet.

This chapter will begin by clarifying what are the key objectives in rewarding employees. Then the current legislative constraints will be detailed followed by suggestions on putting together appropriate forms of pay structure that bring sense into what may be a chaotic and *ad hoc* approach. This is followed by an examination of bonus and performance pay schemes with an attempt to show the key features of successful schemes. The final sections will deal with the wide choice of benefits and non-financial rewards, including share ownership schemes, that can be offered.

What are rewards for?

Traditional thinking has usually regarded pay as a contractual arrangement, a necessary evil to persuade an employee to accept a job and carry it out. In recent years, rewards have been viewed in a much broader and more strategic way. A few examples are shown in Table 5.1.

All of these examples can and do apply to small organisations, as the cases in this chapter will show. What is important is that organisations should regard pay as an investment, not just as an expense, and that employees should understand that they cannot expect a decent pay rate for just turning up to work and doing their basic job.

Effects of legislation

Before establishing any type of payment system, we need to keep in mind the restraints imposed by legislation, which continue to grow each year. The legislation on most of these subjects is complex and continually changing, and only a summary is provided here. You will need to keep up to date with the changes that are announced either in the Budget or through new regulations or primary legislation. Sources for updating are given at the end of this chapter. The main subject areas are the following:

- *Itemised pay statement* (Employment Rights Act 1996). All employees must be given an itemised statement that sets out the content of each weekly or monthly salary. This needs to specify the gross payment, the details of each deduction and the net amount. A deduction cannot be made unless it is authorised by law (such as National Insurance) or by agreement in the employee's contract. In retail organisations, employers are allowed by law to make deductions from wages to make good any cash deficiency in the till or shortfall in stock, but the total deducted must not exceed 10 per cent of the wages due.

Table 5.1 Examples of ways that reward systems can be used strategically

Strategic Intent	Using Rewards	Type of System
Most organisations want to place a great deal of emphasis on employees performing well.	To distinguish between those employees who perform well and those who do not.	Performance pay or type of bonus scheme.
For many organisations, competitive advantage depends on employees possessing certain skills, attributes or behaviours (competencies).	To encourage employees to learn those skills and adopt those behaviours.	Skills- or competence-based pay.
Innovation is vital in most organisations.	To encourage employees to think up new ideas and be innovative.	Recognition schemes.
For many small businesses, it is important to recruit and retain key employees.	To aid recruitment and retention.	Attractive pay and benefits package.
Employees need to be really involved in the business so they can demonstrate a clear commitment.	To encourage employees to become shareholders.	Employee share scheme.
It is essential that employees adopt a flexible approach to their job.	To reward flexibility in working practices.	Flexible benefits scheme.
It is important to encourage a 'one-company' approach.	To apply the same conditions and benefits for all employees.	Harmonised pay and benefits system.

- *Statutory Maternity Pay* (SMP). All qualifying pregnant employees are entitled to 18 weeks of maternity pay. This rises to 26 weeks in April 2003. To qualify, an employee needs to have worked for the employer continuously for at least 26 weeks before the qualifying week (ie the 15th week before the expected week of childbirth). The employee also needs to have average weekly earnings in the eight weeks up to and including the qualifying week over the lower earnings limit for National Insurance contributions (in 2001, this was £72). SMP is 90 per cent of the employee's average weekly earnings during the first six weeks of maternity leave, and the remaining weeks are paid at a flat rate. (In 2001 this was £62.20 per week. This rate rises to £75 a week in April 2002 and £100 in April 2003.) The employee needs to have notified her employer at least 21 days beforehand of the date on which she intends her maternity leave period to begin and to have provided evidence of her pregnancy and her expected week of confinement (EWC).

  Employers can reclaim 92 per cent of SMP from the government, provided the complex rules of the scheme have been applied. They can claim the remaining 8 per cent through Small Employers' Relief, plus a further 5 per cent if they have paid less than £20,000 gross National Insurance contributions (employees' and employer's share) in the last complete tax year before the qualifying day.

  It is possible for employers to enhance the amount of maternity pay, and some larger employers do this as a benefit and to encourage employees to come back to work after maternity leave ends. Details of maternity leave and the right to return will be covered later in the chapter in the section on benefits.
- *Paternity leave*. Plans were announced in April 2001 for a right to two weeks' paid paternity leave to be introduced in April 2003, set at £100 per week.
- *Equal pay and equal value*. The details of this legislation are set out in Chapter 7. Suffice to say here that none of your reward systems or the resulting pay rates should be discriminatory in

any way. It is worth carrying out an exercise to compare the average male rate of pay in the organisation and the average female rate. If it is very different, then you need to consider how that can be justified. It may possibly be because men take up the overtime on offer more than women. On the other hand, it may be because men predominate in more senior positions and better-paid skilled positions and receive higher bonuses based on performance. If this is the case, then the organisation runs the risk of being considered discriminatory.

- *National Minimum Wage* (NMW). The National Minimum Wage was introduced in April 1999 and was increased to £4.10 an hour from October 2001 for employees over 22. It will rise to £4.20 from October 2002. For employees aged 18 to 21, the rate is £3.50 an hour from 1 October 2001. There is currently no minimum wage for employees under 18. Employers have to keep records to which employees have the right of reasonable access.
- *Guarantee pay.* In the absence of any express term to the contrary, employers do not have any implied contractual right to lay off employees without pay or put them on short time. Such a right has to be included under the employment contract by inclusion in the employee handbook (see Chapter 4). Assuming the employer has included that right in the handbook, the *minimum* payment, set out in the Employment Rights Act 1996, is five days' pay within any three-month period for workless days at the guarantee rate (in 2001 this was £16.70 per day). Employers can, and generally do, pay much more in practice, most making the rate up to between 75 and 100 per cent of their normal day's pay.
- *Employer's Statutory Sick Pay* (SSP). The rules for SSP are exceptionally complex, and reference to a guide on the scheme is essential. SSP is not payable until the fourth consecutive day of absence, although any days of the week count towards this four-day period, whether or not they are days on which that employee would be required to work. One or more periods of incapacity for work can be linked to form just one period (in other words,

the employee does not have to wait a further three days without pay) as long as each absence is four days or more and the absences are separated by no more than 56 days in total including weekends.

The maximum SSP entitlement is 28 weeks. Certain employees are excluded from the scheme including those over 65 and under 16, those whose earnings are less than the lower earnings limit (in 2001 this was £72 a week), those engaged on a fixed-term contract of three months or less and those on strike.

SSP is only paid for days when the employee would normally be at work. The standard rate for SSP in 2001 was £62.20. When an employee leaves employment, the employer must generally give the employee a statement of any period of incapacity for work (PIW) over the previous eight weeks. SSP may be withheld by the employer if it is believed that the employee was not ill or the employee failed to notify the employer of the absence according to the employer's rules. Any dispute over payment is made through the Board of the Inland Revenue.

SSP cannot be recovered from the government (National Insurance contributions were reduced when SSP was introduced) except under the Percentage Threshold Scheme, which was introduced to help employers with exceptionally high levels of sickness absence. The scheme provides for full reimbursement of an employer's costs paid in any month where these exceed 13 per cent of the employer's gross NIC (both employer's and employees') for that month. SSP paid above that threshold is recoverable in full. To make such claims, records must be kept. Form SSP2 has been issued by the DSS for this purpose.

Creating a salary structure

Working in chaos

Many small organisations do not have a pay structure as such. Employees are taken on by the organisation's founder or owner and paid the spot rate necessary to persuade those people to join the organisation. They are unlikely to know what other employees are paid. In time individual employees may request a pay rise, arguing on the basis of their performance, the success of the organisation or a vague promise made when they were taken on. This request will be granted (or not) depending on the personal whim of the owner, the organisation's ability to pay or some unscientific and subjective review of individual performance. Periodically, the owner will review everybody's salary and may also award bonuses, based on discussions with the chief accountant and a consensus of the views of the top two or three directors. Generally, little explanation is given to the employees concerned.

With very small organisations, working with informal pay arrangements is inevitable. It would be pointless to construct complex pay systems such as job evaluation or performance-related pay to deal with only a handful of people. However, such informality does have its problems:

- *Lack of consistency.* It is all too easy for decisions to be made without a consistent or logical basis. A pay increase can be granted because business appeared to be looking up that week or denied because work had been slack for a few days. The case for a pay increase itself may not have been examined. Similarly, bonuses may be awarded or not on the basis of the performance of an employee over the last few weeks, rather than being a measured response to performance over the whole year. It may finish up that two people doing an identical job with the same level of performance receive different rates of pay.
- *Inequitable dealings.* Treatment of individual employees can appear very cavalier. Favouritism may seem to be rife where pay progression is fast for some and not for others. Employees who shout the loudest may seem to get bigger pay increases.
- *Lack of transparency.* Without any clear payment system, employees cannot be certain how their rewards are worked out, and this can be demotivating.

There are some minimum standards that should apply even in the smallest of organisations. We saw in Chapter 3 that regular individual discussions with all employees on their performance are essential to guide and motivate employees. It is natural to link these discussions to the way employees' pay may progress, taking into account the development and success of the organisation. This is essential to reduce any perception of inequitable treatment. In Chapter 6, we will see how regular and structured communications with all employees on the company's performance provide the realistic backcloth to salary reviews and help to improve transparency. Consistency can only be achieved if the pay of all the employees is firmly in the mind of the owner when any salary revision is being considered. This should not be too difficult with 30 or less employees, as they can be summarised on one page with easy reference on the palmtop.

Developing a simple salary structure

Once an organisation gets beyond 30–50 or so employees, it ought to have some form of salary/wage structure to help to avoid a continuing ongoing worry over consistency, equity and transparency. The essential feature of a salary/wage structure is that it divides the employees into grade levels. The next few sections show how this is arrived at, with an example shown of a final version in Table 5.5.

The structure can be constructed with or without the help of a **job evaluation** process, understanding the **market rates** for jobs and deciding on the general **positioning on pay** for the organisation.

Should there be job evaluation?

Job evaluation attempts to value the relative worth of jobs, using criteria drawn from the content of the jobs themselves. It does not value the people doing the jobs or their performance. It simply examines the work that needs to be done and the elements, such as responsibility, that go along with that work.

There are two types of job evaluation scheme. There are **analytical** schemes, which carefully examine each part of the job, awarding points for various aspects. The second group of schemes are called **non-analytical** and they simply examine the job as a whole. Analytical schemes, as we will see, are unsuited to small organisations so we will deal with non-analytical schemes first.

Non-analytical schemes

These schemes look at jobs as a whole and do not break them down into component parts. They can be carried out swiftly, cheaply and easily by the owner and a couple of colleagues, working confidentially using their own knowledge of the jobs concerned. The types of schemes include:

- *Job ranking.* Jobs are simply ranked in order of importance by the evaluation team.
- *Paired comparisons.* Each job is compared to all the other jobs. Two points are awarded for the more important of the two jobs and one point each if the jobs are regarded as being of the same rank. An extract from a simple example is shown in Table 5.2. In this example, the owner and fellow directors have discussed each of the jobs and decided that the Wages Clerk is at the same level as the Receptionist (1 point each) but less than the Senior Secretary, Customer Services Clerk and Purchasing Clerk (no points) and more than the Stores Clerk (2 points) and Accounts Clerk (2 points), giving a total of 5 points.

The table can be converted into a set of grades as follows:

Grade 1	Stores Clerk	0 points
	Accounts Clerk	2 points
Grade 2	Wages Clerk	5 points
	Receptionist	5 points
Grade 3	Customer Services Clerk	9 points
	Purchasing Clerk	9 points
Grade 4	Senior Secretary	12 points

Table 5.2 Paired comparison job evaluation scheme

Job Title	Wages Clerk	Receptionist	Senior Secretary	Customer Services Clerk	Stores Clerk	Accounts Clerk	Purchasing Clerk	Total Points
Wages Clerk		1	0	0	2	2	0	5
Receptionist	1		0	0	2	2	0	5
Senior Secretary	2	2		2	2	2	2	12
Customer Services Clerk	2	2	0		2	2	1	9
Stores Clerk	0	0	0	0		0	0	0
Accounts Clerk	0	0	0	0	2		0	2
Purchasing Clerk	2	2	0	1	2	2		9

- *Job Classification.* Under this scheme, each job is put into a grade category by reference to the set descriptions for that grade. A simplified version is shown in the box below. In this example, the jobs could be slotted, following discussion, into the four grades as in the paired comparison scheme. Some jobs, however, may not slip easily into one particular grade description, having elements of two or more.

Job classification scheme – grade descriptions

- *Grade 1.* Simple clerical operations using basic administrative procedures. Essentially routine work with in-built checks. Little contact with customers.
- *Grade 2.* More complex clerical operations dealing with non-routine queries and analysing data to produce simple reports. Errors can present important short-term problems. Some freedom to act on own initiative. Some contact with customers.
- *Grade 3.* Regular complex administration. Can be responsible for small number of staff. Operation of basic budgets. Errors could be costly and significant. Regular contact with customers and some contact with senior management.
- *Grade 4.* Constant variety of work or work of higher technical nature requiring qualifications and/or considerable experience. Significant contribution to objectives of department with large responsibility for decision taking. Contributes to budgeting, and errors can be very damaging. Regular contact with customers and senior management.

Summarising non-analytical schemes

With a limited number of jobs involved, it is relatively easy to operate the schemes and to come to a consensus conclusion. However, there remains a considerable amount of subjectivity in the ways decisions are taken, and the job holders are not involved in any way. It is difficult to publish the results without having to justify each decision individually. A further, rather important difficulty remains. This is that such schemes do not provide any defence at tribunals under equal value claims because of the subjectivity involved (Chapter 7 gives more details here). So a disgruntled employee who considers that his or her job should be valued the same as that of an employee of the other sex on a higher rate of pay can apply to a tribunal under equal value regulations.

Analytical schemes

It has to be said at this early stage that there is simply no point in carrying out a formal *analytical* job evaluation exercise unless you have a minimum of 30–40 different jobs to insert into a grading scheme. That means, as a rough rule of thumb, that organisations with less than 200 or so employees can do without them. On the other hand, if you employ 600–700 or more employees, you are likely to have well over 40 different jobs, so a job evaluation of some type is probably required. In between, say 200–600 employees, it may or may not be worth while, depending on your working context, the number of different jobs and the satisfaction with pay amongst the employees.

This is said with some conviction because you do not enter into a job evaluation scheme lightly. For a scheme to be worth while, it needs an investment of time and effort that is not inconsiderable. It needs an experienced human resources manager or consultant to manage the design of the scheme, oversee the actual evaluation and lead the process of conversion into a salary structure. To ensure that the job evaluation team have a thorough idea of the nature of each job, job holders need to be interviewed, and all job descriptions need to be up to date. An analytical scheme will take, on balance, around six months minimum to design and carry out. Because the time involved is so great, consultants are often brought into the process, which can add substantial costs. Furthermore, the results are not always welcome (some employees will be losers, of course) unless they are sweetened with a reasonably sizeable general pay increase or generous compensation for those employees who lose out.

Because analytical job evaluation schemes are appropriate for few small organisations, it is not intended to go into detail into what are, actually, rather complex processes in a fully fledged scheme. Instead, the box below provides a brief summary of the stages that are required.

> ### Stages in formal analytical job evaluation scheme
> 1. Select a job evaluation committee. It should include employee representatives to enhance its credibility. Four or five members in total should be sufficient.
> 2. Decide on the factors that are important to your organisation in distinguishing between jobs (see Table 5.3 for examples – others can include financial knowledge, physical demands, computer literacy, etc). It is best to limit the total to no more than six factors.
> 3. Decide on the number of levels – usually between four and six for simplicity
> 4. Decide on the points against each level for each factor. More important factors have the most points. Be careful that the way you allocate points is not sex-related (factors such as physical requirements getting too many points).
> 5. Make sure all job descriptions are up to date.
> 6. Make sure committee members know what they are doing by going through a dummy run and carrying out training where gaps are obvious.
> 7. Chose benchmark jobs to evaluate first – these are usually the most crucial jobs with the highest numbers of job holders.
> 8. Evaluate these jobs.
> 9. Evaluate the remainder of the jobs.
> 10. When completed, go through all the results to ensure earlier decisions are in line and that no evaluations stand out 'like a sore thumb'.
> 11. Announce the result and allow any appeals under agreed appeals procedures.

An alternative approach to designing a scheme from scratch is to use a proprietary scheme, such as the well-known Hay guide chart profile or the KPMG Equate scheme. These are well tried and tested (Hay has been around for 50 years) but are generally much too expensive for small organisations to use. The initial training costs, for example, can be very substantial, and there are ongoing scheme maintenance costs that may well exceed the value the scheme adds to the organisation.

Table 5.3 Job evaluation factor point grid

	Levels				
Factors	**1**	**2**	**3**	**4**	**5**
Experience level required	100	200	300	400	500
Complexity of post	80	160	240	320	400
Staff supervised	80	160	240	320	400
Responsibility	100	180	260	340	420
Innovation required	50	100	150	200	250
Financial accountability	60	120	180	260	400

Searching for market information on pay

Once a form of evaluation has produced a grade structure, you need to be confident on the wages/salaries to put against those grades, and an important element in this decision is the current market rates for the jobs on the list.

Information comes from many different sources but it has to be said that few are both specific to your needs and very reliable. Table 5.4 sets out some of the sources and the advantages and difficulties associated with the information provided.

Carrying out your own surveys or being part of a local 'pay club' are generally the best sources. When carrying out your own survey of local organisations, you need to ensure that you take into account the following:

- Make sure you are comparing jobs that are as identical as possible. One materials controller may be very different in terms of role and responsibilities to another.
- Find out whether pay includes additional payments such as bonuses, guaranteed overtime or special benefits like a company car.

- Find out when the pay was last reviewed – if the review is imminent then the current figures are not so reliable.

Sources of pay information on the Web are shown at the end of the chapter.

Table 5.4 Sources of information on pay rates

	Advantages	**Disadvantages**
Government data on labour market trends	Reliable data on national trends. Useful for year-end pay reviews. Free information.	Local trends may vary. No data on sector or individual jobs.
Incomes Data Services	Reliable data by sector with good commentary.	You need to subscribe. Data not local.
National and regional surveys (by Reward Group or Computer Economics, etc)	Reliable, up-to-date information. Regional and sector surveys can be valuable.	Expensive – can cost up to £200. Go out of date quickly.
Selection of current newspaper/ magazine adverts	Full range for comparable jobs. Free information.	Only tell you what is on offer, not whether candidates recruited at that rate.
Information from local agencies	Up-to-date, free information.	Can possibly have small degree of bias towards higher end.
Carrying out your own survey	Focused, up to date and reliable.	Very time-consuming. Returns not guaranteed.
Being part of 'pay club'	Sharing relevant information. Free and up to date.	Sharing pay information with local competitors.

Your organisation's attitude to pay

The last piece of the jigsaw before putting a pay structure together is to identify where your organisation stands on pay generally. This will be influenced by:

- *How much can your organisation afford to pay?* What has the performance been like of late? Is the cash flow in a healthy state? When do you next meet your bank manager?
- *Do you want to be known as a poor payer?* You can recognise these organisations because they are constantly advertising for staff. Few organisations want this sort of reputation, with a few notable exceptions such as McDonald's, which has the ethos of providing jobs for students who quickly move on. 'If you pay peanuts, you get monkeys' can be a very true statement. These organisations place themselves at the lower quartile of the pay range. Cost saving through low pay makes good accountancy but rarely good people management. Some specialist small organisations, for example in advertising, high-tech or research, make a point of paying at the top end of the range because they need the very best specialists on board and need to keep them there. These organisations place themselves at the upper quartile. For most organisations, finding the general market rate and paying that is the adopted policy. In other words, they place themselves at the median.

Simple pay structure

Having carried out some type of job evaluation and some market research, a salary structure can now be put together. An extract is shown in Table 5.5.

How employees' actual salaries within the range are determined will depend on a number of factors:

- *Service.* The employee may be relatively new so the salary is towards the bottom of the range, as with Jones (see Table 5.5).

Table 5.5 Basic salary structure (extract)

Grade	Salary Range	Jobs	Employees and Salaries
Grade 1 Basic clerical	Under £11,000	Post clerk Sales clerk Invoice clerk	Kenn £8,950 Gee £9,250 Winn £10,450 Band £10,800
Grade 2 General clerical	£11,000 to £13,499	Personnel clerk Receptionist Purchasing clerk Secretary	Jones £11,250 Tong £11,450 Madge £12,450 Brick £13,100
Grade 3 Specialist/ advanced clerical/admin	£13,500 to £18,000	Credit control clerk Purchase ledger supervisor Wages supervisor Buyer	Brown £13,600 Sugg £14,500 Lang £14,650 Dross £16,500
Grade 4	Over £18,000	General office manager Personnel/training manager Sales office manager	Hall £20,000 Jedd £21,000 Roberts £26,000

As she becomes more experienced, she will get higher pay increases than her colleagues and move up the scale. Traditional pay systems, such as those for teachers and civil servants, have emphasised loyalty by automatically increasing pay for the first few years of service, irrespective of performance. In recent years, however, there has been a movement away from this system and greater emphasis on paying for performance.

- *Skills.* Some employees may possess specific skills that have a premium in the market place or that affect the performance of the organisation. These skills need to be reflected in the employees' salaries. An example is an employee with specific skills in interactive Web design. Some organisations, especially in manufacturing, have a formal system of skills-based pay where additional supplements are paid to employees who gain accreditation in a series of skills. This can be through the NVQ system, and encourages employees to develop themselves and become more flexible. An example of skills-based pay is shown in Case 5.1.

- *Performance.* Some employees simply perform to a higher standard than others and deserve to be paid more. This can be paid as a bonus but the majority of organisations reward good performance through the basic rate as well as through bonus additions.

None of this is rocket science. However, in small organisations, the basis of salary decisions is often not thought through sufficiently and certainly rarely recorded. This is a mistake and can lead to confusion, difficulties and disappointment at subsequent review times unless the reasons for individual pay decisions (and any future promises) are clearly recorded.

Case 5.1 Skills-based pay at Ormerod Home Trust

The Community Care Act 1992 gave the opportunity to charitable trusts to change many of the practices in employing staff who looked after long-stay residents with learning difficulties. When Roseina Flannery joined as Chief Executive of Ormerod Home Trust in 1994, she found that few staff were qualified in care roles and many had simply transferred from a summer job at Pontin's. The first step was to identify common values within the trust and agree a mission statement, after consultation with staff: 'working to ensure that disability does not become a handicap'.

To raise the quality of care skills, a training programme based on national vocational qualifications was agreed, with additional funds provided through the local Training and Enterprise Council (now the Learning and Skills Council). Funding was also helped by registering the trust as an assessment centre as soon as a handful of team leaders had gained the important D32 and D33 qualification units. The trust could then gain valuable income by helping with the training and assessment of other organisations in the care environment. With these initiatives and by raising local authority fees, the trust managed to increase its training budget to £50,000 for its 75 staff by 1998.

The rates of pay were increased by linking the hourly rate with the NVQ qualifications achieved. This was an encouragement for all staff to obtain the qualifications and has acted as a successful means of staff retention. Previously, staff could only see a pay increase through working extra hours, and such an opportunity was almost eliminated by the arrival of the Working Time Directive.

Moreover, staff gained new skills and specialist knowledge and understood how their contribution affected the business as a whole. They passed their very positive attitude to training through to the residents, who were slowly trained to take more control of their lives by having responsibility for keeping their rooms clean, taking part constructively in house meetings, working together to build a float for the local carnival (they keep winning prizes) and obtaining and holding down part-time jobs in the community. (Source: Littlefield, 1999)

Do bonus schemes work?

Introduction

In Chapter 3, we looked at the various methods of trying to improve performance, including the role that motivation plays. Encouraging employees to work harder through offering a financial incentive has been around for hundreds of years, and bonus schemes, in all their varying forms, have always been controversial. Most people agree with the principle of paying for performance, but getting it to work in practice is far more difficult. Few schemes have been an all-round success; even fewer have lasted beyond three or four years. This is not to say that they should not be attempted, but they should be well planned and handled with great care, and their potential shortcomings should be recognised from the outset.

There are two main types of bonus schemes: **outcome-related**, which are linked to clear measurable outcomes such as production or sales figures, and **combinations of input- and outcome-related**, which operate where outcomes are not always clear cut or measurable and where an employee's input is recognised as important. The latter type is most prevalent in office, service-industry and technical environments, and includes various forms of performance-related pay (PRP) schemes.

We will look briefly at examples, and at the benefits and difficulties of each of these groups.

Output-related schemes – production

Let us imagine a small production unit of 40 employees making widgets. They are paid £300 a week on a 40-hour week. Current output is 32,000 widgets a week for 1,600 production hours, and it is planned to increase this output, keeping the labour force at the same level. A simple bonus scheme would work as follows:

Example 1

Output per week	Bonus
Up to 32,000 widgets	No bonus
For each 1,000 widgets between 32,000 and 44,000	2p per hour bonus
For each 1,000 widgets over 44,000	4p per hour bonus

- No bonus is payable until the existing output is exceeded.
- An accelerator is included to encourage employees to increase output above 44,000 widgets.
- If output rises to 48,000, then employees earn a bonus of 40p an hour (12,000 widgets at 2p per 1,000 = 24p and 4,000 widgets at 4p per 1,000 = 16p). This means a bonus of £16 a week.

This would work well if the hours remained constant but, as this rarely happens, an adjustment has to be made to take actual hours into account. An example of the revised scheme is as follows:

Example 2

In this example, the output for the week is 48,000 widgets and the total hours 1,600.

Output	48,000	
1,600 hours at basic charge of 20p an hour	32,000	
Surplus	16,000	
Bonus calculation		
First 12,000 widgets @ 2p per 1,000	12,000	Bonus 24p per hour
Remaining surplus	4,000	
Next 4,000 widgets @ 4p per 1,000	4,000	Bonus 16p per hour
Total bonus		40p per hour

Example 3

In this example, the output has risen to 50,000 widgets but the hours have increased to 2,000 as more staff have been taken on and some overtime has been worked.

Output	50,000	
2,000 hours at basic charge of 20p per hour	40,000	
Surplus	10,000	
Bonus calculation		
First 10,000 widgets @ 2p per 1,000	10,000	Bonus 20p per hour
Remaining surplus	0	
Total bonus		20p per hour

Although the output has risen, it has not risen in proportion to the hours being worked so the bonus has fallen back to 20p per hour.

Advice on production schemes

- *Always* operate a group scheme. Individual piecework may have worked after a fashion for 150 years but production processes have moved on and individual schemes no longer work. Team

working (see Chapter 3) is so crucial to successful integrated production work that any divisive payment system will inhibit the team from pulling together.
- *Always* include quality in your calculations or you will find that increased production is at the expense of quality. Credit must not be given for poor quality output so this must be reduced from the total if discovered on-site and reduced from the next week's total if rejected by the customers.
- *Only* pay a bonus for hours worked, not when employees are sick or on holiday, although an average bonus could be conceded for holidays when the scheme is working well.
- *Don't* limit the target to production only. You must include other measures, especially quality, but also consider measures of producing on time, waste, and health and safety. These can take the form of add-ons if over target or penalties if below target. Experience shows that there is a considerable support to improvements in these areas if they are built into a scheme.
- *Avoid* giving allowances at all costs. If you give allowances for, say, poor material, machine breakdowns or late supplies, not only will employees (and supervisors) find ways to allocate more hours into these categories than you ever expected, but you will spend all your time arguing against giving more allowances for other reasons. Allowances do not make money – they lose money and, by granting them, you are, in a sense, rewarding failure. You need to build into the targets an unspoken global allowance so good bonuses are earned when things do not go wrong. Employees will then be encouraged to overcome problems, not find excuses. The only time you may wish to include an allowance is where a major new product or process is introduced and this may be phased in over a number of weeks with a fixed cut-off date.
- *Communicate* progress, even if the news is not good. Put up large noticeboards and ensure results are put up every day.
- *Encourage* ideas through a regular meeting, walking the floor and a recognition scheme (details were given in Chapter 3).

Output-related scheme – sales

Many of the same principles of bonus schemes apply to a sales scheme, including using an accelerator and avoiding special allowances.

Because most sales staff work on their own, individual payments are most common, although it is worth including a team-based element as an add-on.

An important consideration is the **balance between basic salary and bonus**. In extreme cases, such as some organisations in double glazing and financial services, there is no basic salary, just commission or bonus. This may sort out the good salespeople and can provide them with the potential of very high earnings, but it has led to many high-profile complaints from customers of mis-selling and unpleasant high-pressure tactics. It is best avoided unless a visit to court or to the regulator is welcomed! For most businesses, the rough balance is that the basic salary can be augmented by between 20 and 50 per cent through a performance bonus.

A simple scheme for a company with 15 sales staff operating in the office equipment sector is as follows:

- Basic salary £18,000.
- For sales over £600,000, a commission of 5 per cent is paid.
- Additional targets are given for existing customer retention and winning new customers.
- Commission is deducted for any contracts cancelled.
- Team targets are set for sales in excess of £8 million (budget less 5 per cent).

Example

Commission for a salesperson selling £760,000	£8,000
Commission deducted for cancelled contract	(£500)
Customer targets bonus	£700
Team sales bonus	£1,000
Total bonus	£9,200

Total income for the year for this salesperson is £27,200. The scheme was adjusted to pay individual sales bonuses on a monthly basis and team sales bonuses on an annual basis.

The idea of a team bonus is to encourage the sales team to work together, co-operate across sales boundaries, pass on leads to one another and carry out with enthusiasm any cross-boundary activity, such as sales promotions or helping to train new staff.

Pitfalls with sales bonuses
- Uncertain and fluctuating earnings can be a demotivator.
- Step down hard on unethical selling – it can spread like wildfire.
- Ensure that all the non-selling activities are spread fairly and evenly around the sales force.
- Take care you adjust price increases into the commission structure – you should be able to link them with salary increases to ensure the effect is neutralised.
- Take care with the situation of a salesperson earning more than the sales manager. It can happen and it can be fair but it is a very sensitive situation.

General points on bonus schemes
- *Never* have a ceiling on the bonus. Employees will always see this as a barrier.
- *Feel free* to make changes in the scheme. It should be made clear at the start of all schemes that circumstances will always change – new products, new markets, new ideas – so the scheme will need to evolve. You will need to be quite sure that the changes as a whole benefit both parties and are not seen as ways for management to stifle earnings. Too many changes will confuse the workforce so only make changes that are really necessary.
- Keep *communicating* the results, even when they are not as good as hoped. Try to give some interpretation or commentary from time to time. Remember, not everybody understands the bald facts.
- *Do not* use the incentive scheme as a replacement for managing the individuals or teams – it can never be that effective and you will lose touch with your staff.
- *Keep an eye* on possible ways to circumvent the scheme. It will always be attempted and it needs to be nipped in the bud quickly.

- Consider the effect of a successful scheme giving high earnings on those associated with the employees, such as managers, supervisors and administrative support. It is probably better not to set up separate bonus schemes for those staff (except, perhaps, for managers). Give a bonus allowance that recognises their contribution and make sure they join in any celebrations – you leave them out at your peril.

Performance-related pay

PRP is a system that attempts to rationalise performance payments to managers, supervisors, technical and administrative staff for whom a conventional bonus scheme, such as that for production or sales staff, is inappropriate. Essentially, it converts the ratings made under a performance review system into payments, which are either added to an individual's salary or made as a one-off bonus. In general, these payments range between 2 per cent and 6 per cent at most. An example of a summarised scheme is shown in Case 5.2.

Case 5.2 Performance-related pay scheme

This is a summarised PRP scheme for a financial services organisation employing 300 staff.

Stage 1: ratings

Employees are rated through their performance review system in two ways: 1) by a measure of their achievement of personal objectives, which can earn them a maximum of 60 points; 2) by an assessment of their personal contribution through improving their competencies in a number of critical areas, which can earn them up to 40 points. Both measures are made initially by their manager with the results being reviewed by a panel of three managers.

Stage 2: conversion into pay

Performance payments are made in two ways: 1) a one-off bonus payment; 2) a salary increase. Bonus payments are made as follows:

Ratings	Bonus
Under 60	no bonus
60–69	£50
70–79	£100
80–89	£200
90–100	£300

Salary increases are paid on the basis of the following salary grid:

Rating	Lower part of salary grade	Middle of salary grade	Upper part of salary grade
Under 60	Zero	Zero	Zero
60–69	2%	1%	Zero
70–79	3%	2%	Zero
80–89	5%	3%	2%
90–100	8%	4%	3%

As an example of how this operates, consider an employee whose personal objectives are rated at 50 and personal contribution at 35, making a total of 85 points. The employee receives a one-off bonus of £200 and, as his or her current salary is on the lower part of the salary grade, the employee receives a salary increase of 5 per cent.
(Source: author's research)

Schemes are quite widespread in the private sector and have spread to many areas of the public sector in recent years. They were introduced into the teaching profession in 2000, despite furious opposition from teachers and their representatives. The problems associated with performance reviews have been set out in Chapter 3 and, although most staff regard the principle of differential payments based on performance as a good one that they would support, in practice the experience is very mixed indeed.

Research has shown that employees find the schemes unfair, divisive, difficult to understand and not worth the effort for the money involved. Managers find the schemes bureaucratic and time-consuming. Certainly most schemes are complex and are based on doubtful data or managerial opinion. On balance, therefore, PRP is not recommended as relevant or appropriate for the smaller organisation. The effort and resources required to introduce a formal scheme are unlikely to produce much in the way of employee satisfaction.

That is not to say that these groups of staff should not have the opportunity to earn performance payments. It is simply that awards should be made on a more informal basis avoiding the complexity of PRP schemes. Awards should be made at the time of annual reviews of salaries.

Implementing annual pay increases

If you do not have a formal system of PRP, this leaves a dilemma. If you believe that some of your staff perform better than others, how do you reward differentially? Let us take two different groups – the managers (and supervisors in smaller organisations) whom you know personally and whose pay increases you decide, and other administrative and technical staff. You are about to award a general pay increase but you want some staff to be paid more than others.

For managers, the starting point is to question the belief that some perform better than others. Why do you consider the performance differs? Is this a consistent view of your senior colleagues? Is it based on any evidence? You need to be quite sure in your mind because you will need to explain to them why they are getting more (or less). So you should have in place some type of performance system, as detailed in Chapter 3, that will give you information from which to draw reasonable conclusions. With a senior colleague, you should draw up a list of managers under the headings set out in Table 5.6.

For other staff, many of whom you may not know, you should ask their managers to present a case for those they are recommending, using the same format, which can then be considered with your senior colleagues.

Salary increases should be communicated personally to all employees. Calculating all the increases, checking that they appear fair across the board and then ensuring that they are all communicated on the same day is quite a logistical exercise, especially as, in many cases,

Table 5.6 Implementing the annual pay increase

Name	Current Salary (a)	Standard Increase (b)	(a) + (b)	Suggested New Salary	Justification

it coincides with Christmas or Easter. It does have to be done properly, however. Employees will not forget if the process is handled cack-handedly, with some employees hearing one day and others having to wait till a few days later, or some being told personally and others simply being handed a piece of paper. It may be better, given the shortage of time, to have short discussions at the time of the announcements and organise a time for a more detailed talk the following week when plans for the next year can be worked out and training needs analysed.

Organisation-wide bonuses

Personal bonuses can be divisive, setting individuals against one another as they compete. If you want to give greater emphasis to co-operation and team achievement, then an organisation-wide bonus may be appropriate. You may also feel, when the business has had a good year, that some of the rewards ought to be shared with your staff.

Sharing out profits, through formal **profit-sharing schemes**, used to have considerable tax advantages, but many organisations abused this situation and the government was forced to abolish the tax concessions in the late 1990s. Research has indicated that employees are rarely motivated by such a bonus because the payments often do not bear any relation to the efforts they have put in personally and also because they do not know how the profits were arrived at. (They may, however, be upset if they hear a rumour that profits have been very good and they do not get any part of the action!)

An organisation-wide bonus, then, has to be thought out carefully. A scheme that informs employees of the organisation's financial performance is a good vehicle for communication in general but questions need to be answered first. What will the bonus be based on? Will a share of the profits be on a fixed formula, such as 5 per cent, shared out on the basis of salary? Will employees be informed during the year of the way profits are heading? How long after the end of the financial year will it be paid out? Finally, will it be much of a motivator, with employees feeling they can really influence events?

An alternative approach is to introduce some form of gain-sharing scheme. These have a US origin and remain rare in the UK but one or two smaller organisations have attempted differing formats. Here, specific organisational targets are set out and, when these targets are exceeded, the resulting benefits are shared between the organisation and staff. A simple example is shown in Case 5.3.

Case 5.3 An example of gain sharing

Schett (not the real name of the organisation), a small engineering company with 120 employees, changed its bonus arrangements in 1996 to introduce a scheme that was linked much more closely to the organisation's objectives. The bonus became more focused on production on time, customer satisfaction, waste reduction and improved health and safety rather than simply high output.

The calculation is as follows, showing an example of the budgeted bonus and the actual for 2000:

(Figures in '000s)	Budgeted	Actual
Sales	£10,000	£10,600
Bonus pool at 2.5%	£250	£265
On-time shipments	90%	92%
On-time factor		
Adjusted bonus pool	£225	£244

Production/labour cost targets	100%	106%
Productivity factor		
Adjusted bonus pool	£225	£259
Customer satisfaction index	80%	76%
Customer satisfaction factor		
Adjusted bonus pool	£180	£197
Waste reduction index	100%	102%
Waste reduction factor		
Adjusted bonus pool	£180	£201
Health and safety index	100%	110%
Health and safety factor		
Adjusted bonus pool	£180	£221

Budgeted pay-out per employee per annum = £180,000 divided between 120 employees = £1,500 per employee.

Actual pay-out per employee per annum = £221,000 divided between 124 employees = £1,782 per employee on average.

An adjustment to individual payments was made to take into account absenteeism (20 per cent deduction for each absence in excess of two in the year) with deductions redistributed amongst the pool. Payments were made initially every six months but, after two years of operation, a monthly payment on account was made with the final adjustment made at the end of the year.

The calculation for 2000 shows that productivity, on-time production, waste reduction and health and safety measures improved, with only the customer satisfaction index being below target. The company's profits and reputation in the market place have improved since the scheme began and employees are much more aware of the company objectives, especially in relation to customers.

(Source: author's research)

The right collection of benefits

The right benefits can make some difference to the decision by individuals to join or leave an organisation. This is especially true when employees wish to join a business but will have to give up a benefit that the business does not provide. The employees will have to weigh up the advantages of joining against the disadvantage of losing the benefit. There are some benefits, especially company cars, that employees will not normally be prepared to sacrifice, although this could change as governments of all shades continue to increase the taxes on perks such as cars.

Company cars

It is not clear why the UK, almost uniquely, provides so many company cars. This policy does not apply to anywhere near the same extent in the rest of Europe or the United States. It provides a headache for most companies, and an inordinate amount of time is spent by senior management to try to get the policy fair yet efficient. Decisions need to be taken in the following areas:

- Which jobs should have a car allocated because of the need to travel or the status of the job?
- What range of car models is appropriate against each job?
- Should employees have a choice of models?
- Should employees be able to upgrade their model by making an additional contribution?
- Should cars be bought outright or provided through a leasing company?
- Should petrol be provided free for private use?
- How often should cars be replaced?
- Who is eligible to drive the car?

From April 2002, the new government policy provides an even more complex regime with the tax charge both set against the car's price and linked to carbon dioxide emissions. The cleanest cars, those with an emission rating of 165 grams per kilometre, will attract the lowest tax rate of 15 per cent of the car's list price, although this will go up to 17 per cent in 2003/04 and 19 per cent in 2004/05 as 155 grams per kilometre and 145 grams per kilometre respectively become the lowest ratings. For every 5-gram-per-kilometre emission, the scale of payment goes up by 1 per cent. So a car with an emission of 265 grams per kilometre will have a tax charge of 35 per cent. Diesels incur an additional 3 per cent charge because diesel emissions have been linked to respiratory illnesses such as asthma. It is quite clear that tax charges will rise annually for most drivers for the foreseeable future. It is likely, therefore, that employees will become more amenable to giving up their company car and receiving a cash allowance instead.

For more detailed information on all areas relating to company cars, see the Web sites listed at the end of this chapter. You will clearly have to keep a close watch on changes that take place each year in this area.

Holidays

The Working Time Directive established the right of employees to four weeks of paid holiday, although this can be interpreted as including days of public holiday. The law changed in 2001 so that this entitlement takes effect from week one of employment. It is quite common for holiday entitlement to exceed four weeks, although the gradual extension of holidays appears to have largely stopped. When holidays can and cannot be taken needs to be specified in the contract of employment.

Family-friendly benefits

Some benefits that encourage flexibility, such as flexitime and job-shares, have already been discussed in Chapter 3. There are a few additional benefits that are either legal requirements, such as maternity leave, or benefits that help recruitment and retention, such as childcare vouchers.

Maternity leave and the right to return

All pregnant employees are entitled at law to time off for antenatal care and to a minimum of 18 weeks' unpaid leave, starting in the 11th week before the expected date of confinement, regardless of length of service and hours worked. This counts as continuous service, and holiday entitlement continues to accrue while contributions should continue into the pension scheme if the employee is a member of one. At the end of this period, the employee has the right to return to her old job or be offered one that is equivalent. She will need to give notice as set out in the section on maternity pay earlier in the chapter. In 2003, maternity leave will increase to 26 weeks and, in addition, unpaid maternity leave for employees with 26 weeks' employment at the notification week will be 26 weeks, making a total break of a full year.

If the employee is sick at the time of her return, she is able to retain her position as long as she has provided acceptable evidence of her sickness. There is uncertainty concerning the right to return to work on a part-time basis. A number of tribunal decisions appeared to extend the law in this direction but it is not clear cut. The indications are that employers should listen to such a request and see if it is practicable. If the result is that the costs and inconvenience of such an arrangement would appear to outweigh the benefits, then there is no obligation on the employer to accede to such a request.

For developments in government policy in this area, see the list of Web sites at the end of this chapter.

Childcare vouchers

Childcare vouchers are being offered by a small but growing number of employers to employees in positions where the market is tight to encourage parents to work. Over 50 per cent of women with children under five now work compared to less than a third in 1980. Employers provide vouchers varying from £20 a week to £80 a week or more and they are currently exempt as a benefit in kind from National Insurance contributions.

Another family-friendly scheme allows employees to take career breaks of up to five years with a right to return to the same, or equivalent, job on their return plus the opportunity to work two or three weeks a year to keep up to date.

Share ownership schemes

Various governments have encouraged employee share ownership schemes since the mid-1980s through providing tax incentives. The essential feature of share-save schemes is that employees commit to buying shares in their organisation through a regular deduction from their salary. The price of the shares is set at the start of the contract so, when the contract period is completed, usually in three or five years, the employees exercise their contract and gain the benefit of any price increase of the shares over the period.

There are a number of motivational aspects to the scheme:

- Research has shown that employees who own shares in their organisation show a higher level of commitment to that organisation.
- Because employees cannot exercise a right to purchase the shares if they have left the organisation, such schemes are an encouragement to staff retention.
- By owning shares, employees are more likely to have a better idea of the organisation's overall performance and to take more interest in the company's developments.

On the other hand, it should not be forgotten that, on a minority of occasions over the last 20 years, share investments have proved far from satisfactory and employees have lost money over the investment. It could also be argued that employees should not be too encouraged to have all their eggs in one basket by both having a job and owning shares in one organisation.

For a smaller organisation, there are special problems. Although the schemes detailed below allow organisations whose shares are privately owned to operate schemes, employees may not see the benefits if they cannot readily trade the shares. A way round this is to set up a trust that will buy back the shares when employees wish to liquidate their holdings, although valuation of the shares will have to be transparent.

In 2000, the government introduced two tax-efficient share ownership schemes with the aim of specifically appealing to smaller companies. These schemes are detailed in the following paragraphs.

All-Employee Share Ownership Plan (AESOP) regulations appear complex but the essential idea is to allow an organisation flexibility in the way the scheme is operated. An AESOP can consist of up to three separate modules. Up to £3,000 of free shares can be awarded to eligible employees each tax year and these are free of income tax and National Insurance. The awards can be linked to performance criteria based on individual, team, divisional or business performance. With partnership shares, employees can buy shares up to £1,500 per annum out of pre-tax salary. Finally, under the matching share regulations, an employer can gift up to two matching shares pro rata to each partnership share an employee buys, up to a value of £3,000 a year. In terms of offering these benefits, an employer can differentiate between employees on the basis of grade, length of service or hours worked provided that it treats all employees consistently within the rules it lays down. (It is possible these regulations may be challenged by part-timers who would appear to be under a potential disadvantage.)

Enterprise Management Incentives (EMI) allow an organisation to grant share options to up to 15 of its most important members of staff, with each person eligible for a maximum of £100,000. No tax is payable when the option is granted or exercised. While capital gains tax is payable when the shares are sold, there are special rules that can potentially reduce the rate payable to only 10 per cent. It is up to the company to decide how long employees must wait before they exercise their option, with a maximum of 10 years.

With both schemes, the publicity for the scheme is crucial to ensure that employees understand what are the main features, benefits and risks of the scheme. A number of specialist companies exist to advise small organisations on how to set up a scheme and produce a publicity pack. Details are provided at the end of the chapter.

Pensions

Every year, pensions become more complicated and more difficult to summarise in a short section. Prior to the arrival of stakeholder pensions, organisations had three choices:

- To offer no pension at all.
- To offer a final salary scheme (defined benefits) where employees can calculate the pension they will receive based on their length of service and their expected final salary. For example, an employee on a final salary of £30,000 with 20 years' service will receive an annual pension of either £10,000 (based on a generous 60th scheme) or £7,500 (based on a less generous 80th scheme). Employees' contributions are fixed but the employer has to make contributions to the pension fund that are sufficient to ensure all the pensions can be paid.
- To offer a money purchase pension (defined contribution scheme) where the employer puts in a fixed contribution (usually between 3 and 8 per cent) and employees also put in a contribution, which they may be able to top up. When an employee retires, the resulting fund is invested in an annuity to yield a pension.

Today, with much lower expectation in returns from investments, and depressing demographics, few small businesses can afford to set up a final salary scheme, because it is much more expensive, so most have set up money purchase schemes, assuming that they have decided that a pension scheme is essential as an aid to recruitment and retention. For employees, a money purchase scheme is less advantageous. They will not know the level of their pension until very close to retirement time, as this will depend on the performance of their pension fund and especially on stock market returns.

The arrival of stakeholder pensions from October 2001 has complicated the picture further. All employers with five or more employees (who can be full time, part time, temporary or permanent) must provide access to a stakeholder pension for employees who have no access to a company scheme. Employers do not need to make any contribution but they must arrange for contributions to be deducted from payroll. Stakeholder pensions will have low charges and other features controlled by law. Employers need to consult employees as to the designated provider. Further details are available from the Occupational Pensions Regulatory Authority (Web site detailed below).

Reference

Littlefield, D (1999) Independence Day, *People Management*, 11 November, pp 52–54

Further information

For share ownership schemes, contact Smith & Williamson, 1 Riding House Street, London W1A 3AS (tel: 020 7637 5377).

A useful Web site for updating on employment legislation is www.tiger.gov.uk.

For details on company car taxation see:

- www.cartax.co.uk;
- www.vcafuelcardata.org.uk;
- www.cashorcar.com;
- www.companycar.com.

Details on stakeholder pensions are available from the Occupational Pensions Regulatory Authority (tel: 01273 627600). Their Web site is www.opra.gov.uk.

Sources for pay information include:

- www.incomesdata.co.uk – a database of 380 pay and benefits surveys, which is only available to subscribers to Incomes Data Services;
- www.salarysearch.co.uk – for a fee (currently £45), Reward Group allow you to search their database of information for salaries, although you are limited to three options, such as size of company or location;
- www.celre.co.uk – the Web site for Remuneration Economics and Computer Economics providing a wide range of salary information.

For updated information on government policy on maternity and paternity pay, see www.dti.gov.uk/er/hot-topics.htm.

6 Communication, consultation and involvement

Introduction

There is extensive research showing that a high level of employee involvement, backed up by effective and regular communication, pays off in terms of organisational performance. In a 1998 report by the Involvement and Participation Association, more than 65 per cent of organisations that allowed their workforce full involvement in all business activities stated that they believed they were gaining a competitive advantage. Furthermore, their employees backed up the findings by confirming that there were greater levels of trust between management and employees and performance was better.

For many large organisations, greater openness has been essential to being able to compete effectively. Stephen Dunn, Head of Group Human Resources at Scottish Power, is quoted in this report as saying: 'Increased competition has forced all the parties to think in new ways and to work for business advantage. It is about looking for solutions to things that, in the past, may have led to conflict. By opening the books and involving everyone in the business, it is now possible to see how business decisions impact on us all' (Walsh, 1998).

Many organisations have followed the lead from household names such as IBM, ICL and Ford in entering into long-term campaigns to improve the total communication process and wean employees on to more positive viewpoints as to the company's direction, purpose and success. For smaller organisations, this process should be much easier as communication can be much quicker, more direct and, often, out of the mouths of the owners themselves.

We have looked in Chapter 3 at specific methods of improving performance, and this chapter will show some further ideas on the communication and involvement **structure** that should help these performance improvement methods to flourish.

Communication, **consultation** and **involvement** are all interlinked. Communication often implies a top-down approach – we are telling you things – but good communication always allows the opportunity for a two-way process to take place. Getting employee feedback (if only in terms of searching or awkward questions!) is effectively a consultation process – finding out what employees think and getting their ideas. A number of the ideas may be robust enough for the organisation to take on board and implement in some form, in which case employees have had an influence on future policy or practice and have got closely involved.

A final factor relating to communication, consultation and involvement is that research indicates a positive effect on **employee stress levels** if these areas are handled effectively and sensitively. One of the main sources of stress is a strong sense of lack of control. When employees have little idea of the direction of the organisation, how their job contributes or what is going on around them, then it is no real surprise that they have little sense of control and stress levels can rise. Dealing with workplace stress is covered in more detail in Chapter 8 under health and safety.

Table 6.1 is a useful checklist to keep as a reference for all communication purposes.

Table 6.1 Communication checklist

What Do We Want to Communicate?	Why Do We Need to Communicate?	Who Needs to Be Involved?	When Do We Need to Communicate?	What is the Best Way to Get the Message Across?
1				
2				
3				
4				
5				
6				

What is there to communicate?

There are five main areas of communication, as shown in Figure 6.1.

Organisational vision

In Chapter 1, the importance of having a vision for the organisation was emphasised. Employees like to believe that their organisation is important, knows where it is going and has a clear view of how to get there. This can help to make their own jobs feel important and improves their self-esteem. It is even better when they believe that the future of the organisation includes themselves – that they can see a career path developing in line with the success of the organisation.

Creating and communicating the vision is important for two groups of organisations. Household names that have developed brands over many years can afford to spend millions of pounds with consultants to continue their vision of an all-conquering set of branded products. It then becomes relatively easy to transfer this vision to employees, who

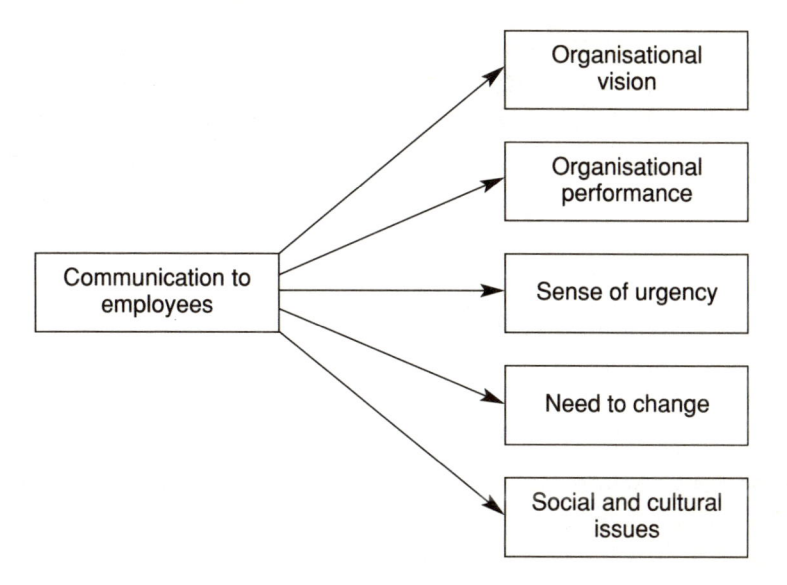

Figure 6.1 Communication to employees

```
Communication to employees →
    → Organisational vision
    → Organisational performance
    → Sense of urgency
    → Need to change
    → Social and cultural issues
```

can identify with the brand. Luxury goods (Gucci, Jaguar) or goods associated with specific markets (Nike, Virgin) generally do not have problems in recruiting or retaining staff.

The second group for whom communicating the vision should be easy is small organisations. To be in business, owners have had to have a strong vision and the confidence to take it forward with all the inherent risks involved in the enterprise. Communicating this vision to a small number of employees with whom they will usually work closely should be far from difficult. It is often forgotten, however, in the rush of the daily struggle to survive and prosper.

It is also an easy assumption to make that there is no need to formalise the vision – to write it down or even discuss it – because it is so obvious to all who work in the organisation what it is. This can be a big mistake. New employees will gain only a garbled version from fellow employees who, themselves, may not be up to strength with the latest directional plans, especially if the organisation exists in a fast-changing environment. So it is necessary to have a simple version summarised and written down. It needs to be in the employee handbook and it is worth putting the essentials on prominent noticeboards. It needs revisiting at least every year, and reference should be made to it (especially if there is a memorable slogan) each time a general communication, verbal or written, goes out to employees, especially if the intention is that the communication should be inspirational.

Organisational performance

Regular updates on how the organisation is performing help to keep the employees in the picture. This can include:

- sales summaries;
- output figures;
- financial performance – annual reports;
- large contracts won;
- progress on expansion plans – new store openings or sales offices in a foreign country;
- health and safety performance;
- attendance performance and other measures of labour productivity.

Are there problems here? Many organisations have traditionally been very wary of divulging much information, beyond the occasional snippet of good news. Their reasons are a combination of the need to retain commercial confidentiality – some of the figures or news can be very market-sensitive – and the worry that too much good news will lead to demands for higher pay and bad news will lead to a reduction in staff morale and employees departing in droves.

Both of these views are misplaced. Let us take the latter view first. Of course there is anecdotal evidence that some key employees, having heard rumours of the organisation going downhill, may decide to up and leave for greener pastures. There will also always be employees who need to find ways to back up their individual claims for a pay rise. Overall, however, what little research there is in this area indicates that there is no evidence to support the view that organisations which take a much more open approach all round have higher employee turnover or have to pay higher salaries than they would wish. In fact, the contrary appears to be the case. Employees who are in possession of the real facts, openly presented, are more likely to act rationally and co-operatively.

We have seen in Chapter 3 that employees like to be treated in a mature fashion. They commit a good part of their lives to their work, the organisation makes considerable demands on them and the least it can do is keep them in the picture. 'Nobody tells us anything!' is the commonest of cries at work.

Confidentiality is a more difficult problem and a balanced view on this a little more elusive. Firstly, for quoted companies, disclosure to the market of information on turnover and profit is a listing requirement. Employees who are shareholders have a right to that information, so why not provide it to everybody? However, that information only needs to be provided annually or every six months and then may be a few months old. It is better to provide more regular and up-to-date information, perhaps monthly. Some of your employees, those who work in the accounts and IT departments, are likely already to have some access to that information. Can employees be relied on to keep this information confidential? They will have signed their employment contracts agreeing to do so and the risk of an individual feeding this information to a competitor is remote. I have been told from a number of sources that most businesses have little problem in obtaining reasonably accurate current trading information on their main competitors from informal sources in the industry.

Taking all this into account, is it worth deliberately keeping such information from your employees? If effective communication in this area works for large organisations, why not for small ones? Most owners of small businesses who have experimented on disclosure have been generally surprised and pleased with the outcome. One business owner in a manufacturing establishment has told me that a more realistic and enlightened discussion in regular management meetings has come about because the managers sitting round the table all possessed the same information. They 'sang from the same hymnbook', so to speak. More ideas have been generated, more processes have been put in place to avoid the same mistakes being made and there has been a genuine increase in commitment all round.

A final point made to justify giving little or no information is that employees are simply not interested, being turned off by a regular barrage of statistics. Again, that may well be true of a good proportion of employees but many, a majority even, will find some of the information of continuing interest. Providing the information costs very little and the total benefit of so doing greatly outweighs any difficulties.

Sense of urgency

Small organisations have to react quickly to the business environment – it is one of their strengths and explains their survival in a harsh business world. It is no surprise that the most successful creatures (in terms of numbers and habitat manipulation) in current evolutionary times are beetles, and the least successful are larger mammals, excluding humankind. Regularly having to evolve and alter the ways of working are the norm for most small concerns. Regular communication can help employees to internalise this situation and help them make greater sense of it. If they possess more facts, they will realise why changes have to be made and made quickly, why products and services that were best-sellers one moment have to be jettisoned the next and replaced with something different, why a business entered one year with great hopes has to be closed down the next and why a rush of business for an unlikely product has to be responded to very urgently as it may be the sign of the organisation being a market leader, perhaps unexpectedly, in a new and profitable market.

Need to change

There will, inevitably, be constant changes that need to be communicated. Handling this process is so important that Chapter 10 has been set aside to concentrate on this issue.

Social and cultural issues

The final subject area to communicate is news and celebration. Social elements substantially aid the integration of the workforce. Events, sporting and social, that are being organised (small companies organise almost as many as large ones) and celebrations to share – marriages, births, TV appearances – all serve to cement the fabric of the business. No organisation employing more than 50 employees should be without a five-a-side football tournament or a 10-pin bowls evening. There should always be a Christmas 'do', even if it's cheaper and more convenient to hold it in March. One small media company organises a summer day out for employees and partners and never tells them where it is going to be till they arrive. The employees love the anticipation and complaining about it afterwards. For some, the cost seems a waste of money. A day out for 60 people can cost £3,000 or more. But when looked at as a percentage of payroll, it is tiny – less than a fifth of 1 per cent. The benefits in terms of employee morale can be high. Without it, the fun of working for the organisation is much diminished.

EasyJet take the social dimension a stage further. Right from the start of their business when they employed 40 staff, they had a weekly barbecue starting at 4 o'clock on a Friday, and the tradition has continued. Attendance is, of course, optional. Some staff use it to complete unfinished business, others network, which is vital because events move so quickly in the low-cost airline industry, and everybody enjoys themselves. To easyJet, the weekly cost is insignificant compared to the satisfaction it brings to staff and the way it maintains morale.

Communication methods

Communication methods can be divided into two main groups – **one-way and two-way communication**. Both have their place and can be effective if operated properly.

One-way communication

The purpose of one-way communication is to impart information that employees either need to know or may find useful. It can take a number of forms, and these are summarised, together with the requirements to do it effectively, in Table 6.2.

You will be aware that circulating the newsletter through the intranet is a faster and cheaper process than printing and circulating a paper-based version.

One-way communication puts the organisation on the right track but it does not always get the best results, as is seen in Case 6.1, Beverage Company.

Case 6.1 Beverage Company

Beverage Company (not its real name) manufactures intermediary products for the food and drinks industry, employing 150 staff in the Manchester area. Up until the early 1990s, the company adopted a paternalistic policy towards employees, but the harsh realities of increased competition and declining profits caused a sea change and a more strategic form of managing people was introduced.

Alongside performance pay, a new appraisal scheme and some empowerment of production staff, a new communication policy was introduced. This was centred on a series of downward communication formats. A quarterly newsletter was introduced, and formal presentations to all staff twice a year by the managing director and monthly team briefings were brought in. This was backed up by e-mail communications and electronic message boards across factory work areas. The underlying objective was to inform employees about new products, encourage quality and share financial information.

However, these initiatives were met with some suspicion among employees. Team leaders who held monthly briefings were regarded as 'supervisors on the cheap', who simply passed on the briefings compiled by the personnel department. The site-wide meetings with the managing director were regarded as partial, with little opportunity for discussion or questioning and an apparent reluctance to show the whole picture. The electronic noticeboards, which showed actual production and planned production, absenteeism rates and customer complaints, were regarded as gimmicks and intrusive. 'There was no getting away from management

Table 6.2 One-way communication

Advantages	Disadvantages	Requirements to Operate Effectively
Noticeboards		
– No need to circulate everybody. – Cheap and easy to carry out. – Permanent reminder.	– Not everybody looks at them. – Can easily become outdated and untidy.	– Place in prominent position (by the lift is best). – Update very regularly. – Ensure they are always tidy.
Company newsletter (including through intranet)		
– Good medium for rapidly updating everybody. – Cheap to produce. – Immediate interest for staff. – Quality versions can be produced using desktop publishing techniques.	– The news you want to circulate may not coincide with planned circulation dates. – If gap between is too long then information can get out of date. – Can often be bland and lifeless.	– One person must have responsibility with sufficient content authority. – Must have lively content. – Must invite feedback. – Special editions must go out when important events occur.
Company video		
– Gives opportunity for managing director to talk to everybody.	– Expensive to produce. – Results can look amateur.	– Avoid altogether.

messages,' complained one employee. Another commented that there was 'Too much communication in one sense – we've forgotten to use general conversation. They try to make things too formal, thinking it's a better way, which isn't always the case.'

When an employee survey was carried out, the response was very disappointing, with 81 per cent believing that management did not involve employees in decision making and only 25 per cent agreeing that management regularly sought the views of employees. Even more worrying, a series of sabotage attacks began shortly after the initiatives began, which caused considerable damage to the reputation of the company.
(Source: adapted from Dundon, Grugulis and Wilkinson, 2001)

Two-way communication

Meetings with all staff

There is no doubt of the positive effect of a regular meeting between the managing director and all the staff. Information can be communicated with the right balance and emphasis, questions can be answered with authority and a positive slant can be put on even the direst news through an enthusiastic delivery. For most small organisations on one site, it is relatively easy to organise, and staff appreciate the updating process, the opportunity to ask questions and the fact that the managing director takes time to carry this out. As a rough rule of thumb, meetings should be around once every six months or once a quarter (unless it is considered important news that needs to be conveyed very quickly to everybody on a personal basis, such as a major acquisition). They should last no more than an hour at most with a maximum 20-minute talk, and with a one-page handout to reduce misunderstanding of what was said. One of the meetings should coincide with the annual results announcement so the results can be briefly interpreted within the organisation's policy on disclosure.

If more than 100 employees are on one site, then the meeting can be split into two. Given the need to retain normal service during the meetings, then splitting them may be a sensible idea anyway. Where more than one site is involved, a representative from each site can attend the meeting and feed back to the rest of the staff.

Briefing groups

Briefing groups (sometimes called team briefings) are more appropriate for larger organisations where whole-site meetings are not feasible, but they can also play a part in organisations employing 150 to 500 staff. They are a vehicle for the cascading of information quickly and effectively down the organisation. In the case of an organisation 400-strong, the cascade will normally have three steps, as shown in Figure 6.2.

```
Managing director
       ↓
   Board members
          ↓
      Heads of department
              ↓
            Staff
```

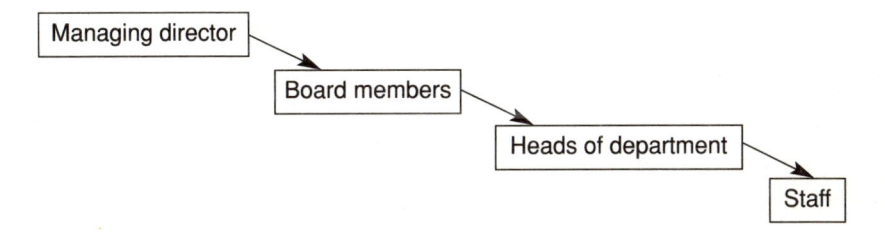

Figure 6.2   Cascading information down the organisation

Each month (sometimes more frequently) board members talk to their heads of department using a common prepared brief, and heads of department, in turn, brief their own staff. Questions and discussion are invited and, where those briefing cannot answer a question, they guarantee to obtain an answer within a specific period of time, such as three days. The briefings should all take place at the same time to prevent muddled messages spreading round the organisation. To operate briefing effectively requires some discipline, especially in preparing the brief and keeping to the specified briefing times. However, many organisations and their employees have found it highly effective in improving two-way communication and supporting the motivating process. The briefing group is also a good forum for consultation on new ideas and for finding out employees' views on subject areas without the formality of a statistical survey.

Staff forums and works councils

The discipline, time, effort and cost of talking to all staff on a regular basis has influenced many small organisations who take communication seriously to set up some form of staff forum or works council. The European Union Directive on Works Councils affects few, if any, small companies at the time of writing, as it applies to multinational businesses that employ over 1,000 people in the EU or at least 150 people in each of two different EU member countries. However, more Directives are in the pipeline for 5 to 10 years ahead, which may affect the consultation and communication processes in small businesses, so this position may change. The important question of union recognition is dealt with later in this chapter, so at this stage guidance is directed at non-union organisations.

The membership of a staff forum or works council will be decided locally but will normally consist of representatives from each major department plus some managers and supervisors. It is usually chaired by a senior manager or board member with a secretary to take minutes and organise the formalities. This role is often taken by a member of the HR department or somebody who has a similar role.

The business of the council/forum can consist of the updating of information (of the kind detailed earlier in the chapter), plans for the future (changes in products, plant layout, health and safety, staffing, overtime, shifts) and major issues where consulting the employees is a sensible idea. This can involve issues concerning terms and conditions – such as pensions, sick pay, rotas, innovation on flexible working – and ways of improving productivity – such as changes in team working, skills development and others set out in Chapter 3. A sample agenda is set out in the box below.

Sample agenda for works council/staff forum
- Minutes of last meeting.
- Matters arising.
- Statistics on sales, production, productivity, attendance, waste.
- Updating on future plans:

Communication, consultation and involvement

- investment in new production facilities;
- improvements in car parking;
- changes in maintenance schedules;
- new policy on harassment.
• Consultation on:
- proposed new bonus scheme;
- revisions to suggestion scheme.
• Health and safety issues.
• Pensions and share-save scheme – talk by Jim Brown, HT Investments.

A forum or council can be a very useful vehicle for communication, consultation and involvement. It has the potential to encourage employees to participate in decision-making processes whilst in possession of the key relevant facts. It can demonstrate that the organisation encourages an open approach to information sharing. It can also be a great disappointment, turning into a talking shop where representatives fail to see the big picture and look to win points relating only to their own department. Management appeals for more attention to absence, waste and productivity increases fall on deaf ears. It becomes a 'tea and toilets' sideshow that satisfies nobody. Worse still, it may raise the cynicism level of some representatives so that they turn to a trade union to represent them. There are a number of difficulties that need to be resolved to ensure a successful outcome:

• *Representation.* Employees representing departments need to be good at this role:
  - They need to be able to gather their colleagues' views and reflect them accurately.
  - They need to be able to report effectively on the information and decisions from the meetings. (Minutes, by the way, should come out as soon as possible, preferably within two days.)
  - Finally they need to be able to take a broad view of the company's position so that their contributions are positive, constructive and realistic.

This is quite a role. Representatives, ideally, should have a clear understanding of what they are taking on and some basic training. On election or appointment, a role description should be drawn up and explained to them, they should have some elementary training in existing information systems (productivity, output, etc) and they should be given time to communicate and consult with their colleagues. This takes up time and management effort but it is a necessary investment.

- *Signs of success.* Representatives will easily become discouraged if their ideas, advice and serious proposals are rejected. It needs a careful hand on the tiller to make sure that some constructive ideas are drawn out and successfully implemented, and credit given appropriately. Sometimes this means spending money that may not have been planned – it will annoy your accountant – but, again, it is an investment to ensure that ideas and support keep coming. It is also important that the skills and experience of representatives (which includes managers and supervisors) are valued, and this can occur through setting up one or two subcommittees to look at specific problems that stretch across the organisation – absenteeism, staff turnover, car parking and waste are subjects where most employees can contribute in producing a report.

    It is important that such a report leads to some action and, it is hoped, a successful outcome. It needs to be constantly remembered (I make no apology for repeating this more than once) that employees who have taken part in the decision-making process will be much more likely to support the implementation of changes and to try their hardest to make these changes work.

    Finally, the managing director needs to attend the council occasionally to provide input and recognise the work of the committee. A note of congratulation to the members of a project group costs nothing and may yield substantial benefits.

- *How far are terms and conditions discussed?* You need to be certain whether any subjects are off limits, the main one being pay. This is not the forum for *negotiating* terms and conditions, although there is plenty of room for consultation on many elements of conditions. The most open of organisations will be content to start indicating the likely pay increases two or three months before the event, based on organisational performance and the economic environment, including the retail price index and local demand for labour. By doing so, they hope that the actual award will bring no surprises.

Checklist for operating a works council/employee forum
- Make sure it includes representatives covering all sections of the business.
- Try to encourage proactive, enthusiastic employees to take part.
- Meet regularly – every month or six times a year, planned in advance.
- Have a competent, respected chair.
- Make sure all members have a chance to have their say and that it is not dominated by one group or a loquacious employee.
- Listen to ideas from employees and respond to them.
- Issue informal but accurate minutes quickly to all employees.
- Make sure actions promised are carried out between meetings.
- Create project groups; make sure they have the resources they need, that they report on time and that useful action is taken.
- Ensure the chief executive attends one or more meetings a year.
- Call a special meeting when news needs to be communicated quickly.

Should trade unions be encouraged or recognised?

One of the more durable legacies of Margaret Thatcher's government was the legislation introduced to curb the power of the unions. This policy was extremely successful in reducing the incidence of strikes (the number of days lost fell from 12 million in 1972 to barely 200,000 in the early 2000s) and also assisted in reducing the attractiveness of trade union membership, which fell from around 13 million in 1979 to below 8 million in 2001.

The main thrust of the Conservative legislation from 1980 to 1995 was to make strikes illegal unless they met strict situational or procedural requirements. The legislation included provisions to make secondary picketing illegal, ensure strike ballots took place, give notice of impending strikes to employers, allow employers to dismiss strikers selectively and increase the powers of individual trade union members to take action against their own union.

The Labour government from 1997 has only made minor alterations to these controls (strikers cannot now be dismissed in the first eight weeks of their strike nor selectively thereafter), but it has introduced legislation that supports the inroads of trade unions into organisations where they have not previously been recognised. This departure was introduced in the Employment Relations Act 1999, which provides that the employer must allow a union membership ballot if 10 per cent of eligible employees call for one, and must recognise the union if 40 per cent of eligible employees vote in favour. Recognition must occur without a ballot if more then 50 per cent of eligible employees are already members. Recognition includes these rights:

- the right to negotiate terms and conditions of employment, including pay;
- the right of representation at disciplinary hearings;
- the right to be consulted over changes in working practices.

Businesses with less than 20 employees are exempt from the legislation. It is not certain how effective this legislation will be in increasing union penetration. By 2001, there was considerable evidence that voluntary recognition was increasing, with the GPMU union claiming 60 voluntary agreements alone within a year. However, in the first year of operation, the Central Arbitration Committee (CAC) had received only 84 applications and had granted only seven statutory union recognition agreements, far fewer than expected. One of those companies was Saudi Arabian Airlines with 200 members while another recognition claim was made on behalf of 30 clerical staff at Union Bank of Nigeria. Case 6.2 details the union recognition experience of Statex Press.

Case 6.2 Union recognition

Statex Press, a small printing firm in Newcastle, is an example of a business forced to recognise the union. GPMU claimed that more than 50 per cent of the workforce were union members, which was denied by the company. The company had told the CAC hearing that it would accept recognition if a ballot showed a majority in favour. This disagreement left CAC to make a decision. They sent a case manager to make an impartial investigation that resulted in CAC accepting the union claim and insisting on the company recognising the union without the necessity of a ballot.

Statex was unconvinced that there was a clear majority in favour and has since claimed that recognition has meant a deterioration in employee relations.

(Source: Hammond, 2001)

A simplified guide to the process of handling a union recognition claim is shown in Figure 6.3.

An organisation without unions needs to think carefully about its general strategy towards employee relations and act accordingly. Trade unions (and some commentators) have put forward the following reasons why trade union recognition can be beneficial for employers:

- Communication with employees is far easier through recognised, representative sources.
- Terms and conditions are much easier to enforce and police when reached through formal negotiations leading to solid agreements.
- Employees prefer to work under an employee relations set-up where there is some counterbalance to management's prerogative. They feel more confident and secure so will work better.

Stage 1 Voluntary union recognition (30 days)
Trade union makes a formal, written claim for recognition in respect of a specified bargaining unit. Union must have 10 per cent of members of proposed bargaining unit. Employer has 10 days to respond. If it agrees to negotiate, a further 20 days are allowed for a voluntary agreement to be reached. If no agreement reached, claim goes to CAC.

Stage 2 Identification of bargaining unit (30 days)
Once CAC decide that a claim is admissible, parties have 20 days to agree a bargaining unit – it could be all the employees or a section. If no agreement, it goes back to CAC, which decides on a unit within 10 days.

Stage 3 Campaign and ballot
Parties agree date for ballot, which must be overseen by a qualified independent person (a solicitor perhaps). Access arrangements for the union must be agreed within 10 days (if no agreement, CAC makes an order). A 20-day access period (a sort of 'hustings') then takes place. Union needs to obtain 40 per cent of votes of bargaining unit to obtain recognition.

Stage 4 Setting up of bargaining structure (30 days)
If ballot is successful, parties have 30 days to negotiate their own collective bargaining structure. If no agreement reached, six-stage, 50-day standard structure will be imposed by CAC (claim, explanation, response, first negotiation, final negotiation, ACAS conciliation).

Figure 6.3 Handling a union recognition claim

- In recent years, trade unions have been happy to work with the organisation to make changes that lead to greater productivity and profitability because this leads to better long-term security of employment. They no longer resist change and, when agreed, will give every support to make it work.
- In disciplinary and grievance procedures, it is preferable for the organisation to deal with an experienced representative (shop steward) so as to help avoid wrong decisions by management that can lead to unrest or a tribunal.

Most organisations, especially small ones, find these arguments unconvincing, and union penetration in workplaces employing less than 100 employees is around half that recorded at workplaces employing over 500. Counter-arguments include:

- Unions need to be consulted on a wide range of plans and activities, a list that is likely to be extended by further European Directives over the next few years. This is a very time-consuming process.
- Despite the apparent willingness to accommodate change, trade unions appear reluctant in practice and attempt to exact a high price for any agreement. It also takes too much time when urgent action may be imperative.
- Recognition leads to additional rights for union representatives, including paid time off for official trade union training and preparing for negotiations, and the provision of reasonable facilities, which can include an office, meeting room and telephone.
- It is difficult to provide a responsible job for an elected shop steward if he or she has to keep breaking off to deal with union business. Managers do not like having shop stewards in their department for this reason. If a shop steward is moved to a less responsible job then experience shows a gradual slide towards shop stewards having an increasing amount of time off the job.
- Disputes can often simmer and relationships deteriorate between shop stewards and management over rights and responsibilities.

- Having trade unions can polarise the workforce, emphasising the degree of conflict between management and employees. Employees' loyalties may gradually move from supporting the organisation to supporting the union.
- Management has to spend much more time in preparing for and carrying out negotiations, activities that produce little added value and divert management away from productive areas such as gaining work and improving inefficiency. Countering what is regarded as trade union propaganda can be especially time-consuming.
- Strikes, which are disastrous for business, can only take place in a unionised environment.
- Communicating is a key management responsibility. It should take place directly with the workforce, not through the medium of a trade union.

Given these convincing arguments, what can a small organisation do to avoid being faced by a recognition claim? It has to be remembered that when a claim has been made, the battle is half-lost. At that stage, a proportion of employees have decided that their grievances are so great that they would be better served by having a union on the premises. So the crux of the matter is to try to prevent employees developing long-standing and important grievances.

Handling grievances

There are two methods here: 1) a reactive approach, which deals effectively with grievances when they arise; 2) a proactive approach, which tries to prevent them in the first place.

Reactive approach

There are numerous incidents or situations that can lead to employees holding a grievance. They can be extremely serious, such as a sexual assault or a severe safety hazard. They may be less serious but still of great concern to employees, such as a new shift rota, a failure to consider an employee for promotion, a critical appraisal report, a lack of opportunity for overtime or too much pressure of work.

A grievance is like an infection. Unless it is dealt with quickly and efficiently, it will fester and may spread quickly, causing unnecessary pain and suffering (lower productivity or reduced co-operation and commitment). A procedure, then, will seek to ensure the following:

- that the employee's case is heard quickly;
- that the employee concerned will have a fair hearing with the opportunity for full discussion to take place;
- that a response from management will follow without too long a gap;
- that the decision taken appears to be a fair one that has been considered carefully.

The procedure should make clear to whom the grievance should be addressed, who should accompany the employee if he or she requires somebody to help in the process, and specific time limits for the meeting to be held and the decision given, plus the stages of any appeal. The box below shows a typical progression. It is always wise for a clear record to be made of the grievance and the outcome.

Typical grievance procedure for a small organisation

1. The employee raises the grievance informally with his or her immediate superior.
2. If the employee is not satisfied with the outcome, a meeting is convened between the employee and the manager, normally with the supervisor present unless the employee requests otherwise. A record is made of the main issues and the decision.
3. If the employee is still not satisfied with the outcome, then the matter is referred to a director, who will convene a meeting, listen to the parties and take a decision within three to seven days. A record is made of the main issues and the decision.

Note The employee may nominate a colleague to accompany him or her at stages 2 and 3.

Making use of ACAS

If there is a long-standing grievance involving the workforce as a whole or an important segment and the resolution of this dispute has proved very difficult, then it is worth considering using the services of the Advisory, Conciliation and Arbitration Service (ACAS). This is a government-funded but independent service that can provide a free mediation or arbitration service. It was asked to assist in over 500 cases in 1999–2000, most of which were resolved in this way. ACAS is a goldmine of information on all aspects of employee relations, including the effects of legislation. It received 715,000 calls for advice in 1999–2000, nearly half from employers.

Proactive approach

Avoiding grievances is always better than having to react to them. There is no sure-fire way to avoid them altogether but a checklist to help you down this road is shown in the box below. Most of this advice has been dealt with earlier in the chapter.

> ### Checklist of a proactive approach to avoiding grievances
> - Communicate effectively and regularly so that employees are rarely faced with unpleasant surprises.
> - Create some form of consultative forum so that employees have the opportunity to give their views and you have the chance to test the water.
> - Talk informally to employees to find out if there are any issues festering that nobody has the courage to raise, as they are fearful of the effect this may have on their jobs and futures.
> - Consider using an **employee attitude survey**. This is a confidential report that can be carried out for you by a professional body such as MORI (it is expensive but not as much as you may fear) or through the local college where a student on a management or human resources course could carry one out for you free as a course project. It does not need to be long or complex, just focusing on employees' attitudes towards certain key areas of

relationships between management and staff. Areas covered could include:
- management style;
- quality of consultation and communications;
- working practices;
- level of pay and benefits compared to that of other employers in the locality;
- quality of training and career opportunity;
- level of trust between management and employees;
- whether overall the organisation is a good employer.

Research has shown that employees respect the employer more for giving them the opportunity to comment, and they generally do so with honesty and balance. It can certainly help in the relationships with employees. On the other hand, carrying out a survey has its dangers. You may be disappointed with the results or find difficulty in interpreting them. (If you use MORI, you will be able to compare the results with other results on their database.) Employees will expect some feedback in generalised terms and some action to follow from the results – you cannot just forget the outcome and expect everybody else to do the same.

- Try to involve employees through some of the motivational methods suggested in Chapter 3. These include identifying employees who are good team players and giving them responsibilities in teams. Ensure that employees' career opportunities are regularly considered. Pick out employees with potential and involve them in project work across departments. Use an employee recognition scheme to reward those who have made an effort to come up with good practical ideas or have made an outstanding contribution over and above the call of duty.

A reminder of the legal interventions

The law has intervened in the consultation process in a number of ways. The major areas are in the necessity of creating works councils, the requirement to recognise trade unions and the requirement to consult employees where redundancies are planned (see Chapter 9). You should remember that you cannot dismiss employees because of their union activities, even if you have not recognised trade unions. This is automatically unfair.

References

Dundon, T, Grugulis, I and Wilkinson, A (2001) New management techniques in small and medium-sized companies, in *Contemporary Human Resource Management*, ed T Redman and A Wilkinson, Financial Times Prentice-Hall, London

Hammond, D (2001) CAC made relations worse, *People Management*, 25 January, p 6

Walsh, J (1998) Report finds partnership equals profit, *People Management*, 19 March, p 13

Further information

For advice on handling grievances, see Jackson, T (2000) Handling Grievances, CIPD, London.

Web sites worth visiting are:

- www.acas.org.uk – the Web site for ACAS, which includes a list of their publications, some of which can be downloaded at no charge;
- www.tiger.gov.uk – the Tailored Interactive Guidance on Employment Rights site, which is an excellent site for updated legal advice;
- www.incomesdata.co.uk – the Web site of Incomes Data Services, which provides a wealth of fortnightly information on employment legislation and other employment issues (details of subscriptions are provided on the site).

7 Equal opportunities

Introduction

Not a week passes, it seems, without news on equal opportunities. If it is not a new act or regulations being implemented, then it is new tribunal interpretations and large awards and settlements being made. Sometimes the figures are dazzling, such as £300,000 being awarded to a female City banker for discrimination, or the results are confusing, such as the varying rulings on uniforms for men and women. Often it is small organisations that get into trouble, especially in the rapidly changing area of sexual harassment.

Equal opportunity issues permeate all areas of managing people, and mention has been made in Chapters 2, 3 and 5 of some of the applications in the field of recruitment, selection, performance and reward. This chapter brings all those issues together, describing the underpinning legislation, explaining why it is important, how the main problems can be avoided, the main management actions that need to be taken and how it can be turned to the advantage of a small business.

Legislation

Table 7.1 is a summary of the current legislation.

Table 7.1 Equal opportunities legislation

Legislation	Subject Areas	Body that Oversees the Legislation
Equal Pay Act 1970, amended by the Equal Value Regulations 1983	Deals with equal pay for men and women for like work, work rated as equivalent and work of equal value.	Equal Opportunities Commission
Sex Discrimination Act 1975	Deals with discrimination between men and women on the grounds of sex and marital status. Sexual harassment is also covered.	Equal Opportunities Commission
Race Relations Act 1976	Deals with discrimination on the grounds of race, colour, nationality and ethnic origins.	Commission for Racial Equality
Disability Discrimination Act 1995	Deals with discrimination against disabled people.	Disability Rights Commission

An important point to remember at this early stage is that, unlike in unfair dismissal cases, there is *no limit* to the amount of compensation that can be awarded in cases of discrimination.

The role of the overseeing body is to monitor the operation of the Acts, investigate organisations where discrimination appears to continue strongly, draw up codes of conduct, commission research and support the tribunal cases of individuals and groups where important issues are at stake.

There is *no* legislation yet on age discrimination, but a recent European Union Directive requires such legislation to be in place before 2007.

What is discrimination?

Discrimination occurs where a person is treated less favourably and suffers a detriment because of that person's sex, race, marital status or disablement. **Direct discrimination** is usually easy to spot, for example where a woman doesn't make the short list for a sales position because the manager wants to keep an all-male sales team, where a black person's application is refused because 'black people would not fit in' or where a company's policy is not to take on young married women because they will leave to have families.

It is not always straightforward to identify **indirect discrimination**. This is where someone suffers a detriment because of a requirement that disproportionately excludes the particular group to which the person belongs. Here are a few examples:

- job requirements on height and weight that clearly discriminate against women;
- excluding candidates from a specific area of a city where the ethnic population is high;
- insisting on a higher level of spoken and written English than the position warrants;
- requiring applicants for a professional position to be 'between 27 and 35 with successful relevant experience', as many women who have left work to bring up their families are unable to meet these requirements;
- recruitment being carried out only by word of mouth when the employees are predominantly white.

It is possible for discrimination to be allowed in two situations, but these are very limited. Firstly, discriminatory job requirements may be 'genuine occupational qualifications' (GOQs). These apply only in modelling, acting and when privacy and decency in the provision of personal services are concerned (for example, a personal care worker for a severely disabled older lady). Even these areas are being whittled away, for example ethnic restaurants can no longer insist on ethnic waiting staff! The second situation is if the discrimination is 'objectively justified' by the employer but few such claims by employers have succeeded at tribunals.

Disability cases

The Disability Discrimination Act added additional requirements on employers in that they have an obligation to make 'reasonable adjustments' to the workplace to accommodate the needs of disabled people. This applies in all establishments except those where fewer than 20 employees work.

A number of decisions by tribunals have been very favourable towards the claimants. Examples are:

- An employee with back pain asked for adjustments to be made to a bench (costing £500) but this was refused and she was subsequently dismissed for poor attendance. She won her case, and the tribunal heavily criticised the company for not making the adjustment (*Palmer* v *Caradon Mira*, 1998).
- A job applicant was appointed as a social worker but, when medical reports showed that she had a history of mental illness that had involved hospitalisation and psychotherapy, the offer was withdrawn. The Employment Appeal Tribunal found that the organisation had made no effort to consider adjustments to her work and awarded her compensation (*Farnsworth* v *London Borough of Hammersmith and Fulham*, 1999).
- A supermarket manager was diagnosed as HIV-positive. After treatment, he considered himself fit to return to work, but the employer refused and made insufficient effort to make adjustments to his work. A settlement of £300,000 was reached ahead of the tribunal hearing (*Hedley* v *Aldi*, 2000).
- An employee had irritable bowel syndrome and her doctor recommended less stressful work. Her employer refused and she was placed on a busy counter. She went long-term sick and was

eventually dismissed. Her claim for disability discrimination was successful and she was awarded £14,600.

In disablement discrimination cases, the tribunals have grown increasingly generous, with awards made for 'injury to feelings'. Five-figure sums are not unknown in this category.

Equal Pay Act

The legislation lays down the principle that men and women are entitled to the same rate of pay if they are carrying out broadly the same work. This can be 'like work', work that is rated the same under an internal job evaluation scheme, or work that is of 'equal value'.

It is best to explain equal value with an example. In your organisation, you have a small canteen run very efficiently by a cook/manager called Ellen. She has been in post full time for 15 years and earns £12,000. She works with three part-time staff. One day, you promote Tom, one of the stores assistants aged 28 with two years' service, into the newly created position of stores supervisor in charge of one other member of staff. Ellen finds out on the grapevine that he is being paid £14,000 and she gets angry about this. Although she likes Tom, she has known him in the village since he was in shorts and believes that the job she does is worth at least as much as his job. She believes it has 'equal value' and she would be able to put in a claim to a tribunal, if she found no internal remedy.

The procedure is very long-winded. At the initial hearing, the tribunal will usually appoint an independent expert who will take about four to six months investigating the claim and coming up with a recommendation. The tribunal considers the recommendations but it is often faced with reports commissioned by both the claimant and the organisation concerned (some equal value cases have been so complicated, they have taken up to 10 years to complete by the time they have gone through every court and off to the European Court of Justice and back). The difficulty for employers is that any concessions made to the claimant will normally have a knock-on effect for other staff. It is certainly best to avoid such claims if you can.

Practical advice

It is better to be proactive

You have three choices where equal opportunities are concerned. You can ignore the whole subject and carry on discriminating, whether openly or covertly. This is not a risk worth taking, of course, because you will undoubtedly one day have to face the traumas of tribunal claims and bad publicity. A second approach is simply compliance. This means complying with the letter of the law but without much enthusiasm. You can design and follow the correct procedures, keep out of tribunals and regard the whole business as an unnecessary and regrettable set of bureaucratic rules. Most small companies, if they think about the subject at all, follow this approach. However, this does nothing to add value to the organisation. If the legislation is there, it is worth trying to see if it can be put to an advantage. This can be done by looking at what is called the 'business case' for equal opportunities.

The starting point here is the forecast of a **long-term shortage of labour**. This is not caused just by economic prosperity and the fall of unemployment but, more importantly, by the rapid demographic changes occurring in the UK. Birth rates are continuing to fall and more and more young people are going into higher education, so the traditional sources of labour (young, white, full-time males) are much reduced. Organisations therefore have to rethink their employment policies and try to widen the pool of employment to look for untapped sources of expertise. This means adapting the jobs to match the labour available, such as:

- changing standard full-time hours to accommodate part-time work that may be more attractive to women, students and the semi-retired;

- changing working conditions and benefits to allow wheelchairs, career breaks, childcare facilities, prayers and language classes;
- changing unnecessary requirements such as height, strength and age.

Customer relations are a second important factor. Women make up 52 per cent of the population, ethnic minorities and disabled people over 5 per cent each and the elderly around 20 per cent. You cannot afford to put off any of these groups by having a labour force that is, say, all white or predominantly male. Customers are increasingly looking through the front door of the organisations they buy from and, if they do not like what they see because of the image it reflects, they will go elsewhere.

The same argument applies with the concept and image of a 'good employer'. Organisations that are seen to have high ethical stances, with policies in place on 'dignity at work' that prevent harassment and bullying, and a generally progressive attitude to equal opportunities will be more attractive to both customers and potential employees.

There are a number of cases of larger organisations gaining benefits in this way, including B and Q with its policy of recruiting older employees, Littlewoods with its community recruitment policy and Boots with its much widened career development system. All have gained by increasing their recruitment pool, increasing their staff retention rate and improving their customer satisfaction indexes. Such policies are well worth replicating (albeit in a much less formalised system) in smaller organisations.

If you are still not convinced, perhaps the recent research study showing that people with disabilities have the same productivity levels as the general working population, a better-than-average safety record and lower levels of absenteeism and sickness will help to change your mind.

You must be careful not to be so carried away with promoting equal opportunities that you practise positive discrimination, in other words offering jobs or promoting employees *because of* their sex, race or disability. This is equally against the law.

Some specifics

The following sections give some specific examples of areas where you need to take some care to ensure you do not fall foul of the legislation.

Recruitment and selection

- Do not use job titles such as 'waiter' or 'chambermaid' that clearly indicate one sex. Use sexless titles such as 'operator'. 'Manager' can still be used if it is made clear that applications from both sexes are welcomed.
- If you use a picture in any of your recruitment literature, make sure that it contains a mix of males and females and contains staff of ethnic origin.
- Do not restrict your recruitment to word of mouth or through relatives.
- If you use any selection tests, make sure they are of recent origin (some older tests were standardised on all-white groups) and give special assistance to those applicants whose first language is not English so they are not disadvantaged.
- In interviews, steer clear of questions relating to the home background or marriage/children situation, and do not talk about childcare except in the context of any arrangements you may be offering in this area.

Retention

- All of the proactive flexibility systems set out in Chapter 3 (part-time, flexible hours, job-shares, etc) provide support and assistance to those with family responsibilities who wish to balance the demands of work and home.
- Make sure that promotion opportunities are available to all of your staff and that the selection process is open and transparent.
- Give consideration to any cultural requirements of ethnic-minority staff. These can include special arrangements for food,

prayers, holidays and variations in the dress code. This is a difficult area, and operational needs have to be balanced against employees' requests. There is no straightforward answer here, as tribunals have continued to take each case on its merit. In general, they have supported organisations, especially small ones, that have listened to the requests of staff, made some effort to accommodate those requests and carefully justified why they cannot accommodate everything that has been asked.
- Consider requests for women to work part time. This can be very disruptive for the small business and there is still no legal entitlement in this area. The government in 2001 indicated through a Green Paper that it wished to encourage employers to accept such requests but legislation is unlikely in the short term. However, it makes sense to try to be co-operative where employees have specific pressures that can be exacerbated by working full time. This applies particularly when women are returning from maternity leave. The best approach is not to slam the door but to place the initiative on to the employee to work out a plan as to how the work could be accommodated on a part-time basis. If this plan looks reasonable, agree to the arrangement on a trial basis with an agreed cut-off time – say three or six months. Being co-operative could be a good investment for the future, when the employee may respond to requests for her to be flexible. Slamming the door could lead to the employee leaving or, worse, a tribunal claim for discrimination.

Disability needs

- If any of your employees become disabled through an injury, accident or illness, do not dismiss them out of hand. Give consideration to their situation, get advice on the prognosis from their doctor (you will need their permission for this) and think about any 'reasonable adjustment' you could make to help them get back to some sort of normal work. You may agree with them

that they will come back on a part-time basis or on a trial basis and, if so, it is essential such an arrangement is confirmed in writing. Tribunals judge the 'reasonable' nature of the arrangements by looking at the costs involved against the employer's ability to pay (the size of the organisation is obviously a factor here), as well as the current situation of the employment of disabled people in the organisation.
- Don't reject out of hand applicants with disabilities, especially if you are employing none currently.
- Take special care with cases involving mental disability, which includes the occurrence or reoccurrence of stress-related illnesses. They are particularly difficult to handle for both the employer and any subsequent tribunal. You should get legal advice here before taking any precipitous action.

Sexual harassment and bullying

If there is one area where small organisations have hit the headlines in employment terms, it is through the stories of harassment and bullying that have emerged from tribunal cases. Time and time again, tribunals have heard evidence that male managers, often owners or directors, have behaved in such a way that female staff have felt intimidated, embarrassed and humiliated to such an extent that they have become stressed leading to the onset of physical ailments and clinical depression. Moreover, the perpetrators have often expressed no remorse for their actions or shown a great willingness to settle. They often appear to hold the view that it is their company, they choose how to run it, how they act is their affair and staff who do not like it should leave. In other words, they feel that a culture of sexual innuendo or offensiveness within the small business is fine because it is a closed community. Well, it is not fine – it is against the law. Being a small organisation is not a defence against unacceptable behaviour so it is worth spending a little more time on this area.

What is harassment?

Harassment has been recognised for over 25 years as a form of discrimination carried out by a member of one sex or race against a member of the opposite sex or another race. In recent years, the question of what makes up harassment has been clarified more carefully. In July 2000, the European Commission issued amendments on the Equal Treatment Directive, where sexual harassment was defined as: 'Unwanted conduct related to sex... with the purpose or effect of affecting the dignity of a person and/or creating an intimidating, hostile, offensive or disturbing environment. In particular, if a person's rejection of, or submission to, such conduct is used as a basis for a decision that affects that person.'

Who decides if the action fits into any of these categories? Interestingly, it is the employees involved. If they decide the action is offensive and harasses them, then it *is* offensive. Employees do not have to prove this; they simply have to show it – it is an entirely subjective test. Here are a few examples of various forms of harassment:

- sexual banter, even if it is good-natured and a familiar office or factory activity;
- pin-ups around walls;
- derogatory remarks and nicknames;
- invading body space;
- deliberate bodily contact;
- suggestive remarks in front of other-sex employees;
- unsolicited presents;
- unnecessary checking of work;
- ignoring or excluding an individual.

What should the management do about it?

Firstly, of course, management must lead by example. They must make sure that anybody in a position of authority understands both the legal situation and the harm such behaviour can cause.

Secondly, they need to make it plain throughout the organisation that any action that could be construed as harassment by any employee will not be acceptable. This is best done through the normal communication channels such as an employee handbook or a regular newsletter. It is best to confirm this in a positive way by stressing the pride the organisation takes in being a discrimination-free organisation and wanting to keep it that way. Pin-ups or racially offensive literature of any form need to be banned from the premises.

Thirdly, they have to respond to all complaints of harassment by employees. To avoid a successful claim for harassment, the organisation needs to show that it has carried out a proper investigation. This is not always easy because the question arises as to the stage at which accusations should be addressed to alleged perpetrators. So it is important for there to be a discussion first with complainants as to what action they would like taken. This discussion can be led by an independent manager, or it is possible to bring in a skilled counsellor from outside the organisation. This will vary depending on the nature of the harassment, whether it is overt or covert, a one-off incident or a long line of continuing actions. Possible options that can be put to a complainant include:

- *Doing nothing*. The complainant, having talked through the situation, may recognise that it is not a threat or that he or she has misread the situation. However, the harassment may continue unabated.
- *The complainant raising the matter with the offending person*. The complainant, having been counselled over the matter, may feel more confident in raising the issue with the perpetrator and getting the person to stop. A trusted third party could be present. There are numerous examples of perpetrators simply not being aware of the harm caused and, when this is pointed out, being willing to apologise and change their ways. However, this might be a risky and daunting action where success is not guaranteed.
- *The complainant moving jobs*. This may be an easy solution and one that would satisfy the complainant but could be demoral-

ising for that person and lead to longer-term problems should the reason for the move leak out.
- *The organisation investigating.* Witnesses would have to be interviewed confidentially and their versions recorded. If there is no supporting evidence from any other sources, then the organisation needs to go back to the complainant to discuss where to go now. In particular, the other actions detailed above could be reconsidered. If the complaint appears to have some justification, then the perpetrator needs to be interviewed, with a colleague if wanted. The seriousness of the matter needs to be emphasised and other processes detailed in disciplinary procedures (see Chapter 9) carried out.
- *Disciplining the perpetrator.* Discipline may take a number of forms from a rebuke (coinciding with an expression of deep regret and a reconciliation with the complainant) through a final written warning to instant dismissal in the most serious cases. Moving the perpetrator to another position has also to be considered.

It is also worth remembering that a tribunal case can be brought against both the company and certain named individuals. For example, an Irish lecturer working at Northumberland College of Arts and Technology in the 1990s was subjected to continuing racial harassment including being called an 'Irish prat' by a fellow lecturer. He was awarded £29,000, of which £13,000 had to be paid by the college, £2,000 by the principal, £6,500 by his line manager (both of whom had taken no steps to bring the harassment to a stop once it had been reported to them) and £5,000 by the colleague who had instigated much of the abuse.

A note on uniform

Although the rulings on whether employers can insist on employees wearing uniforms have shown some inconsistency, it has been shown that separate requirements for men and women are allowed on the following basis:

- They appear to be supported by the majority of the workforce.
- They do not put heavier requirements on one sex than the other.
- They can be objectively justified by the employer and have not been instituted in a discriminatory way.

Further reading and Web sites

Clements, P and Spinks, T (2000) *The Equal Opportunities Handbook*, Kogan Page, London

For a series of articles on the business case for equal opportunities, read Schneider, R (2001) Variety performance, *People Management*, 3 May, pp 26–37. (Interestingly, that edition also reports (p 8) on the Equal Opportunities Commission settling a sex discrimination case brought against it by one of its employees!)

For a practical guide to harassment issues, see Stephens, T (1999) *Bullying and Sexual Harassment*, IPD, London.

The Web site for the Equal Opportunities Commission is www.eoc.org.uk.

For further information on the Disability Discrimination Act, see www.disability.gov.uk.

8 Health, safety and welfare

In the early 1990s, Peter Kite ran a small outdoor activity company. In December 1994, he was sent to prison for three years for manslaughter as a result of the death of four teenagers under his control on a canoe outing off the coast of Dorset.

If you manage a small office-based organisation, you may be tempted to skip this chapter, doubting its relevance. You may regard the whole edifice of health and safety to be top-heavy, bureaucratic and hard on the chequebook. However, ignoring this area is a risk you may not be wise to take, given that a single, avoidable accident in your business could cause you immense damage, both financially and in the time you need to spend in any subsequent investigation and court action. And that is not counting the emotional strain of being responsible for an injury or illness to an employee.

Here are some facts: 1) days lost through injury at work in the UK exceed 30 million; 2) 6 per cent of adults suffer from work-related ill health.

This chapter, then, will explain the main elements of health and safety legislation, will detail your main obligations arising from the legislation and will give some practical advice on actions you need to take.

The legislation and obligation on employers

There are over 100 separate pieces of legislation in place concerning health and safety and it will be impossible to cover all of them. Only the most influential have been selected. Croner Publications produce the monthly *Health and Safety at Work*, which will keep your organisation updated on all the existing and future developments.

Health and Safety at Work Act etc 1974

This all-embracing legislation is best summed up by the confirmation that 'It shall be the duty of every employer to ensure, as far as is reasonably practicable, the health, safety and welfare of all his employees.'

This is the fundamental **duty of care** that has been steadily expanded by the courts over recent years. It extends to providing safe systems of work, equipment and the workplace environment in total. There must be arrangements for the safe storage, handling and transport of all articles and substances. Employee safety must be ensured through effective communication, supervision and training, and welfare provision must be adequate.

The employer's duty of care does not stop at employees; it extends to subcontractors, visitors and general members of the public.

'Reasonably practicable' is not easy to define. It certainly limits the absolute responsibility and allows employers to achieve a balance between the assessed risk of an unsafe practice and the cost of avoiding that risk. You do not have to build a steel casing over a factory to protect it from a light aircraft crashing into it because the risk is small and the cost great. But you do have to make wide walkways in a factory to ensure safe passage of employees and materials and you need to make sure those walkways are clear of cables and the floors are not slippery, for example.

Another provision is for organisations to use the 'best practical means' in examining solutions to safety risks. This is to prevent employers taking short cuts or using cheap botched jobs. Where everyday operations involve safety risks, such as in construction work or many industrial operations, then the law expects organisations at least to have investigated and actively considered modern safety systems.

There are also duties on employees. They have to co-operate in any changes relating to improving safety, they have to follow instructions, they must wear safety gear where required, they must take reasonable care of their own health and safety and they must not be reckless. If they refuse reasonable instructions under headings of health and safety, not only can they be dismissed but if they wilfully ignore safety warnings it is possible for them to be prosecuted individually at the same time as the organisation in the event of a serious accident taking place.

Law enforcement

Under the Act, the enforcement is carried out by the Health and Safety Executive (HSE), whose inspectors mostly deal with factories, and local authority enforcement officers, who deal with service industries – hotels, restaurants, offices and warehouses. They have extensive authority, including the rights to:

- enter premises with or without notice at any reasonable time (accompanied by the police, if obstructed);
- examine books and documents;
- take statements, samples, measurements and photographs;
- direct that work and equipment are left undisturbed.

Their main aim is to assist in prevention of accidents and they can be a valuable source of guidance and advice. They try to visit all premises in their patch on a regular basis, although they will visit more often those places with a poor history on safety or where they have experienced less co-operation. If they see dangerous or unhealthy practices they will exercise persuasion to get the defect remedied. But if this

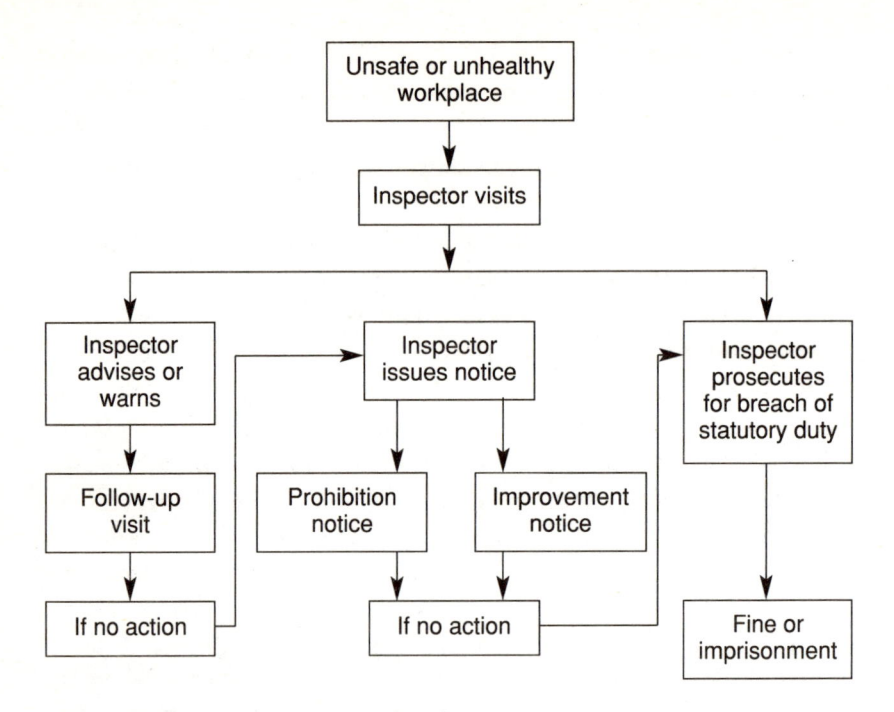

Figure 8.1 Monitoring by inspectors

does not work, they have powers to issue notices, as shown in Figure 8.1.

Improvement notices are issued where the inspector is satisfied there has been a contravention of a statutory provision. The improvement notice will give the employer a certain time within which that contravention must be remedied. Work can continue in the meantime. A **prohibition notice**, which means the work must immediately cease, is issued when the inspector considers that the activity involves a risk of serious personal safety or of a severe safety hazard to the employees or the public. Around 9,000 notices are issued each year and the records of such notices are on public view for up to three years, providing a deterrent to safety transgressors.

For an individual manager to be prosecuted, it has to be shown that the breach occurred through his or her consent, connivance or neglect.

Where disasters have occurred in large organisations, such as the sinking of the *Herald of Free Enterprise*, it has proved difficult to pin the blame squarely on management because responsibility is shared through various layers of management down to the safety officers. In smaller organisations, however, the courts have found it much easier to allocate the blame, especially if local managers or supervisors have attempted to remedy safety defects but these have been obstructed by senior management.

The Act also established rights for internal safety representatives, who can be appointed by management or elected by the workforce – clarified by the Health and Safety (Consultation with Employees) Regulations 1996. Representatives must be involved in the consultation process and given reasonable time off to carry out their duties, together with basic facilities such as use of a telephone and a filing cabinet. Their duties range from investigating potential hazards and complaints made by fellow employees to making representations to management to further improvements in the workplace.

Obligations on employers

Employers must draw up a **health and safety policy** (where five or more people are employed). It is sensible to incorporate the policy within a health and safety handbook for the staff. The policy should set out the major aims (reducing accidents and hazards) and the major roles and responsibilities for safety (for employers and employees). The handbook should continue with:

- operation of any safety committee;
- major safety hazards where employees must taken special care;
- safety rules;
- protective equipment;
- fire regulations, drills and emergency procedures;
- reference to other specialised documents (hazardous substances, for example).

It is important that such a document should be made easy for all the staff to understand. An excellent guide to preparing a policy has been prepared by the Health and Safety Executive (see 'Further information' at the end of the chapter).

A **risk assessment exercise** should take place regularly. (This is a legal duty under the 1992 Code of Practice for the Management of Health and Safety at Work.) The Code requires the appointment of 'competent persons' to assist in this and other safety tasks. For a small business, this can present a problem, although it is usually solved by allocating the role to the person with health and safety responsibilities.

There are three main stages in the process of assessing and controlling risks:

- identifying hazards (the potential causes of harm);
- assessing risks (the likelihood of harm occurring and its severity) and prioritising action;
- designing, implementing and monitoring measures to eliminate or minimise risk.

Hazard identification can be carried out in a number of ways. Observation through, say, a regular safety tour of the plant by the safety officer and safety representatives for the areas will bring to light poor housekeeping such as accumulated rubbish or blocked fire exits, safety equipment not being worn and poor lighting or ventilation. Such hazards have to be considered as much for employees who may be aware of the dangers as for visitors to the site and especially new employees who could be young and completely unaware of potential dangers.

Longer investigations by trained technicians or by external agencies may be necessary to investigate the hazards of pollution, noise or noxious fumes and their degree of danger or to decide where, if at all, smoking can be allowed on the premises. Long-term projects will be needed to identify hazards in planned changes through new equipment, machinery, materials and layouts. A proper investigation here will involve the suppliers of the equipment, machinery and materials.

When it comes to **assessing the risks**, it is useful to attempt to identify the severity of the hazard. A three-part rating scale for risk assessment (see Table 8.1) provides a useful and consistent approach to identifying hazards and also provides help with prioritising safety action. It is not possible to eliminate every conceivable hazard. Where there are budgetary limits, the total hazard rating provides a league table of necessary action where those with the highest points get tackled first.

The final stage is to decide what can be done to **control or eliminate the risks**. Measures to consider include the following:

- Tightening up on housekeeping procedures should make the site cleaner, tidier and, therefore, safer. Supplying better protective equipment will serve to avoid the likelihood of injury to persons exposed to the risk.
- Replacing hazardous materials with safer alternatives will avoid or reduce the need to monitor and protect employees.
- Redesigning the production processes or layouts through such improvements as separating the operator from the risk by enclosing the process, using remote-control equipment, improving guarding and increasing extraction systems is a valuable investment in terms of hazard prevention.
- Automating lifting processes will also tend to reduce the incidence of back injury, although fork-lift trucks and other devices provide a further source of potential danger, which needs to be assessed.

Risk assessment continues to be a matter of balance. The test of 'reasonably practicable' is still used in the context of cost and difficulty balanced against likely danger. It is important, therefore, that organisations have set out policies and procedures that help them to achieve a fair balance and that will highlight actions that they have to take speedily.

Table 8.1 Making risk assessments by rating hazards

Likelihood of harm		
Certain	It is certain that harm will result whenever exposure to the hazard occurs.	4 points
Probable	Harm will probably result in most cases when exposure to the hazard occurs, although there may be exceptions.	3 points
Possible	Harm may occur in some cases when exposure to the hazard occurs, although there are likely to be many exceptions.	2 points
Slight	Unlikely that harm will occur, except in a very small minority of cases.	1 point
Severity		
Major	Death or major injury, as defined by RIDDOR, is probable.	4 points
Serious	Injuries, though not necessarily formally classified as major, are likely to result in absences of more than three days.	3 points
Minor	Injuries may cause some absence but probably for not more than three days.	2 points
Slight	Any injuries are unlikely to result in time off work.	1 point
Extent		
Very Extensive	Likely to affect the whole workforce and/or significant numbers of the public.	4 points
Extensive	Likely to affect a whole work group and might affect some members of the public.	3 points
Limited	Likely to affect only a small number of either employees or members of the public.	2 points
Very Limited	Likely to affect only single individuals.	1 point

(Source: Fowler, 1995)

Control of Substances Hazardous to Health Regulations (COSHH) 1988

These regulations concentrate on the duty of care of employers in respect of the handling and utilisation of hazardous materials.

Obligation on employers

- A risk assessment must be made at least every five years to identify all potentially hazardous substances and to establish and publicise the precautions necessary. Criticisms have been made that all manner of commonplace materials, such as turps and Tippex, finish up on employers' lists but there is no doubt that such products can be misused and cause ill health.
- Systems must be put in place to prevent or control these risks and ensure that the controls are monitored and recorded so that they work properly.
- Staff must be informed of the hazards and trained in the control processes, and regular health surveillance should take place of the staff who are regularly involved.
- Even more importantly, employers should be vigilant in attempting to reduce the risks by replacing materials and substances with less hazardous ones.

The Reporting of Injuries, Diseases and Dangerous Occurrences Regulations (RIDDOR) 1995

This sets out the requirements on keeping records and reporting.

Obligations on employers

- All deaths and major injuries need to be reported by telephone to the Health and Safety Executive immediately after the accident and a written report made within 10 days. Lesser accidents that lead to an employee being off work for more than three days need to be reported using form F2508 within seven days.

- Dangerous occurrences that do not lead to any injury also need to be reported and recorded. An example is the collapse of a machine where employees managed to run clear. The main aim here is for the enforcing authorities to follow up some situations to ensure they are not repeated.
- Any incident including violence by employees in the workplace must be reported and recorded.

The Health and Safety (Display Screen Equipment) Regulations 1992

These regulations have had a major impact on the day-to-day operations of the growing number of employees spending much of their time in front of a screen.

Obligations on employers

- Employers must periodically assess, evaluate and eliminate or minimise the health and safety risks associated with work on display screens. Reflection, noise, ventilation, sitting position, working height and angle should be examined.
- The employees concerned should be trained so that they are aware of the risks involved and can avoid them.
- Employers must arrange for employees to have regular eye tests and ensure that the work is planned to include breaks and changes in activity.

Manual Handling Operations Regulations 1992

These regulations were introduced to try to reduce the increasing amount of absence through back strain and other lifting-related illnesses.

Obligations on employers

- Employees must be trained to lift loads in the correct way.

Health, safety and welfare

- Lifting gear should be provided where applicable.
- Risk assessment should take place to consider whether automation of the lifting process is a possibility.

Other legislation

Amongst the long list of other relevant legislation, the most important are the Personal Protective Equipment at Work Regulations 1992, which impose duties on employers to provide suitable protective equipment and make sure it fits, train people in its use, and maintain and store it properly; the Provision and Use of Work Equipment Regulations 1992, under which employers need to consider carefully a number of aspects when introducing machinery, including training, lighting and protection; and other regulations concerning the protection of young people and pregnant women, and the control of asbestos. Information on where the details of all the legislation are available is given at the end of this chapter.

Practical advice

Providing a culture of safety

A good record on safety does not just happen by chance. Nor will discipline be a wholly successful option. Although there may be an immediate response to actions taken against employees not following safety procedures, research has shown that this response is only short-term and centres on compliance rather than proactive support. In other words, employees will ensure they try to keep themselves out of trouble and especially will try not to be found out for any non-compliance. They will close their eyes to safety hazards that do not personally affect them and they will put little thought or effort into areas where rules and regulations are not spelt out. You cannot be wholly successful by managing health and safety through diktat.

What needs to be encouraged is a culture among employees of

taking a proactive interest in safety and not needing to be constantly reminded. The objective is to achieve a situation where employees willingly train and advise new staff, carefully examine all new materials and equipment for hazards and keep their own area clean and free of hazards.

This can be achieved through three principal vehicles – communication, involvement and zero tolerance.

Communication

Imparting all the facts on safety is a good starting point. How much is needed depends, of course, on the context. For a small manufacturing company, the following should apply:

- Posters should be prominently displayed and regularly changed.
- Instructions on the use of new equipment or materials should be personally disseminated to all employees involved – not just in writing but through a short off-the-job session together with a practical application.
- New employees should have a thorough induction on health and safety issues with some form of informal test before they are allowed on any job with hazards.
- Examples of accidents and injuries that could occur should be communicated through any regular internal communication medium, such as a newsletter.
- Warning signs should be displayed in all areas where hazards apply.
- All employees should take part in a short training session on lifting techniques and emergency drills.

For organisations essentially office-based, communication requirements are more limited but still should extend to general safety posters, induction of new employees in potential hazards and dissemination of accident information. It keeps safety in everybody's minds.

Involvement

This is the next and probably most important stage. The starting point is the safety committee. All but the smallest organisations should have some format where managers and staff can discuss safety issues in a constructive manner. Experience shows that employers being proactive in this area prevents the committee from being either a talking shop or the source of management-worker arguments. Proactive means consulting on new protective equipment, asking for ideas on the safety aspects of new plant or layout, putting right defects quickly that have been identified on a regular safety inspection by committee members and acting responsibly when any accidents or serious incidents occur.

There is no doubt that some safety representatives can see their role as giving them the opportunity to exercise their right to take time away from work. In general, however, few small organisations find this a difficulty, as the absence of a safety representative from the place of work is noticed quickly when there are few employees. In fact, safety representatives can play a valuable role in helping encourage fellow employees to follow safety rules – to wear protective equipment, keep their area tidy, etc. As long as the concept of the safety team is emphasised and put into practice (safety inspections should *always* be carried out jointly by management and safety reps), then a co-operative committee will be the norm.

The committee must not be used to bypass managers and supervisors. They should be equally involved through safety issues being on the agenda of most (or all) management meetings. They can be given specific safety tasks to research and report on, working with a specialist in the organisation (an engineer or chemist, for example). They should also be given opportunities to attend any relevant safety course.

Zero tolerance

This applies principally to housekeeping. There is no more telling evidence of management's lack of interest than a tolerance of a dirty and untidy work area, as Case 8.1 indicates. Actions are essential here and continual vigilance needs to be exercised.

It goes further than this, however. If any short cuts on safety of any type are allowed, it sends a clear message to the workforce. If you turn a blind eye to machines being loaded while operating, in contravention of manufacturers' instructions, it encourages employees to adopt the approach of putting production before safety. The consequences here could be disastrous.

Good housekeeping applies to offices as much as to any other area. You should ensure that cables are not trailing dangerously, filing cabinets are not overloaded and work areas are kept reasonably tidy. Employees who injure themselves by falling over or knocking themselves can make claims against the employer even if partly to blame for their own injuries.

A final element in this discussion on creating a safety culture is the willingness to create a **safety budget** or, at least, to be prepared to spend money when it is necessary. All efforts of getting staff enthusiasm and involvement will founder if it comes against the rock of cost cutting. 'We can't afford safety' is a dangerous slogan and it is far better to develop a list of costed safety improvements, which the safety committee prioritise and which can be implemented when funds are available, than to write off any reasonable suggestion.

Case 8.1 Cleaning up at Zeldan Plastics

Zeldan Plastics (not its real name), a long-established company with 70 employees making lighting components, had been acquired 18 months previously. Working with the existing management, productivity and technical improvements had been made but, when the author first visited the Midlands factory on appointment to the holding company, the working areas had not changed much for 25 years. The floors were littered with extrusion offcuts, packing materials, other production debris and, by afternoon each day, the waste from the fast food brought into the areas from a van that stopped outside the site. Accumulated grime and evidence of small rodents were apparent in the areas beneath and behind machines.

Cleaning was carried out by an external contractor early each morning but the specification was light and the performance unreliable. Employees (those who stayed – there was a high turnover problem) were used to working under these conditions and made no effort to remedy any of the problems. Cleaning up was not in their job description – that was the work of the cleaners. There was a growing concern by the holding company that the quality of work was affected by this culture, and a number of minor accidents had taken place in recent months, the most serious being a bad fall by a 55-year-old employee slipping on the floor. There were rumours that she was threatening action against the company. On top of this, management was hesitant to bring potential customers on to the site because of the conditions.

An important new contract had been signed, which, if successful, could lead to substantial work in the future. This, together with the recent accident and the decision to work towards ISO 2000, acted as the catalyst for action. A management meeting led to a three-pronged attack. Over the forthcoming holiday shutdown, the entire factory would be extensively cleaned and painted. Stores areas would be reorganised to free up an amenity area, and food and drink would no longer be allowed in working areas. A change in the working practices would mean that employees would be responsible for keeping their own work areas clean and tidy.

Discussions took place firstly with all the employees in their work areas to present the outline of the plans and to emphasise the importance of the new contract in terms of job security. Representatives from each department then joined management in drawing up the details. It was subsequently agreed that the extra housekeeping duties warranted a pay increase, which would be taken into account when the next pay increase was due in six weeks' time. The way the cleaning took place would be decided by each of the five department teams, as would the new shift break arrangements to avoid the situation where every department used the amenities at the same time. (An initiative on team working was being introduced simultaneously.) Departments would be 'inspected' by one of the management team on a regular but unannounced basis every six months and a prize awarded to the best department.

The outcome surprised even management. Far from complaining about the extra work they had to do, most employees adapted to the new clean regime with enthusiasm, especially to the interdepartment competitive element. Suggestions of improvements in handling and disposing of the waste were quickly taken up; employees kept their own areas clean with little effort and new employees quickly fell into the new clean culture after it was emphasised during induction. Management made a point of introducing potential customers to the staff when they were brought around – in fact supervisors and key staff were coached on communicating to and handling customers.

This empowerment process (see Chapter 3) was one of the most important elements of the culture change and it led to other improvements. Staff turnover dropped, and quality and material usage measures improved, as did overall productivity, which allowed pay rates to improve. Accident rates were halved in the first year and dropped further in subsequent years.
(Source: author's experience)

Working with enforcement agencies

HSE or local authority inspectors are often seen as 'the enemy', to be kept away from premises as much as possible. This has arisen because they are seen as interfering and overbearing and lead to more money being spent. Of course, there are always some characters who may fit the stereotype but most inspectors are in post because they are dedicated to reducing accidents and injuries. Their experience is that some employers will only move to make necessary injury-preventing improvements when the big stick is waved.

There is increasing experience that a proactive stance with inspectors produces a far more positive approach. Where new layouts or equipment are planned, it is no bad thing to ring the inspector for advice. Human nature is such that inspectors tend to respond much more positively and will regard your organisation as a safety-conscious one. Their knowledge of the safety market is such that they may even save you money!

Work design

Another proactive approach to improve safety is through designing safety into the work. Here the starting point is to try to adapt the work to employees and not try to shoehorn employees into the work needs. Great advances have been made in machine design. For example, guillotine operators in printing now need both hands to operate the equipment, protecting them from the dangers of feeding paper in with one hand. When a new layout is being considered, safety should be of equal consideration with speed and efficiency. The ergonomic needs of employees should be carefully considered – their stance, sitting positions, hand operations and vision should all be reviewed and improved where required. Regular breaks should be built in, especially where the work is gruelling. This seems obvious advice but is often forgotten in the routine of production.

Finally, the macho lifting culture should be avoided. Yes, strong young men are handy to have around but you should not need to rely too much on their strength. Back strain comes easily but is difficult to remedy. Insisting on employees being able to lift heavy weights is seen these days as discrimination against women and disabled people. Take a more realistic and modern-day approach to lifting needs by considering automated storing systems as well as fork-lift trucks. However, you should make sure you train employees in using them properly – misuse of fork-lift trucks is one of the largest single causes of deaths and serious injuries in recent years.

Smoking policy

In a recently published research item, a US factory manager estimated that each smoking employee cost his company around £45,000. This was worked out by calculating the time spent on smoking, absenteeism due to smoking-related illnesses, property damage and additional maintenance.

With the advent of legal claims for 'passive smoking' in recent years, most organisations have adopted workplace smoking policies. These either eliminate smoking altogether from the premises (always the best policy but you may lose some key staff) or limit it to specific smoking areas.

The advent of such policies has been opposed at tribunals by some employees but such claims have been largely unsuccessful, especially if the policy was introduced after a ballot of all employees and a period of adjustment allowed before the new regulations were imposed. Consultation is essential and a majority is rarely difficult to obtain. The more progressive of employers can agree to subsidise employees in their efforts to give up smoking on a limited time basis.

Occupational stress

There has been a huge rise in the interest in stress in recent years – chiefly because it is costing employers so much more money! The CBI estimated that it cost £7 billion in 1998 through absenteeism plus legal and insurance payments, about £310 per employee per year. Claims for compensation arising from mental problems almost doubled between 1993 and 1998.

Stress manifests itself in:

- high absence levels;
- increase in alcohol or drug taking;
- high levels of employee fatigue;
- unwillingness to take on responsibilities or be responsible for decisions;
- increased hostility between employees and against management;
- unwillingness to change practices;
- unpredictable behaviour with mood swings;
- desire to retire early;
- 'early burn-out' with the subsequent loss of talent, skills and experience.

The causes are many and varied, and there can be a mixture of stress in the workplace and personal difficulties, with one kind exacerbating the other.

Workplace stress can arise from:

- increase in work intensity;
- aggressive management styles;
- bullying or harassment;
- over-promotion;
- lack of guidance as to how to do the job properly;
- overambitious objectives;
- excessive computer work;
- too great an exposure to customer demands;

- unpredictable work flows;
- fear of organisational change.

A landmark case in 1995 has opened the floodgates to compensatory claims by employees. John Walker was a social-work manager with Northumberland County Council who had a mental breakdown as a result of his workload. When he returned to work after the breakdown, nothing had changed and he had no positive assistance from his employer to help him cope successfully. He became ill again and had to give up work entirely. He was awarded £175,000 because the court held that the employer was negligent in respect of its 'duty of care' towards him. Psychiatric damage could be regarded as identical to physical injury, and John Walker's eventual breakdown was reasonably foreseeable.

Other cases have followed hot on the heels of the Walker case and make it clear to employers that they must take reasonable steps to ameliorate potential health-damaging situations in the stress arena. This is common sense and has an effect upon the opinion of employees towards the organisation. For small organisations, the issue of 'reasonably practicable' comes into play. The smaller the organisation, the less is expected of it in terms of making appropriate adjustments, and the same applies with disability cases.

Conclusion

A simple message is to take health and safety issues seriously and show the workforce that you regard them as important by the actions you take. You may like to complete the occupational health and safety checklist issued by the Health and Safety Executive, which you will find on their Web site (see below). It may stimulate action in one or more areas.

Reference

Fowler, A (1995) How to make the workplace safer, *People Management*, 26 January, pp 38–39

Further information

Stranks, J (2001) *A Manager's Guide to Health and Safety at Work*, Kogan Page, London

The Health and Safety Executive provides a huge amount of advice and information for small businesses, which is available from its Web site, www.hse.gov.uk. The main publication here is *Health and Safety in Small Firms* and this is backed up with the document *Stating your Business*, which is an excellent guide to preparing a health and safety policy document. The list of other publications deals with all aspects of safety law and practice from COSHH regulations to stress at work.

Information on best practice is available from www.britishsafetycouncil.co.uk.

9 Discipline, dismissal and redundancy

Introduction

In an ideal organisation, this chapter would be superfluous. Employees would all perform well, would follow all the rules and, as the organisation steadily expanded, there would be no need for dismissals or redundancies. Sadly, we do not live in an ideal world. In fact, the pace of change is so great that restructuring and redundancies are becoming more common each year, even in this period of comparatively low unemployment.

So we need processes in place to handle these difficult situations that take into account both good employee relations and the complex law that applies. The Advisory, Conciliation and Arbitration Service (ACAS) gives substantial advice on action in this area. Its Web site is shown at the end of the chapter.

Discipline

An inevitable consequence of employing people is that there must be a set of rules laid down to regulate behaviour and performance. The rules should be set out in the employee handbook (see Chapter 4). We also saw in the opening chapter that successful organisations rely upon employees working proactively and willingly towards helping the organisation achieve its objectives. The most reliable employees exercise self-discipline and work within a framework of a mutually agreed code of behaviour. But there are always exceptions where action of some sort needs to be taken to get an employee back on track.

Most minor disciplinary matters can be dealt with in the day-to-day informal contact between employees and management. A small request here, a word of advice there, an informal discussion that 'clears the air' can solve 90 per cent or more of problems. To find a solution to the other 10 per cent that cannot be settled in this way requires a **disciplinary procedure** to be in place.

Some commentators believe that any disciplinary event can be regarded as a failure on management's part. The wrong employees have been selected; the performance targets have not been made clear; employees have been managed and motivated badly so that their behaviour is faulty. Whatever the reason, it is best to regard discipline not as a contest between the parties or the imposition of management's will but as a problem to be solved with the use of punishment as only one of the solutions.

Disciplinary procedure

For a small organisation, the procedure should be short, simple and to the point. An example of such a procedure is shown in the box opposite. This takes into account the essential recommendations for disciplinary procedures set out by ACAS, which state that procedures should:

- be in writing;
- specify to whom they apply;
- provide for matters to be dealt with quickly;
- indicate the disciplinary actions that may be taken;
- specify the levels of management that have the authority to take the various forms of disciplinary action;

- provide for individuals to be informed of the complaints against them and to be given the opportunity to state their case before decisions are reached;
- give individuals the right to be accompanied by a representative or work colleague of their choice;
- ensure that employees are not dismissed for a first breach of discipline, unless it is gross misconduct (see later);
- ensure that a disciplinary action is not taken until the case has been carefully investigated;
- ensure that individuals are given an explanation for any penalty imposed;
- provide for the right of appeal.

Although ACAS's recommendations do not have the status of law, tribunals are careful to take into account whether such recommendations have been included in an organisation's procedures and take a serious view of any major breach. Even the smallest organisation should not try to short-circuit these requirements.

Example of disciplinary procedure in a small non-unionised company

Objective
The purpose of the company's disciplinary procedure is to ensure the safe and effective operation of the business and the fair treatment of individual employees. The desired outcome of any disciplinary action is for an improvement to take place, and all parties should work towards this end.

Stage 1: informal warnings
Minor breaches of company discipline, misconduct, poor attendance or timekeeping and poor performance will result in a verbal warning given by the employee's immediate supervisor after discussing the matter with the employee concerned. A note of this warning will be made in the employee's personnel record.

It is hoped that no further action will be necessary as long as the improvement takes place. Assuming the improvement takes place, the note of the warning will be removed from the employee's personnel record after six months.

Stage 2: formal warning

Where there is a more serious breach of company procedures or the employee fails to improve and maintain that improvement after an informal warning, a formal warning may be required. A hearing will be convened with the employee together with two members of the management team, including the employee's manager. The matter will be discussed and the employee will be given full details of the disciplinary issue. The employee will have the opportunity to answer the case fully. After considering all the facts of the matter and the employee's contribution, a decision will be made on whether a warning is the appropriate course of action.

If it is decided that a warning will be given, the employee will be informed of the basis of the decision, the details of the necessary action to remedy the situation, the training that may be given and the consequences if no improvement takes place or if the employee's action is repeated. These consequences may include dismissal. This will be confirmed in writing.

It is hoped that no further action will be necessary as long as the improvement takes place. Assuming the improvement takes place, the note of the warning will be removed from the employee's personnel record after 12 months.

Stage 3: suspension or dismissal

If no improvement takes place after the formal warning or if the employee's action is repeated, then dismissal may take place. A hearing will be convened with the employee together with two members of the management team consisting of the employee's manager and another manager who has not been involved previously in this disciplinary matter. The matter will be discussed and the employee will be given full details of the disciplinary issue. The employee will have the opportunity to answer the case fully. After considering all the facts of the matter and the employee's contribution, a decision will be made on whether suspension without pay or dismissal is the appropriate course of action. All mitigating circumstances will be taken into account.

If it is decided that dismissal is the appropriate action, then the employee will be given the reasons and this will be confirmed in writing. The relevant notice will normally be given. If suspension plus a continuation of the warning is deemed to be appropriate, the employee will be suspended without pay for up to seven working days and given the reasons for the decision. Confirmation in writing will be given in each case.

In the case where gross misconduct takes place, the matter will move immediately to Stage 3 and the same procedure on the hearing will take place. Gross misconduct could include:

- serious breach of safety rules;
- refusing to obey a legitimate instruction;
- theft, fraud or deliberate damage to company property;
- violent behaviour or threats of violence to fellow employees, customers or management;
- acts that could be regarded as discrimination or harassment on the grounds of sex, race or disablement;
- being under the influence of drink or drugs on company premises.

It should be noted that this is not a comprehensive list.

In certain cases where an incident of gross misconduct is being investigated, the employee may be suspended with pay.

Where gross misconduct is deemed to have taken place, the employee will be dismissed without notice when procedures have been completed.

Appeal

Employees have the right to appeal against dismissal, suspension or a formal warning. The appeal will be heard by a director of the company within five working days, in the presence of the employee's manager. A decision on the outcome will be made within 48 hours of the hearing.

At each stage of the procedure, the employee may bring a work colleague along to assist in representing his or her views.

Operating the procedure

One of the key purposes in operating the procedure is to identify to the employee where he or she is going wrong, in other words to establish

Table 9.1 Differences between misdemeanour and gross misconduct

Misdemeanour	Gross misconduct
You cannot dismiss without a warning.	You can dismiss instantly without a warning.
When you dismiss, you need to give notice.	No notice is required.
Examples include: – poor performance; – bad timekeeping and attendance; – inappropriate attitude to management, fellow employees, customers, suppliers or members of the public.	Examples include: – theft or fraud; – refusing to obey a reasonable instruction; – fighting; – causing a severe safety hazard (smoking in a non-smoking area); – breaking the confidentiality code.

that there is a gap in the employee's performance or behaviour and to get his or her acceptance that such a gap exists. You will certainly need to distinguish the important differences between a **misdemeanour** and **gross misconduct** (see Table 9.1).

Figure 9.1 shows the three stages in operating the procedure.

```
Identify the problem → Understand the problem → Solve the problem
```

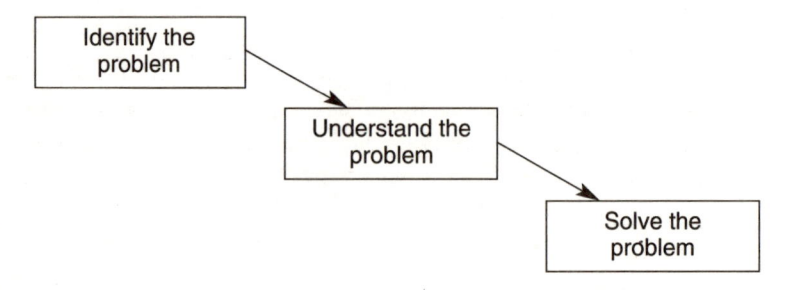

Figure 9.1 The three stages in operating the procedure

Stage 1: identifying the problem

Let us look at a few examples of how you would deal with misdemeanours. You need to find out as many facts as possible about the situation before you take action. Here are a few points to consider, taking each misdemeanour in turn:

- *Timekeeping and attendance.* How often is the employee late or absent, and over what period of time? How does that compare with fellow employees or any level of performance that you specified in the employee handbook? What effect has this poor timekeeping had on the employee's work or the department's morale? Has the decline been sudden or has it occurred over a long period of time? Have you heard about any likely cause of this behaviour?
- *Performance.* How is the performance lacking? Do clear targets exist for the employee that are not being met? Were they realistic targets or have circumstances changed? Is the performance clearly worse than that of the employee's colleagues? Has the relationship with the employee's manager deteriorated? Is the decline in performance sudden?
- *Attitude.* How has the poor attitude shown itself? Is it lack of co-operation? Is it unwillingness to help out when needed? Is it rudeness or unwarranted sarcasm? Is it an argument that turned nasty? Was it a single offence? Did it take place in front of other staff or customers? How did it start and was there any provocation? Were there any witnesses and how reliable are they? Were there any mitigating circumstances? What is the level of damage that has been done – to relationships with managers, suppliers or customers?

In each situation, you need to take the employee's service and experience into account. Employees with longer service and considerable experience generally have less excuse for their actions.

Stage 2: understanding the problem

When you get together with the employee, you need to set out the facts as you see them, backed up with evidence, showing the gap between *expected* and *actual* behaviour. It is also important to set out the damage that the employee's actions may be causing or have caused. Bad timekeeping affects the department's performance, causes difficulties for fellow employees and reduces overall morale. An argument with an important customer will damage future prospects.

You then ask for the employee's side of the picture, listen to the employee's version of events and especially listen to the reasons given for his or her actions. You need to try to obtain acceptance and recognition from the employee that an offence has taken place. It is essential that this discussion takes place in a non-combative way, so the employee may open up and provide personal information that has influenced the action. For example:

- A series of absences may be associated with domestic problems – sick children or parents – or with an alcohol-related problem.
- Lateness may arise from a marriage break-up or caring for a sick relative.
- An attitude problem may arise from a deteriorating relationship with the manager because the employee has been passed over for promotion. A more serious problem may present itself, such as sexual harassment by the manager.

Although each situation is different, there is a consistent line that can be taken. If the facts are disputed, then you need to adjourn the discussion and arrange to meet again, having carefully checked those disputed facts. A proper investigation is important, it must be stressed.

Proper investigations are also essential for more widespread problems, such as company absenteeism levels. An example of such an investigation and the benefits obtained by working out remedies for the difficulties unearthed is shown in Case 9.1.

Case 9.1 Absenteeism investigation at Tollit and Harvey

Tollit and Harvey is a stationery and office supplies manufacturer in Norfolk, employing 170 staff, which found itself with an 8 per cent absenteeism problem in the mid-1990s, together with endemic lateness. The management estimated that this cost them around £90,000 per annum, which came straight off the bottom line, and action was essential to avoid further declines in competitiveness.

Together with an organisation called Healthy Norfolk, an alliance of health authorities and statutory and voluntary bodies in the county, all the employees were invited to complete a questionnaire on job satisfaction, stress levels and other work-related issues. The results provided an interesting picture:

- 30 per cent said that their lighting, ventilation, workstations and rest areas could be improved.
- 30 per cent said that not enough effort was being put into training activities.
- 20 per cent found management communication poor.
- Employees underestimated the time taken off through sickness by 50 per cent.
- Overall, employees confirmed that the factory morale was low.

Managers in the plant suggested that the generous sick leave, which employees considered an entitlement to be taken, and a lack of commitment were the main culprits. Tightening disciplinary procedures and reducing sick leave were seen as the solution. The general manager thought otherwise, focusing on a wider view of managing employees individually more effectively.

The initiatives he installed included:

- multi-skilling the workforce so that employees were less likely to develop upper limb disorders associated with repetitive assembly-line jobs – this also helped relieve the tedium, which had an effect on absence;
- improving the working environment by installing air conditioning throughout the factory and laying special floor matting to reduce the strain of standing at workstations for long periods;
- a formal weekly communication session with supervisors and monthly session with work representatives;

- a switch to a four-day week (suggested by the shop floor);
- return-to-work interviews after each absence – if particular concerns were raised, individuals were referred to the company's occupational health nurse;
- opportunities for training into the role of team leader, which provided career opportunities and covered for any supervisory sickness.

Individuals with the highest absence were also identified for personal counselling and a number of those, who were obviously in the wrong job, left the organisation of their own free will.

The outcome of these actions was that absence dropped to 2 per cent within two years with a saving of around £70,000 together with the cost benefits achieved through productivity increases. A repeat survey of the workforce in 2000 showed a markedly happier workforce with the number of employees who gave a high score for job satisfaction more than doubling since the first survey.

Interestingly, the introduction of the legislation giving employees the right to take time off for family emergencies has not affected the improved absence figures. Employees appear to take up these rights when they are really needed rather than ringing in sick and taking extra days off.
(Source: Arkin, 2001)

Stage 3: attempting to solve the problem

When the facts are accepted, then you need to set the employee down the path of improvement:

- *Set objectives.* Objectives should be made clear and they should be time-based, such as a 10 per cent improvement in performance within three months or an 80 per cent reduction in absence over the next 12 months. Solutions that are suggested by the employee are always more likely to succeed than those imposed from above.
- *Make the consequences clear.* Where there is little or no mitigation then the employee may be given a warning that no improvement will lead to further action under the disciplinary procedure. Even if you decide that a warning is not appropriate, you will need to make it clear that a continuation of the problem is

unacceptable and that a solution is essential. If that cannot be achieved then it may be necessary to invoke the disciplinary procedure eventually.
- *Help the employee to achieve those objectives.* The manager and employee concerned will need to work together to help achieve this improvement. The organisation may be able to assist. For example, where performance has deteriorated, then additional training or guided experience can be very useful; hours can be adjusted on a temporary basis where employees are having to look after an aged relative; employees can be strongly advised to take up counselling if they have an alcohol-related problem.
- *Record.* Take notes on what happened, and what was agreed. Communicate the outcomes (briefly) to the parties concerned. If a warning is given, this will need to be recorded on the individual's file. Most warnings, especially for misdemeanours, do not last for ever. A date should be noted, in a year or six months, when the warning no longer applies and it is deleted from the employee's file.
- *Monitor the situation.* Regularly check the ongoing situation to see if an improvement is occurring. Step in early if a deterioration is evident. Review the situation formally when this was agreed at the earlier meeting. Remember to congratulate the employee (it is likely that this is best carried out confidentially) if a secure improvement has been achieved.
- *Further action.* If no improvement has taken place, then a continuation of the disciplinary procedure is required with a verbal warning followed by a written, final warning. No improvement after a final warning may lead to dismissal.

Formal or informal?

You will see from the typical disciplinary procedure (see the box giving an example of a disciplinary procedure earlier in the chapter) that these actions can be carried out formally or informally. When you have found out the initial facts, you need to decide whether the employee's actions warrant an immediate warning or whether a short, informal word will recover the situation. Except in the case of one bad specific incident of poor attitude or performance, or where the employee has been subject to previous actions, an informal discussion will usually suffice.

The same investigative and problem-solving processes should apply whichever form is used. The main difference is that, under the formal process, the employee is more likely to take up the right of being accompanied by a representative or work colleague, which means that personal elements that have influenced the employee's behaviour are less likely to surface. Another difference with the formal system is that there should be two people present from the management side. Just as in interviewing (see Chapter 2), the second person makes it easier to question and take notes but a second person can also be important should any of the events under the procedure subsequently be disputed.

The way a tribunal responded to the dismissal of an employee whose attitude to management was unsatisfactory is shown in Case 9.2.

Case 9.2 Dismissal of an employee because of his attitude

Mintoft was an experienced sales manager who persistently refused to comply with his employer's paperwork procedures, which detailed the recording of faults and repairs in second-hand cars. This had been introduced so that the garage could give warranties with some degree of confidence. He had been given two written warnings requiring him to follow the procedures and a third final warning six months later stating there had been no improvement and indicating that dismissal would follow should there be another occurrence.

He went home sick a few days later and when he returned was met with criticism about the state of used cars. A heated argument took place with his branch manager in the presence of the managing director where Mintoft restated his dislike of the system and said in clear terms that he was not prepared to operate it. He was then dismissed. The tribunal found that Mintoft's attitude was such that he was never going to change his view about the system and dismissal was an acceptable response.
(*Mintoft v Armstrong Massey*, EAT 516/80)

Handling gross misconduct

These are serious cases (see Table 9.1), so they need to be dealt with formally, fairly and efficiently. In each case, the key aspect is the nature of the investigation both before the hearing and at the hearing itself. The investigation must be carried out thoroughly, taking into account the level of administrative and personnel support available, as will be explained below.

Right to notice

Except in the case of gross misconduct, employees are entitled to notice on termination of their contract. The amount of notice is generally set out in their contract but the legal minimum is: one week's notice for employees whose service is between one month and two years; one week's notice for each year of service, up to a maximum of 12 weeks' notice, for employees with over two years' service. In other words, a person with 18 months' service is entitled to one week's notice, and an employee with 10 years' service is entitled to 10 weeks' notice.

Dismissal

Since 1972, employees have had the right to take up a claim for unfair dismissal at what are now known as Employment Tribunals. They are courts of law, but the intention has always been that they should be more informal and quicker dispensers of justice.

This section will deal with the requirements of a fair dismissal and then detail the tribunal process, indicating a number of examples with their associated lessons for management.

General considerations – natural justice

It cannot be stressed enough that management's actions should be seen as **fair**, **considered** and **consistent**, not abrupt and arbitrary:

- *Fair* means that there is a fair hearing, the employee's case is listened to and a reasonable decision reached, and that the process has gone through appeal. Where gross misconduct has taken place, dismissal can take place without the necessity of a warning and it can apply instantly. However, it must not be carried out on the basis of mere suspicion. Three principles apply here: firstly, the employer must have a genuine belief that the employee is guilty; secondly, the belief must be based on reasonable grounds; thirdly, an investigation must be carried out into the matter such as is reasonable in all the circumstances. For practical purposes, the employer should not unnecessarily delay the proceedings so that recollections fade.
- *Considered* means that the decision is reached after the hearing (management does not make up its mind before the hearing takes place!) and all the facts are taken into account. It should be clear it is not rushed. The employee has the right to a letter detailing the reasons for the dismissal.
- *Consistent* means that the decision does not reverse previous decisions on similar incidents. If you let a couple of employees off with a warning after they are found guilty of petty theft, it is difficult to dismiss the next person to be found guilty of the same offence. In legal parlance, this is called setting a precedent. An example of this is shown later, in Case 9.8. If you want to change the punishment for such offences, you can do so by publicising the change to all employees. An example is that of an organisation that, in the early days of the Internet, lets employees who download pornography off with a warning. Once the seriousness and prevalence of this offence becomes apparent, however, the organisation might decide to change its policy and, after discussion with the management team and employee representatives, circulates all employees with the new policy and puts it up on noticeboards for three months. This is sufficient to change the precedent.

However, there are some difficulties in practice for small organisations in following standard disciplinary procedures:

- ACAS has recommended that an immediate superior should not normally have the power to dismiss without reference to senior management. For a small organisation with very few levels of command, this may mean reference to the managing director on each occasion. Perhaps there is nothing wrong with this, as it does provide a degree of consistency, but it does place a burden on one person and it becomes very awkward if that person is not available for any reason. Tribunals have recognised this situation and, as long as the problems of delay and the options of suspension have been considered carefully and an appeal mechanism is in place, then a decision by an immediate superior has been accepted.
- An appeal must be heard by somebody not associated with the decision to dismiss so the managing director should not hear the appeal. It will be necessary to find somebody (part-time board member, perhaps?) who is sufficiently senior and knows the organisation to take the appeal.
- Investigating the situation can be very time-consuming. Tribunals, again, have recognised the special conditions that apply with small organisations and have differentiated between the full-blown investigation that must take place in, say, a local authority, where resources from a personnel department are at hand to obtain witness statements, take copious notes of meetings, etc, and the investigation in a small organisation where no such resources exist. That does not mean that investigations should be cursory or slipshod but that the overall standard required should be appropriate to the situation and resources available at the time.

Automatically unfair reasons for dismissal

There are certain situations where you simply cannot dismiss fairly and you would automatically lose a tribunal claim. These are set out in Table 9.2.

Table 9.2 Automatically unfair reasons for dismissal

Automatically unfair reason	Comments
Dismissals that involve, race, sex or disability discrimination.	Details are given in Chapter 7. Remember there is no upper limit on the compensation in these cases.
Dismissals connected to the trade union activity of the employee or to his or her activities as a redundancy or pension representative.	You cannot discriminate against a trade union activist or an employee simply because the employee is a trade union member and carrying out trade union activity within his or her rights (see Chapter 6).
Dismissals related to maternity.	You are highly unlikely to be able to dismiss a pregnant employee, even if for example she is consistently absent and her performance drops badly. Again, no compensation limits apply in these cases.
Dismissal for taking some action on health and safety grounds.	For instance, where an employee refuses to carry out work from a platform he or she considers unsafe and has reasonable grounds for thinking this.
Dismissals of a shop worker or betting worker for refusing to do work on a Sunday.	Under legislation relating specifically to Sunday working.

Who can claim unfair dismissal?

Employees are able to put in a claim only after they have served a qualification period of one year's continuous service. This applies to both full- and part-time employees.

It is quite complex determining what an employee is. An employee is not necessarily what his or her contract of employment says,

Table 9.3 What is an employee?

Issue	Employee	Self-employed
Tax	Paid under PAYE	714 or equivalent
Able to work for more than one company?	Usually exclusive to that company	Usually no restriction on how many companies the person can work for
Tools, equipment and transport	Provided by employer	Usually provided by self-employed person
Day-to-day control	Usually work programmed within boundaries	Usually able to organise work within own boundaries
Can the person refuse work?	Very serious to refuse an instruction to take on work	Usually able to refuse work without serious penalty

although that influences the decision. There have been a number of cases where contracts have specified self-employment and where tax and National Insurance payments have reflected this relationship but the individual has successfully claimed unfair dismissal as an employee. This is because the tribunal looks behind the formal relationship and considers the points set out in Table 9.3. If the tribunal decides that on balance the self-employment status is a façade, then it will treat the claimant as an employee and allow him or her to make a claim.

Constructive dismissal

Not all dismissals are carried out by employers. Situations may arise where employees consider that they have been treated so badly that they cannot continue in employment. The situations could include:

- being humiliated in front of their peers;
- being bullied continually;
- being a victim of sexual harassment;
- having a major benefit removed, such as a company car, without due reason;
- being downgraded or moved to a lower-status job.

In each of these cases, employees can claim constructive dismissal. They are, in effect, saying that the employer has indicated by its actions that it no longer wishes to be bound by the mutual contract of employment. However, the action by the employer must be serious; it must, in legal terms, go to the heart of the contract.

An important point here is that employees must take action quickly after the incident (or, in the case of bullying, the final incident that becomes the 'final straw') because, if they take no action, they are appearing to accept the employer's behaviour or decision. An example of constructive dismissal is given in Case 9.3.

Case 9.3 Constructive dismissal

Robinson had been bullied and harassed by her manager and, following her complaint, he had been given a warning and ordered to refrain. She had been assured that he would be moved but he was not. Robinson, who was off sick at the time, met her employer in August 1997 to discuss her return to work but it appeared that she would have to work with the same manager. She remained on sick leave, turning down the offer of an internal transfer. By June 1998, it was quite clear that the manager would not be moved. She was sent two letters, one offering another transfer and the next withdrawing that offer. She resigned, claiming constructive dismissal.

She won her case, as the tribunal decided that there had been a complete breakdown in trust and confidence, with the two-letters incident being the final straw allowing her to act promptly at that stage. This decision was confirmed at EAT.

(*Abbey National v Robinson*, IDS 680 EAT)

How does a claim for unfair dismissal progress?

The stages of a tribunal claim are set out in the following sections.

Stage 1: application and response

Within three months of losing his or her job, the employee needs to complete a form IT1 setting out his or her case. This form is readily available from ACAS, a trade union or consumer bodies such as Citizens Advice Bureaux. There is no fee involved in making the application. A copy of this claim form is sent to the employer, which must respond giving its views on the events detailed on the IT1.

Stage 2: conciliation

Both parties will be contacted by a conciliation officer from ACAS who will try to get the parties to consider settling the case before it goes to the tribunal. Seeing the parties separately, the officer will discuss alternatives to a tribunal. They could include reinstatement, a cash settlement or the claim being dropped altogether. In 1999, of the 53,000 claims received, 21,000 were settled, 12,000 were withdrawn and 10,000 were still to be processed at the end of the year, leaving fewer than 10,000 actually going to the tribunal. If an agreed settlement is reached, it is confirmed through the ACAS COT3 form signed by both parties, which leads to the ex-employee losing his or her right to take the claim to a tribunal.

Stage 3: the tribunal

If no settlement is achieved, the tribunal will go ahead. The time it takes can vary considerably. Most take no more than a day or two but some complex cases have been known to last for up to a month.

The tribunal is made up of three people: a legally qualified independent chair, a person from a list put forward by employers' bodies and a third person from a list put forward by trade unions. The latter two have experience of industry or commerce and act in their own right, not as representatives of their constituency.

Certain aspects of the tribunal are identical to a court of law. Witnesses must take the oath, and the rules of evidence apply. Hearsay is generally discounted. Written evidence is, in general, exchanged beforehand. There are some differences, however. The tribunal takes much more initiative in directing the questions – they are more **investigative** – than in a normal court where the judge generally leaves it to the prosecution and defence to bring out all the important elements in the case. This is to help individuals (and some smaller organisations) who are unused to taking a case and may be daunted by lawyers representing the other side. There is more informality generally. For example, the writer has experience of taking a tribunal in the back room of a pub! In England and Wales, witnesses sit in for all the evidence, rather than being precluded from doing so until they have given evidence themselves.

The tribunal will take a decision on whether the dismissal was fair or unfair based on the balance of probabilities (not beyond reasonable doubt). It will look at the chain of events and the evidence presented to it and decide if management's actions in dismissing the employee were within a 'band of reasonableness'. In other words, the tribunal is not supposed to decide if it would have dismissed the employee in those circumstances but whether this was one of the decisions that could reasonably have been made.

The following points are crucial in coming to the decision:

- Did the offence or offences justify dismissal?
- Did a reasonable investigation take place?
- Were the disciplinary procedures followed closely?
- Did the organisation really believe that the person concerned carried out the offences and was there sufficient evidence to warrant this belief?
- Were any mitigating circumstances taken into account?

If the answer is yes to all of these questions, then the tribunal will generally decide that the dismissal was fair. If the answer to one or more is no, then it can consider the following judgments:

- There may have been some faults in the procedures but these were relatively minor and, on balance, did not cause management's case to fall down, so the decision is still one of 'fair dismissal'.
- There were major flaws in management's handling – perhaps major procedural errors or not taking mitigating circumstances into account. However, there was evidence that the employee had contributed towards the dismissal by his or her actions, for example poor timekeeping or performance, or perhaps it was clear that the employee had carried out the offence, such as minor theft. In these cases, the tribunal may decide that the dismissal was 'unfair' but the fact that the employee contributed to the dismissal leads to a reduction in the compensation (see below) that is awarded to the employee.
- Management did not act fairly in respect of the nature of the offence or the procedures for dealing with it and so an outcome of 'unfair dismissal' is recorded, with the applicant receiving compensation.
- Management's actions were so unjustified and unreasonable that the dismissal is 'unfair' and the employee should be reinstated in the job. This happens rarely, and it is even more rare for the employer to agree with this judgment and take the employee back. If management refuses to do so, then the amount of compensation is increased.

Compensation can be agreed between the parties or calculated by the tribunal. In most cases, the tribunal, having come to a decision, will suggest that the parties reach their own agreement on a settlement. If the parties are unable to do so, then the tribunal's calculation will be based solely on the losses of the employee both up to the time of the tribunal and in the foreseeable future. No legal costs can be claimed, except where the tribunal has decided that the case has been frivolous or that one of the parties has acted 'vexatiously, abusively, disruptively or otherwise unreasonably'. The compensation is made up of three parts:

- *a basic award*, which is essentially the employee's redundancy entitlement with that employer;
- *a compensatory award*, made up of losses or anticipatory losses;
- *an award for damaged feelings and reputations* (this part arose from a House of Lords decision – *Johnson* v *Unisys*, March 2001 – so is very new, and this decision has some long-term implications on the total amount of compensation).

There is a maximum of £240 on the calculation of a week's pay under the basic award. The employee has to make reasonable efforts to find another job and will need to show evidence of these efforts at the tribunal.

Here are examples of the calculations involved, which do not include awards for damaged feelings:

Example 1
An instantly dismissed 26-year-old computer programmer in London with three years' service, earning £26,000, who obtains alternative work within four weeks at a higher salary.

Basic award	3 weeks × £240 per week	£720
Compensatory award	4 weeks × £500 per week	£2,000
Total		£2,720

Example 2
A 56-year-old man in Sunderland dismissed with notice for poor performance, with 12 years' service, on £400 a week, who had no alternative job by the time of the tribunal. Here, the tribunal has to decide when it is likely that he may be successful in finding a job and the level of pay he may receive. Of course, this is speculation, based on realistic information from the experience of the tribunal members. Let us assume in this case that the age and location of the employee will work against him and the tribunal decide that a job is unlikely for 12 months from the date of dismissal and that the pay will be £300 a week, not rising to his original level of pay for a further two years.

Basic award	18 weeks* × £240 per week	£4,320
Compensatory award	34 weeks** × £400 per week	£13,600
Plus	104 weeks*** × £100 per week	£10,400
Total		£28,320

The company would have to pay this sum but the employee would receive it after deduction of the social security payments already received and those likely to be received over the next few months before the anticipated job arises.

* Employees over 41 are entitled to 1.5 weeks' pay for each year of service.
** 52 weeks less the 18 weeks' notice he would have been paid.
*** 2 years' difference between the anticipated new job's pay of £300 a week and old pay of £400 a week.

Where reinstatement has been ordered but the employer has refused to comply, an additional award can be made of between 13 and 26 weeks' pay.

The maximum compensation that can be awarded in unfair dismissal cases was £51,700 in 2001, which is likely to be raised in line with inflation each year.

There are other complications regarding compensation calculation including the treatment of performance and discretionary bonuses, company cars and pension entitlements. Further information about these items is available from the sources indicated at the end of the chapter.

Stage 4: appeals

Either party may disagree with the tribunal findings and choose to appeal. The appeal route is set out in Figure 9.2.

Appeals can be made only on legal issues, not on the finding of fact. So an appeal will only succeed:

- when the tribunal has misdirected itself as to the law; or

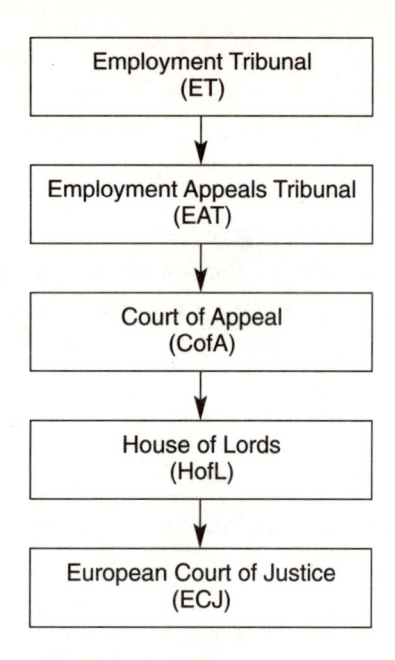

```
Employment Tribunal
        (ET)
          ↓
Employment Appeals Tribunal
        (EAT)
          ↓
  Court of Appeal
       (CofA)
          ↓
   House of Lords
       (HofL)
          ↓
European Court of Justice
        (ECJ)
```

Figure 9.2 Unfair dismissal appeal procedure

- when the tribunal has misdirected itself as to the undisputed facts or ignored factual considerations it should have taken into account; or
- where the decision is regarded as perverse.

If you are involved in appeals at any levels, it is essential to have legal support.

Arbitration scheme

In May 2001, the government introduced a voluntary arbitration scheme providing an alternative forum for an applicant pursuing a straightforward unfair dismissal case who does not want to face a tribunal, providing the employer is also happy to go down this route. The hearings are expected to take place within two months of the parties' agreement to arbitration and to last for only half a day, with lawyers not generally taking part.

The process is informal and held in secret with no procedural rules. Interestingly, arbitrators are not bound by existing law or precedent. Their job is simply to decide whether the dismissal is fair or unfair. Awards are also secret. The arbitrator does, however, need to take into account the ACAS Disciplinary and Grievance Procedure Code of Practice and *Discipline at Work Handbook*. Employers cannot make any 'jurisdictional points'. In other words, they cannot claim that the claim was lodged late or that service was not continuous. After opening statements from both sides, the arbitrator will adopt an investigating role, questioning both sides – but there will be no cross-examination allowed (ie where one side cross-examines the other, as takes place in a tribunal). The arbitrator gives a decision in writing with reasons but does not give a total summary of the facts. There is no appeal against the decision. Time will tell if this informal system will be seen as fair and workable by both sides.

A selection of cases illustrating dismissal for gross misconduct in a number of circumstances is shown in Cases 9.4 to 9.8.

Case 9.4 Smoking

Rogers refused to comply with a smoking ban introduced into his workplace after a four-month notice period. The tribunal considered this to be a 'wholly reasonable' period for smokers to adjust and concluded that the employers had acted wholly reasonably in the circumstance.
(*Rogers v Wicks & Wilson*, 22890/87)

Case 9.5 Dishonesty

Oliphant, a till operator, was dismissed after she failed to register a sale. Dismissal was in accordance with an agreed disciplinary procedure that stated that till irregularities were gross misconduct and that dismissal would usually follow. EAT found that the dismissal was unfair, saying that it was not

reasonable for the employers to impose an extreme sanction of dismissal for a single unexplained departure from the recognised procedure, particularly as the employer did not claim it was specifically dishonest.
(*Laws Stores, Ltd v Oliphant*, 1978 IRLR 251)

Case 9.6 Refusal to work overtime

Kirkpatrick, a service engineer, was contractually required to work overtime but was originally exempted from a stand-by rota because he had no experience of refrigeration maintenance. After attending courses on the subject, however, he was asked to join a 24-hour stand-by roster. He persistently refused because of family commitments and was eventually dismissed. The tribunal held that Kirkpatrick was contractually required to join the roster because of the overtime term and concluded that the employers had acted reasonably in dismissing him. The stand-by roster was necessary for the company's interests and, after training, he was competent to carry out the work. EAT upheld the decision, affirming that the nature of a service engineer's job meant that some overtime was inevitable.
(*Kirkpatrick v Lister-Petter Ltd*, EAT 363/89)

Case 9.7 Loyalty

Laird was the editor of a newspaper whose employment contract expressly prohibited him from having any interest in any competing business. He was dismissed when his employers discovered that he was involved in the publication of two free regional newspapers. A tribunal held that the dismissal was unfair, pointing out that the employers had made no enquiries into the circulation of the two free newspapers, the area that the papers covered or their advertising rates. Had they done so, they would have discovered that the employee's outside interests were of a relatively minor nature that could cause only minimal harm to his employers. EAT agreed that no reasonable employer would have dismissed without making proper enquiries as to the extent and circumstances of Laird's involvement with the other newspapers.
(*Scottish Daily Record and Sunday Mail Ltd v Laird*, EAT 1164/94)

Case 9.8 Violence
Fennell, a Post Office worker, was summarily dismissed for assaulting a fellow employee in the canteen. In his defence, he alleged that a number of employees had been treated differently in the past for similar offences. The tribunal accepted this argument, pointing out the inconsistent behaviour by the Post Office, and this was supported in the higher courts.
(*Post Office v Fennell*, 1981 IRLR 221)

If you are faced with a tribunal

If an IT1 form suddenly arrives on your desk, this is unfortunate but not unusual considering that over 100,000 tribunal claims are made each year. Tribunals can sometimes be quite complicated with many arguments over the exchange of information beforehand, and this book cannot detail all the possible twists and turns. However, here are a few decisions for you to take:

- *Representation.* This is a key decision that influences all the others. Given that you and your staff are not likely to be experienced in handling tribunals, you will be looking for legal assistance. It is possible to handle it yourself and some tribunals can be sympathetic to your case but you are, on balance, more likely to tumble into one of the many pitfalls that occur regularly throughout tribunal hearings. Legal help is available from either a local solicitor or a human resources consultancy. Before choosing, check how experienced your representative is and obtain a reference from a 'satisfied customer'.
- *Trivial pursuit.* If you consider that the claim is trivial or vexatious or has been made completely without foundation and just to cause you annoyance (or in the hope that you will settle handsomely) then it is possible to try to persuade the tribunal to take some action. If the tribunal agrees with you, then it has the right to warn the applicant that costs could be awarded against him or her (the limit was raised to £10,000 in 2001) and the tribunal

may also insist upon a deposit of up to £500. Such actions by the tribunal have been very rare but, if you have strong convictions, then it is certainly worth making representations to the tribunal in writing at an early stage.

- *Do I settle before the tribunal?* Over half the tribunal claims made are settled before tribunal takes place. Although the settlement amounts in such cases are confidential to the parties, anecdotal evidence is that most settlements involve comparatively small sums, certainly less than £2,000 and many less than £1,000. If a settlement can be achieved around these levels, it is eminently sensible to do so. Tribunals take up a great deal of management time and worry. Few issues of principle are involved and the risks of losing generally outweigh the ultimate pleasure of being proved right. However, if the settlement being claimed is much more substantial and you are confident that you have acted correctly throughout, then it is right to stick to your guns. You may get some indication from the ACAS conciliation officers as to where a possible settlement may occur although they do have a duty to remain scrupulously impartial and retain confidences. Also, be prepared to negotiate a settlement on the morning of the tribunal – it is generally a low point for both parties where will-power is fading and a sensible settlement appears much more attractive!

Redundancy

Since the 1970s, redundancy has increasingly been regarded as a necessary evil. Jobs are no longer offered for life and the pace of change has become so rapid that a group of employees rarely fits the organisation's requirements for extended time periods. In Chapter 1, the point was emphasised that a good employer should take positive action through training and personal development to enhance the skills and employability of staff. Such an investment is good business. However, even the best organisation will face some downturn or need to carry out a structural change where there is simply no alternative but to declare some redundancies.

The first thing to recognise is that this can be fairly devastating for most of the employees concerned. If they are young, then chances are that they will be able to find another job fairly easily. However, it can hit their self-esteem and confidence, and there is a considerable weight of evidence that the incident influences their behaviour for many years. For older employees it can be much worse in that alternative opportunities may be hard to find and, if they have enjoyed the job, it can herald the end of a satisfying and rewarding period of their lives. There are, of course, a minority of employees for whom it is less of a problem, as they may have been planning to leave or to retire. Whatever the situation, it is only sensible to approach it with great care and respect for the feelings of all the staff.

The most difficult problem when faced with a decline in business is to decide if this is a temporary or permanent situation. If it is purely temporary, then holding on to your workforce is important and redundancies should be avoided. A more extended downturn will produce an inevitable requirement to reduce staff numbers. (See Figure 9.3.)

Mitigating the redundancy situation

It goes without saying that you should make every effort to avoid

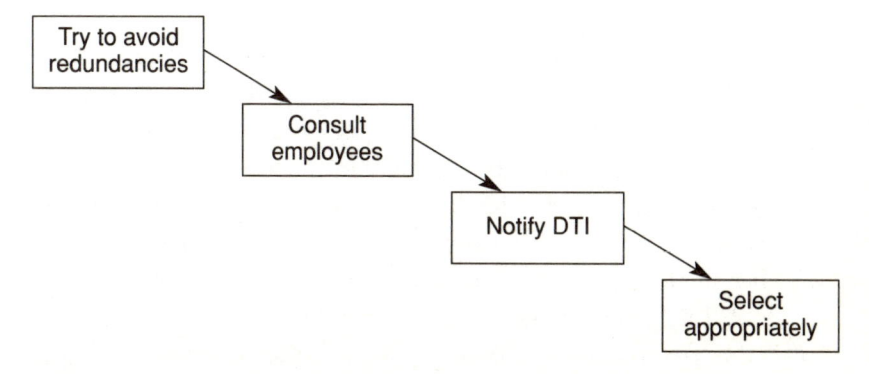

Figure 9.3 Approaching and implementing redundancies

having to make **compulsory** redundancies. This can be done through methods such as:

- Eliminating all overtime and sharing available work around the organisation.
- Reducing or eliminating temporary and agency staff.
- Freezing all recruitment.
- Transferring staff and retraining them to carry out alternative work.
- Offering full-time staff the opportunity to work part time, with perhaps two operating as a job-share. This can have its attractions for certain staff, particularly those approaching retirement age. You cannot unilaterally impose this, however.
- Offering early retirement. Depending on your pension scheme (if you have one) and individuals' circumstances, this can involve a considerable loss to the employees unless the employer makes a contribution to their pension fund. You will need advice here from your pension broker. Again, it may suit some staff who may have been looking for an opportunity to leave early and where a relatively small inducement could persuade them to accept.
- Bringing work into the organisation. You may have outsourced work that it is possible to bring back in without too much of a financial penalty.
- Offering your employees to an associated company, local supplier or customer. You may have built up a very close relationship with a number of local contacts and a mutual arrangement of transferring labour can be very beneficial. It is certainly worth trying as long as commercial security is not involved. Arrangements need to be made over who pays the employees (it is best if they remain on your payroll) and any changes of terms, but employees will tend to accept such a temporary arrangement rather than being made redundant.
- Offering voluntary redundancy under suitable terms. This will be discussed later.

A more drastic proposal is to agree with the staff a reduction in their working hours and their pay on a temporary basis. Perhaps this would involve working a staggered four-day week, and the company would make the gesture of reducing their pay by only 10 per cent to help mitigate the losses involved. This is costly but it might save the costs of redundancies, and the goodwill it engenders may be advantageous. It does need to be thoroughly discussed with the staff and have an end date when the contracts revert to normal.

Compulsory redundancies and the law

If these measures prove inappropriate or unsuccessful and compulsory redundancies are required, then the law intrudes in a number of ways, as detailed in the following sections.

Definition of redundancy

The Employment Rights Act 1996 (section 139.1) has a complex definition of redundancy but essentially it means an actual or expected reduction or cessation of work or a major change in the business operation that leads to fewer employees being required. This is drawn very broadly and tribunals have rarely interfered with the employer's decision to declare redundancies. However, the Act does not cover the situation where the sales manager is 'made redundant' and another person recruited to do the same job. That is not a redundancy situation, but a simple dismissal. There has to be a substantial change in the work done by that person, the salary and the responsibilities for it to be considered a true redundancy situation.

Consulting with the workforce

There is a general requirement on employers to consult with the workforce and especially those who may be affected by the redundancies. Where 20–99 employees are to be made redundant, consultation must take place at least 30 days before the redundancies will take effect (90 days where 100 or more redundancies are involved). The law demands that consultation should take place with trade union representatives or elected representatives of employees but common sense demands that, in a small organisation, it is important to keep everybody in touch and be very proactive in meeting with those closely involved on a regular basis. The situation will change from week to week so fixing regular meetings is vital. Subjects to be discussed include the timings, selection procedures and payments.

If you fail to follow the legal requirements, then a tribunal can make a 'protective award', in other words can insist on the amount of payment made being increased.

Proper consultation is vital, as the tribunal ruling in Case 9.9 illustrates.

Case 9.9 Consultation on redundancies

Scotch Premier Meats Ltd decided to close a slaughterhouse, involving the loss of 155 jobs. It was seeking a purchaser but did not tell staff – it merely offered them voluntary redundancy. Nor were the elected representatives, who were being consulted, informed of the intention to sell the business. EAT awarded a protected award because of the failure to disclose this vital information. EAT also concluded that the volunteers for redundancy had been dismissed because the court was convinced that, had the volunteers known of the probability of being transferred to another employer on the same terms, they might not have volunteered for redundancy.
(*Scotch Premier Meats* v *Burns*, 2000 IRLR 639 EAT)

Notifying DTI

It is a requirement to inform the Department of Trade and Industry on form HR1 where over 20 redundancies are involved, with a fine of up to £5,000 if you do not do so. Findings of DTI research indicate that consultation has led to a considerable reduction in the number of redundancies actually occurring.

Selection for redundancy

It is a legal requirement that selection for redundancy is made on a fair basis. If an employee believes that he or she has been selected unfairly then that employee can apply to a tribunal in the same way as for unfair dismissal and will be able to obtain the same form of compensation. The set of criteria that an organisation uses for selection purposes is therefore crucial. The most common methods of selection are choosing volunteers and last in, first out (LIFO) but many organisations are switching to systems that help to define which are the valuable employees and which are employees who make little or no contribution to the organisation. Here is a short word on each of the systems:

- *Choosing volunteers.* This would appear on the surface to satisfy everyone. It provides no trouble and pleases both those chosen and those remaining with a job. However, the situation often presents itself where a number of those who volunteer may be very valuable employees with specific marketable skills, who will have no trouble finding alternative jobs. Those are just the employees you want to keep, of course. This is a dilemma with no easy answer. If you accept all who volunteer then you may leave yourself vulnerable in a competitive market place. If, on the other hand, you turn those employees down and make others compulsorily redundant then you would appear to most of the workforce to be acting unfairly and there would be an additional drop in morale and goodwill towards you that would be remembered for some time. You might be more likely to face tribunal claims on this front. Moreover, it is likely that many of the high-quality employees would leave in the future anyway, having indicated their willingness to move. So, on balance, it is probably better to accept all the volunteers on the basis that you can begin hiring again when business starts to pick up.
- *Last in, first out.* LIFO is a very transparent process and rewards good service, but it may involve making redundant relatively new and enthusiastic employees with considerable potential and leaving an ageing workforce without the required skills.

- *Identifying skills and performance measures.* Under these systems, a set of criteria is established against which each employee on the list of possible redundancies is assessed. An example is shown in Table 9.4. It looks quite complicated and is only appropriate where you have to be truly selective. Let us take an example. You may have a production line of 20 employees and, because of a fall-off in demand, you have to cut that in half. You may be able to relocate two employees to other work but that still leaves eight employees to make redundant. To choose those fairly you have to adopt some form of objective measures, such as those set out in Table 9.4. The eight employees with the lowest number of points will be the ones made redundant. The measures you adopt will be appropriate to your own situation. You may want to include length of service, for example, and the points you apply will reflect the relative importance you place on those measures.

    A further advantage of using an objective method of this sort is that it allows you to 'bump'. This is where you transfer a person in a redundant job to another position and you make that job holder redundant instead. The fact that you have gone to the effort of setting out selection criteria emphasises the importance you place on retaining crucial skills and know-how and will help to lessen the criticism of 'favouritism'. Where an employee has been offered an alternative position with the organisation, that employee has, at law, the right to a four-week trial period during which his or her redundancy rights are protected. So if the employee finds the job unsuitable within the four-week period, he or she can take redundancy instead.

It is important to disclose the methods of selection for redundancy to the representatives in the period of consultation and to let representatives see the results of such a process. In the case of *John Brown Engineering Ltd* v *Brown* (1997 IRLR 90 EAT), the policy decision to withhold all marks used in the selection process resulted in the dismissal being held to be unfair because the employees had no oppor-

Table 9.4 Example of selection criteria for redundancy

Measure	Criteria	Employee 1	Employee 2
Timekeeping	20 points maximum with 2 points lost for each lateness over period	14	12
Attendance	24 points maximum with 2 points lost for each absence	24	18
Current skills	Ranked on set of 6 skills – maximum 40 points	30	20
Potential	Ranked by supervisor – maximum 20 points	18	14
Quantity of work	Ranked by supervisor – maximum 15 points	13	10
Quality of work	Ranked by supervisor – maximum 15 points	11	12
Warnings	No warnings – 10 points; one warning 5 points; two warnings 0 points	10	5
	Maximum = 144	120	91

tunity to know how they were assessed. The court found that any subsequent appeal procedure could be regarded as a 'sham'.

Redundancy payments

The law lays down the minimum payments that employees are entitled to when they are made redundant. This is on top of their statutory right to notice. The entitlements are:

Age under 18   no entitlement to redundancy payment
18 and over but under 22   half a week's pay for each complete year of service
22 or over but under 41   one week's pay for each complete year of service
41 or over but under 65   one and a half weeks' pay for each year of service

Employees need to have at least two years' service before any payments are due and, for 64-year-olds, the entitlement is reduced by one-twelfth for each month they are over 64 (a person aged 64 years 6 months would have the entitlement reduced by a half, for example). A further limit is that there is a maximum figure for a 'week's pay', which in 2001 was £240.

Table 9.5 gives two examples of the calculations.

These are minimum payments, and many employers choose to augment them. Some leading blue chip companies, such as BT and Glaxo, have very generous redundancy payments that more than double the statutory entitlement. Many small organisations are simply not able to afford the extra cost involved. However, it is worth considering improving the deal because it does help to sweeten the blow and indicate that the organisation has the best interests of the employees at

Table 9.5 Calculating redundancy pay

Employee	Age	Years of Service	Salary (week)	Calculation
1	26	10	£300	2 weeks at zero (16–17) 4 weeks at £120 (18–21) = £480 4 weeks at £240 (22–26) = £960 Total = £1,440
2	51	20	£400	10 weeks at £240 (31–40) = £2,400 10 weeks at £360 (41–51) = £3,600 Total £6,000

heart. One common improvement is to ignore the week's pay limit and base the calculation on the employee's actual pay, as most employees earn more than the current limit of £240. Another option is to make all payments at the rate of one and a half times a week's pay. A third option is to guarantee a minimum amount (say £2,000), which helps to protect those with short service. A final option is to make a terminal bonus to employees who have effectively served out their notice period.

Helping employees declared redundant

Where an employer can really help to ease the blow of redundancy is in giving substantial help to the employees concerned in obtaining another position. This can be basic help or wider help.

Basic help

This includes:

- Making sure the local Job Centre is aware of the redundancy situation and has details of the staff affected.
- Circulating all the major local employers, giving them information about the staff being made redundant including the skills available.
- Helping employees draw up CVs and giving them essential advice on preparing to look for a job and for interviews.
- Allowing time off to look for alternative positions. Employees have the statutory right to reasonable time off with pay to look for alternative positions. What is 'reasonable', however, has never been formally defined. It clearly covers attending interviews.

Wider help – outplacement

You may want to consider using an outplacement agency, which will provide professional job search services on an individual or group basis. The services are used mostly for employees at the managerial level and include helping employees come to terms with the redundancy and its implications, working with the employees in working out their next step, devising a job search strategy and supporting each step they take from then on. This is carried out on a confidential basis. The fees will vary depending on the amount of support and the length of the period of job search. A rough guideline is around £2,500 for a manager who takes four months to find a suitable position. It is costly, but it is worth considering the undoubted benefit that it brings to the individuals concerned at a time when they are at their most vulnerable.

Should redundant employees work their notice?

There are varying strands of thought here. An unhappy employee serving out three months' notice can be very disruptive and, if in crucial customer-facing, IT or accounting functions, can cause positive harm. In practice, however, employees rarely act in a vindictive manner. They are concerned that, if they do so, they will not be given a reference. On the other hand, if you really want to be regarded as a heartless employer, then call in employees one by one, tell them they are redundant and ask them to clear their desks in the next hour. (Or, as in the case of one or two employers, clear their desks for them and leave them to collect black plastic bags with their belongings at the gate – yes, there are documented cases of this really happening, especially in US-owned companies!)

A compromise could be to allow staff some choice as to when they leave with payment for their unserved notice to be 'paid in lieu'. In many cases, such as closing down a unit, you will want a good proportion of your staff to work right to the end so each solution will have to be adjusted to the circumstances.

Protection of survivors

It is all too easy in the rush and activity of a redundancy situation to ignore those employees apparently not involved – the survivors. For them the situation is far from easy and it is not a happy time. They may immediately have a sense of relief and even satisfaction that their jobs are safe for the time being but they will have to work with employees serving out their notice and they may well wonder if the business is on the skids and their turn will come next. Alternately, they may believe that their workload will increase and wonder if they will be able to cope. It is essential that efforts are made to try to maintain their morale. Regular communication is important and methods should be used to involve them in future planning. Asking employees to suggest how work can be reorganised, efficiency improved and relationships with customers enhanced, and following up some of their ideas often works wonders in turning round an unhappy work group at this time.

Reminder of what you should do

- Try to keep employees in the picture as much as possible – the picture often changes from week to week and rumours always travel fast – so go out of your way to let them know as soon as any decisions have been made.
- In the event of selecting employees for compulsory redundancy, make sure each person involved in the process knows about the criteria for selection.
- Ensure there is a process of appeal against selection.
- Give as much help as you can to those being made redundant.

What you cannot do

You cannot discriminate in your selection – you cannot choose the difficult union representative or part-timers (who are likely to be predominantly women), nor should your choice result in a predominance of employees from an ethnic background or those who are disabled.

References

Arkin, A (2001) A Norfolk broadside, *People Management*, 19 April, pp 36–39

Further information

For more guidance on employment law, see Chandler, P (2001) *Waud's Employment Law*, Kogan Page, London.

Advice on handling absence is given in Evans, A and Palmer, S (1997) *From Absence to Attendance*, CIPD, London.

Redundancies are dealt with in Fowler, A (1999) *Managing Redundancy*, CIPD, London.

For discipline, see Fowler, A (1998) *The Discipline Interview*, CIPD, London.

The ACAS Web site is www.acas.org.uk. It includes an extensive publication list – some publications can be downloaded at no cost.

The Web site for Incomes Data Services www.incomesdata.co.uk has extensive coverage of employment law issues.

The CIPD publishes a set of guides on dismissal in association with Hammond Suddards (solicitors). It also publishes *Guide to Redundancy* (1996).

For a useful resource in training managers in discipline and grievance handling, see *Managing Discipline and Grievance: 21 practical activities*, Fenman (www.fenman.co.uk).

For an article on how to deal with absence in a small organisation, see O'Donnell, J (2001) Sacking slackers can be hard work, *Sunday Times*, 29 July, p 12.

10 Getting the changes you need

Introduction

The ability to change fast is one of the strengths of most small organisations. To carry your employees with you in this change is not always done so well, and staff are sometimes left confused and dispirited by the changes. So it is important to understand how the change process works and what you can do to mitigate the adverse effects rapid changes can cause. This chapter deals with some of the theories of change, advises on how it should be carried out and then gives some major examples of successful change programmes in small businesses.

Understanding the change process

Changes are not all the same. They are carried out in response to the external and internal environments. Externally, the pressures may come from changing economic patterns, government legislation or the arrival of new technology. Internal pressures can come from the arrival of new competitors, the development of new ideas, products or services, or higher requirements from customers. Some pressures require fast, radical change, others slow and deliberate. Don Young, of change consultancy YSC Ltd, has produced a model indicating four different approaches, as set out in Figure 10.1:

- *Crisis management.* Major changes will be required following an event such as a merger or acquisition, a fire or some legal or commercial disaster. They need to be driven through immediately and go to the core of the organisation.
- *Transformation.* Changes may be just as serious here, in response to economic or social pressure, but a longer time span is available for planning.
- *Fine-tuning.* Minor changes are needed all the time to achieve day-to-day improvements over a short time period.
- *Building the business.* This is the best situation in which to plan where no fundamental changes are needed and a long time span is available – not very common for small businesses!

	Major serious change	
CRISIS MANAGEMENT		**TRANSFORMATION**
Short time span		Long time span
FINE-TUNING	Incremental change	**BUILDING THE BUSINESS**

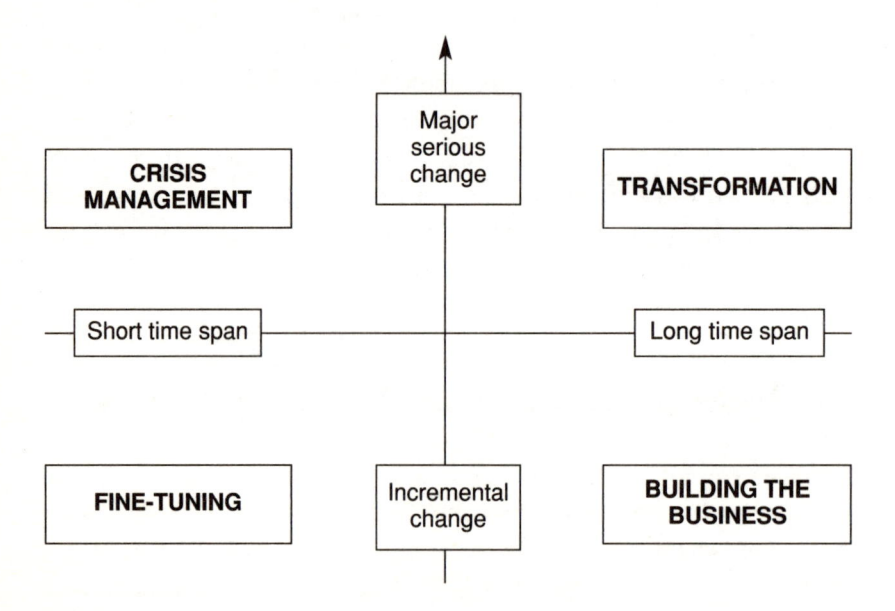

Figure 10.1 Young's model of change

There will always be resistance to change but different types of change are likely to bring about different types of resistance. Fine-tuning and business building can find their opponents but they are likely to be isolated and have special pleadings. Transformation and crisis management are a different matter, where resistance, both active and passive, can be substantial and very damaging unless handled effectively.

Where change is easiest to achieve is where the forces driving change are greater than those resisting it. See Lewin's (1951) force field analysis shown in Figure 10.2.

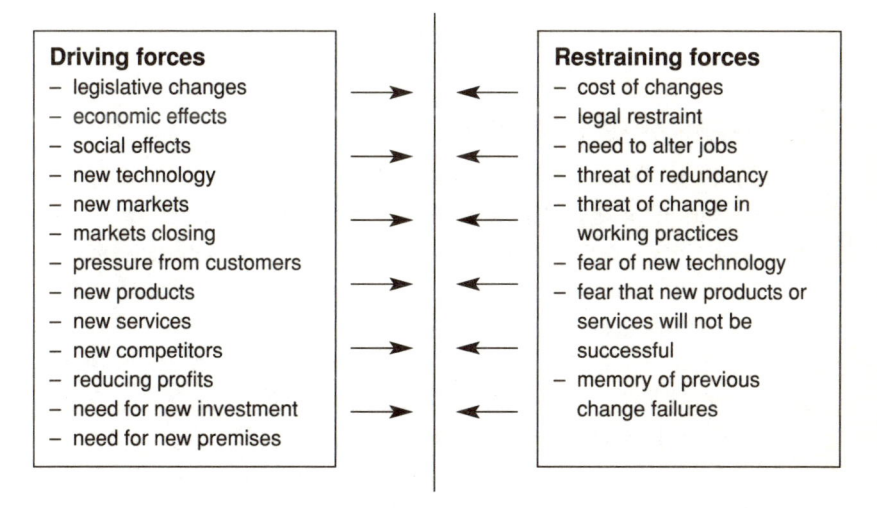

Driving forces	**Restraining forces**
− legislative changes	− cost of changes
− economic effects	− legal restraint
− social effects	− need to alter jobs
− new technology	− threat of redundancy
− new markets	− threat of change in
− markets closing	working practices
− pressure from customers	− fear of new technology
− new products	− fear that new products or
− new services	services will not be
− new competitors	successful
− reducing profits	− memory of previous
− need for new investment	change failures
− need for new premises	

Figure 10.2 Lewin's force field analysis

It is the job of management to ensure that the driving forces weigh more heavily in people's minds than the restraining forces. So the change process has four parts to it (see Figure 10.3):

- *unfreezing the current situation* – convincing everybody that a change is required;
- *introducing the change programme*;
- *refreezing the new situation* – so that the changes stick;
- *evaluating the changes*.

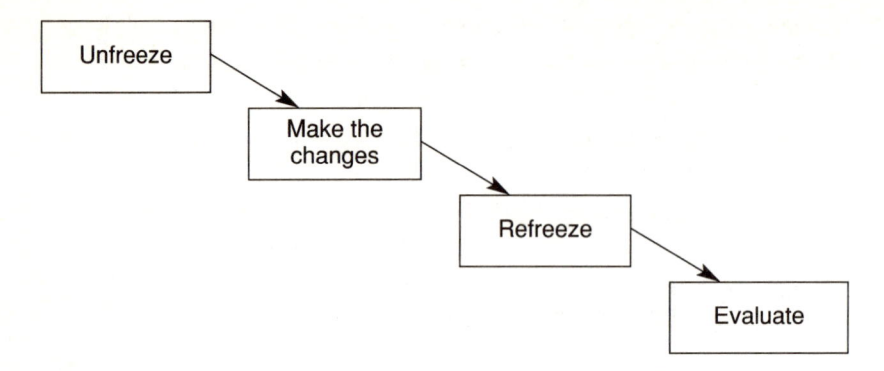

Figure 10.3 Lewin's model of change

The unfreezing process

Convincing employees of the need for change takes two forms. First is the presentation of the facts and figures that justify the change. This may be convincing on the surface, but dry facts, figures and arguments are unlikely to cause the change to be welcomed enthusiastically. This needs the second approach, which is the winning of hearts and minds through emotional and personal appeals. This emphasises what the change can offer for the employees. It may involve some pain in the short run but will bring better benefits long term.

The more consultation there is, the more employees will feel that they own the change, rather than having it foisted upon them. Producing a sense of crisis can, surprisingly, help in focusing employees' minds on providing a positive contribution in the consultation process. One medium-size manufacturing business, when faced with the withdrawal of a large customer contract, set up three project groups with the job of finding alternative work or other solutions to the situation within four weeks. The pressure seemed to work, as all three groups produced some workable solutions accepted by the directors and immediately put into effect with some success.

This whole process is made much easier if there is a culture of accepting change in the organisation. If change is more or less normal, such as in the fashion or media industries, then employees can be convinced of the need for any sort of change quite easily (up to a point). This cultural aspect needs to be worked on, then, through consistent communication with all employees.

From the board viewpoint, the unfreezing is completed when the various options that emerge from the consultation process are considered and evaluated, and decisions taken on the best course of action.

Introducing the change programme

Having consulted over the change, which also helps to make sure that the changes are not completely unexpected, the next stage is to sell the change programme that has been decided. Here **inspirational leadership** must re-emerge to convince employees that the changes decided upon are essential and the correct ones to meet the short- or long-term needs. A vision has to be painted to show where the organisation is now moving towards and how the situation will improve when the vision is met. Active commitment from the top (and that means *everybody* at the top) is an essential ingredient. Sometimes a **code word** is devised if the changes are substantial and long-term so that everybody can have the same focus. This also can create a feeling of excitement.

Each employee should receive details of the changes and how they will affect the employment situation. If redundancies or major changes in terms and conditions are involved, then they need to be spelt out early on. How to handle redundancies is detailed in Chapter 9.

Refreezing the situation

This means building the changes made into the culture in such a way that they become the norm. This process involves **effective training** for all staff involved in the changes so they incorporate the changes in their normal way of working. If there is a major change towards empowering employees or working more flexibly, for example, it will not be effective unless employees are shown how it can be operated and given the chance to practise it in theory before moving to the real situation. This can be achieved by using role-plays in the training or working from case studies. New documentation will also need to be produced, such as employee handbooks, quality manuals or operating/sales handbooks.

More important, employees need to be chosen who will act as 'champions' of the change – those who carry other employees along with their enthusiasm and keep their eye on how the changes are working, stepping in when necessary to put things right. They do not need to be managers – it can be a good career role to develop promising employees with potential to move into management.

Evaluating the change

As with all plans, it is vital periodically to evaluate how progress has been made and to celebrate success that has been achieved, especially where employees or departments have put in a lot of work to make the change a success.

Who is in favour of change?

Michael Armstrong (1993) has identified certain groups of employees who may be for or against changes. Those against change are:

- *Preservers*. They have a high need for security and low curiosity, and are in favour of consistency and stability. 'It's working well now, so why change it?' is their motto. They have reached the position they want, enjoy their job and do not want the situation altered.
- *Drifters*. They have little interest in the organisation or the future so have little curiosity or need for security. They are indifferent to change so will not support it, although may not be too active in opposing it.
- *Worriers*. They have little self-confidence and find changing a major challenge. They have a genuine concern that all changes

will work against them, perhaps because of their age or low intellectual or social abilities.
- *Doubters*. They actively resist change and can always find a good reason for not doing something, such as 'It didn't work last time' or 'It will cost too much.' They have a cynical view of the organisation and of the change process, having seen many cases of considerable effort being put into changes that have not worked out successfully. They will make a major effort to frustrate the changes.

The groups in favour of change are:

- *Leapers*. They regard change as the norm and welcome it at every opportunity. They see every problem as a challenge and have a low boredom threshold. They are usually the visionaries who have benefited from change programmes, although they may not be good at converting change into a reality. They may act without much research, planning or thought and can certainly ride roughshod over people's feelings.
- *Steppers*. They see the logical reason for change and are quite prepared to accept and welcome it as long as it is thought through properly. They like it to be taken a step at a time with risk aversion built in and are not happy at walking into the unknown.
- *Facilitators*. They enjoy helping with the change process, although they are not great visionaries and rarely help much in the planning. They simply like action and working with people who inspire them. In turn, they are good at inspiring people towards making the changes work.

Handling the change process, in Armstrong's view, is a matter of enlisting teams of leapers, steppers and facilitators, and ensuring that the objections put up by those opposing the changes can be overcome (see Figure 10.4). Leapers are, of course, the prime movers of change but they do not always reside in management roles. They need to be

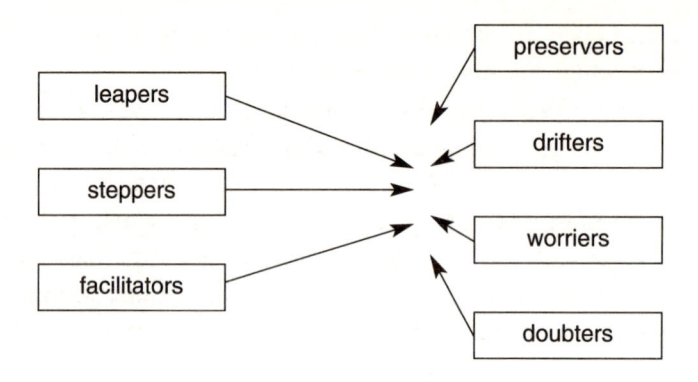

Figure 10.4 Armstrong's model of change

identified and their visions harnessed, and they should be put in charge of creative thinking groups at an early stage of the change programme, sometimes to 'think the unthinkable'. Steppers are the backroom staff who take those ideas and lick them into shape, help discard the truly unworkable ones and set out realistic plans to put the changes into action. Steppers must stay on hand to help make revisions when they become necessary (and they will!). Facilitators are the main change agents. They help to implement the plan, ensuring they carry people along with them. This involves training, coaching and working with staff on the detailed implementation.

All three groups need to be represented on any change project team. Without one of them, the project is unlikely to succeed, so identifying the employee types is crucial.

Overcoming the opposition is not always easy. Preservers may have much to lose from the changes so they have to be brought on board at an early stage and convinced that there are benefits for them. They bring a realistic approach and may have a good historical perspective so their views on what may or may not work can be useful and valid.

Drifters may not have a part to play as they may drift away from the organisation during the changes. On the other hand, the changes may create a spark of interest in them that could lead to a more positive approach. Attempts should be made to involve them and they should not be ignored or they could turn hostile and even destructive.

It is important to find out what the real fears are of the worriers. It may be possible to allay them at an early stage or to make special efforts to overcome them, such as additional help with the retraining. Special interest in their fears can help convert a worrier into a firm supporter of the changes. A responsibility for helping in the planning process can be a good move.

Doubters can be a major obstacle because cynicism is very difficult to remove. Sometimes they may not be persuadable but efforts must be made, as their opposition can be brutally destructive in its effect on morale. It may be wise to give them some responsibility for a part of the change programme but they need close supervision, clear targets and an understanding that excuses cannot be accepted.

As with any successful programme, it is the teamwork aspects that are crucial. A dedicated, committed and inspired team can overcome a fragmented opposition to make the changes successful. Two cases follow of successful changes in small organisations.

Case 10.1 Pindar Set

Pindar Set is a small, family-owned Yorkshire business, employing around 250 staff and, until the mid-1990s, their only business was with *Yellow Pages*, designing and typesetting the directory advertisements under a profitable 10-year contract. The arrangement was very stable, the process had not changed significantly for many years and the business structure and operations, based in Scarborough, were very traditional.

Everything had to change when *Yellow Pages* decided to move to a shorter-term contract with tighter margins and greater responsiveness to customer demand, which involved using *Yellow Pages'* own design studios in Birmingham, Bristol and Manchester. The new contract transferred 80 *Yellow Pages* staff, based in the studios, into Pindar Set, almost doubling the workforce. The problems faced included:

- staff at the different sites working on very different employment contracts;
- sharply reduced profit margins;
- a rolling one-year business contract creating some business uncertainty;

- advertising production having to be turned round in 5 days, rather than 25;
- traditional skills demarcations with very limited flexibility;
- peaks and troughs of work from 2,000 ads one week to 600 the next.

Improving occupational flexibility

The first area tackled was improving the skills and flexibility of the workforce. Staff needed to be able to tackle more than just one part of the production process so a multi-skilling programme got under way that eliminated unskilled jobs. Employees were grouped together into teams and learnt all the tasks in that team so they could, where necessary, follow a job through from start to finish. A testing and accreditation process was used to ensure consistency across the business.

Team working

Running the empowered, multi-skilled teams needed skilled team leaders, and Pindar set up an in-house development programme spread over 18 months that involved 30 days' training for each team leader. This cost £3,000 per person and was considered much better value for money than simply sending team leaders on an outside training course. It enabled them to put learning into practice and to take on responsibilities gradually, acting as deputies to existing supervisors while taking part in the training. The courses were run as a series of modules including:

- communication;
- personal stress management;
- problem solving;
- recruitment;
- negotiation;
- presentation skills;
- managing change;
- discipline;
- assertiveness;
- production and financial planning;
- staff appraisal;
- health and safety.

This allowed the 21 team leaders trained under this programme to become very broadly competent, dealing with all people issues and day-to-day responsibilities.

Temporal flexibility

All four sites had been operating institutional overtime for a number of years, which could not continue. In 1997, after some experiments, the company started a twilight shift from 4.30 pm to 1 am. Initially staffed by new recruits, the shifts were successful, which led to the setting up of six such shifts, manned by a combination of new and existing staff.

A second major initiative was an annualised hours scheme to help deal with the peaks and troughs. Employees are given one week's notice of the hours they will work in the following week with built-in safeguards so they can balance their work and home life. Staff work between 25 and 45 hours a week over four or five days (more if they want to) to make up a total of 1,680 hours in the year. Once employees have reached this total, they can take off the rest of the year as holiday. This scheme was started on a 12-month trial for volunteers only but, once the initial difficulties were overcome, it achieved general agreement from the workforce with 85 per cent taking part, for which a supplement of £500 is paid. Agreement was not reached, however, with the print unions in the original Scarborough plant.

Improvements achieved

The organisation has been able to measure the following improvements:

- overtime costs cut by two-thirds;
- 50 per cent increase in availability to customers;
- increase in productivity from 1.2 adverts per hour to 1.9;
- customer complaints down from 123 a month to 10 a month;
- absence rates down to 2 per cent;
- success in five-day turnaround in advertisements.

An attitude survey has also shown that there has been an increase in job satisfaction and concern over quality plus the appreciation of increased job security and opportunities for promotion and development. This has all led to the decline in profits being halted and steadily improving results in recent years in a scorchingly competitive market place.

(Source: *People Management*, 9 November 2000, pp 29–36)

Case 10.2 Hindle Power

The main driving force for change for Hindle Power, an engineering company employing 32 staff in Peterborough, came from its main customer, Perkins Engines, which told Hindle Power in 1996 that it would have to meet much tougher customer service targets or have its contracts terminated. The main focus of company improvement was directed at training employees to do their job better. A training budget was set up for the first time, and staff were trained and encouraged to determine their own training needs through a revised appraisal system. The emphasis in the new scheme was to encourage employees to stretch themselves, rather than looking back and focusing on past results. This enabled employees to clarify their own career goals and request up to 26 days a year training to meet them. One junior manager extended his skills from servicing engines to running the stock control and parts provision. Four supervisors completed an NVQ4 in business management while another took an Open University degree in science that has helped her in problem diagnosis and finding solutions.

Suppliers were drawn into the training by running product awareness programmes, and short internal courses were run in IT skills and customer care. A formal induction course was started for the first time. Altogether, 700 days of training took place over a three-year period, an average of nearly 10 per employee.

Communication systems were also overhauled with monthly financial results being posted and staff invited to attend performance briefings every three months. The general manager recalls that staff were a bit cynical for a time but slowly and surely they began to realise that the business was sincere in trying to get employees more involved and committed.

A further initiative was to embark on Investors in People, which was considered the bedrock of this transformation, forcing managers to plan more effectively, communicate to their staff and consider all the people issues involved in performance improvement. The result has been an increase in the labour force to 49, an expansion in the areas of work and numbers of customers, turnover up two and a half times and losses turned into profits, producing a Christmas bonus for staff under a new profit-sharing scheme. The link between training and bottom-line performance was quite clear to all concerned.

(Source: *People Management*, 3 February 2000)

References

Armstrong, M (1993) Devil's advocate, *Human Resources*, Autumn, pp 10–14

Lewin, K (1951) *Field Theory in Social Science*, Harper, New York

Further information

Further information on managing change can be found in Leigh, A and Walters, M (1998) *Effective Change: 20 ways to make it happen*, CIPD, London.

Index

Adams, J 69
advertising, recruitment 28, 29–31, 32–37, 42
Advisory, Conciliation and Arbitration Service (ACAS) 188, 225, 226–27
 Discipline at Work Handbook 249
 dismissal 239, 243, 252
All-Employee Share Ownership Plan (AESOP) 162
Armstrong, Michael 270–72

Beeby, Peter 12–13
Belbin, Meredith 93
Blackpool Pleasure Beach 113–14
blame, culture of 10–11
British Psychological Society 56
Business Links 125

Central Arbitration Committee (CAC) 182
change 172, 268–70
 case studies 273–76
 models of 265–68
 supporters and doubters 270–73
Citizens Advice Bureaux 243
Clamason Industries 96
communication 3–4, 166–68, 172
 attitude surveys 188–89
 briefing groups 177
 grievances 186–89
 health and safety 216
 one- and two-way 173–76
 organisational performance 170–72
 social and cultural issues 173
 staff forums and works councils 178–81
 trade unions 181–86
 vision of organisation 168–70
conflict 94
 see also discipline
Control of Substances Hazardous to Health Regulations 213
crisis management 266–67

Davies, Robin 62–63
decision-making 3–4, 46–48
development and training 13, 90, 108–09, 145–46, 269
 coaching and mentoring 118–20
 external providers 120–21
 government-sponsored 125–26
 identifying needs 116–17
 induction 110–15
 Investors in People 122–24
 needs analysis 20
 NVQs 121–22
 planning 117
Disability Discrimination Act 192
discipline 225–29
 appeals 229
 formality 235–7
 gross misconduct 230, 237, 249–51
 operating procedure 229–35
Discipline at Work Handbook (ACAS) 249
discrimination 193–94
 disability 192, 194–95, 199–200
 Equal Pay Act 192, 195–96
 ethnicity 200–03
 legislation 131–32, 191–92
 practical advice 196–200
 recruitment 46, 48–49
 sexual harassment 200–04
 unfair dismissal 240
dismissal
 arbitration schemes 248–51
 claims against 243–48
 compensation 245–47
 constructive 241–42
 discipline procedure 228–29
 facing tribunals 251–52
 fair and unfair 189, 237–41
 notice 237
 see also redundancy
DTI Work-Life Balance Fund 125
Dunn, Stephen 166

Index

EasyJet 58
employees 14
  agreements 15–16
  costs of 21
  empowerment 72–73, 74
  grievances 186–89
  handbooks 15–16, 114–15
  indivdual importance 69
  involvement in safety 217–18
  retaining 62–64
  staff forums and works councils 178–81
employment agencies *see* recruitment agencies
Employment Relations Act 182
Employment Rights Act 111, 129, 131–33, 255
Enterprise Management Incentives (EMI) 162
Equal Pay Act 192
European Foundation for Quality Management (EFQM) 94–95
European Union directives 178, 192, 201
Everest Double Glazing 4–5
executive search agencies 28, 29–31

fairness 8, 69
  dismissal 237–41
  in feedback 86–90
  pay, skills and promotion 90–91
  feedback
    fairness 86–90
    motivating employees 79–81
    sources 88–90
flexible working 12
  discrimination 198–99
  geographical/teleworking 101–03
  hours 97–100, 199
  numbers of employees 100–01
  occupational 103–04
  for small businesses 96–97
  things to avoid 104–05

goals
  fairness 86–87
  motivation 68
  SMART performance plans 75–77
  teamwork 92
government assistance 125–26

harassment and bullying 200–04, 241–42
Harvard Business School 81
Hay guide 140
headhunters 28, 29–31
health and safety 205, 215–20
  employers' obligations 209–11
  enforcement agencies 220
  induction 111
  legislation 206–11, 213–15
  occupational stress 222–23
  risk assessment 210–12
  smoking 221, 249
  teleworkers 102
  work design 220–21
Health and Safety Executive (HSE) 207–08
Herzberg, F 68
Hindle Power 276
Holbeche, Linda 11
hours
  flexible working 97–100, 199
  part-timers regulations 100
  teleworking 102–03
Internet recruitment 43, 45
interviewing 63
  preparation and structure 49–54
  what can go wrong 46–48
Investors in People (IIP) 9, 122–24

Job Centres 28, 29, 31, 261
job descriptions 24–27
  analytical and non-analytical 135–41
  broadening 71–72
job satisfaction 2–3
John Brown Engineering Ltd v *Brown* 258
Jukes, Michael 96

Kepner-Tregoe 81
Kite, Peter 205
Kohn, A 69
KPMG Equate scheme 140–41

leadership 6–13, 87–88
Learning and Skills Council 122
Lewin, K 267–68
loyalty 6, 63, 250

Manual Handling Operations Regulations 214–15
Martin, P 6
Maslow, Abraham 68
meetings *see* communications
motivation 7
  fairness 88–91
  feedback 78–81
  goals and challenge 68, 73, 75–78
  keeping interest 68, 70–73
  needs of employees 66–70
  recognition 68–69, 81–86
  teamwork 91–96

National Vocational Qualifications (NVQs) 121–22, 146
Nichols, J 6
Northumberland College of Arts and Technology 203

Omerod Home Trust 145–46
organisational climate 12

Part-Time Workers Regulations 100
pay and benefits 143

pay and benefits (cont'd)
   analytical and non-analytical schemes 135–41
   annual increases 154–55
   bonus schemes 146–52
   child care 159, 160
   company cars 158–59
   current market rates 141–42
   equality and discrimination 131–32
   fairness 90
   holidays 159
   legislation 129, 131–33
   maternity and paternity 131, 159–61
   minimum wage 132
   pensions 163–64
   performance-related 152–54
   recruitment 35
   salary structure 133–35, 143–46
   shared profits 13, 155–57, 161–62
   sick pay 132–33
   teleworking 102–03
   see also rewards
pensions 163–64
performance 73, 75–78
   assessing training needs 116
   feedback 79–81
   motivational needs 66–70
   organisational 170–72
Peters, Tom 79
Pindar Set 105, 273–75
promotion 90–91

Race Relations Act 192
recognition 81–86
   feedback 78–81
   motivation 68–69
   see also rewards
recruitment 19–23
   attracting applicants 27–37, 42–45
   CVs and application forms 37–42
   defining the job 24–27
   discrimination 46, 48–49, 198
   interviewing 46–54
   offering the job 60–62
   references 58–60
   reorganising vacancies 23–24
   shortlisting 45–46
   temporary employees 32
   testing 54–58
   unsuccessful candidates 61–62
recruitment agencies 28, 29–32
redundancy 252–55
   consultation and selection 255–59
   helping employees 261–62
   legal requirements 255–61
   payments 259–61
   surviving employees 262–63

Reporting of Injuries, Diseases and Dangerous Occurences Regulations 213–14
rewards 12, 13, 128–30
   bonus schemes 146–52
   extrinsic and intrinsic 67
   organisation-wide 155–57
rights, employees' 14–15
risk assessment 210–12

Saudi Arabian Airlines 182
self-employment 241
Sex Discrimination Act 192
Simpson, Steve 95
skills 71, 103–04
small organisations 3–5
   performance 170–72
   vision 168–70
SMART mode 75–77
Sportasia 12–13
Statex Press 183
stress 222–23
Swift Construction 98

teamwork 91–92
   Belbin's team types 93
   conflict 94
   human resource planning 20–21
   improving performance 92–96
   motivation 67
teleworking 101–03
temporary workers 32, 100–01
testing 8
   advantages and disadvantages 55–57
   assessment centres 57
   types of 54
Thatcher, Margaret 181–82
Tollit and Harvey 233–34
trade unions 183, 184–86
training *see* development and training
Transfer of Undertakings (Protection of Employment) Regulations (TUPE) 15

Union Bank of Nigeria 183
University for Industry (UfI) 125–26

Van Hage Garden Company 123–24
Vesuvius 94–95

Walker, John 223
Watkin, Chris 11–12
Welch, Jack 2–3
Windsor (D W) manufacturers 103–04
Workplace Employee Relations 3
works councils 178–81

Young, Don 266